Tracing Topographies: Revisiting the Concentration Camps Seventy Years after the Liberation of Auschwitz

Each of the contributions collected in this volume attempts, in various ways and from various perspectives, to trace the relationship between Nazi-occupied spaces and Holocaust memory seventy years on from the liberation of Auschwitz, considering the multitude of ways in which the passing of time impacts upon, or shapes, cultural constructions of space.

Accordingly, this book does not consider topographies merely in relation to geographical landscapes but, rather, as markers of allusions and connotations that must be properly eked out. Since space and time are intertwined, if not, in fact, one and the same, an investigation of the spaces – the locations of horror – in relation to the passing of time might provide some manner of comprehension of one of the most troubling moments in human history. It is with this understanding of space, as fluid sites of memory, that the contributors of this volume engage: these are the kind of shifting topographies that we are seeking to trace. This book was originally published as a special issue of *Holocaust Studies: A Journal of Culture and History*.

Joanne Pettitt is an Associate Lecturer in Comparative Literature at the School of European Culture and Languages, University of Kent, Canterbury, UK.

Vered Weiss is a Lecturer at the Department of Multidisciplinary Studies, Sapir Academic College, Israel.

Tracing Topographies: Revisiting the Concentration Camps Seventy Years after the Liberation of Auschwitz

Edited by
Joanne Pettitt and Vered Weiss

LONDON AND NEW YORK

First published 2017
by Routledge
2 Park Square, Milton Park, Abingdon, Oxon, OX14 4RN, UK

and by Routledge
711 Third Avenue, New York, NY 10017, USA

Routledge is an imprint of the Taylor & Francis Group, an informa business

© 2017 Taylor & Francis

All rights reserved. No part of this book may be reprinted or reproduced or utilised in any form or by any electronic, mechanical, or other means, now known or hereafter invented, including photocopying and recording, or in any information storage or retrieval system, without permission in writing from the publishers.

Trademark notice: Product or corporate names may be trademarks or registered trademarks, and are used only for identification and explanation without intent to infringe.

British Library Cataloguing in Publication Data
A catalogue record for this book is available from the British Library

ISBN 13: 978-1-138-70156-4

Typeset in MinionPro
by diacriTech, Chennai

Publisher's Note
The publisher accepts responsibility for any inconsistencies that may have arisen during the conversion of this book from journal articles to book chapters, namely the possible inclusion of journal terminology.

Disclaimer
Every effort has been made to contact copyright holders for their permission to reprint material in this book. The publishers would be grateful to hear from any copyright holder who is not here acknowledged and will undertake to rectify any errors or omissions in future editions of this book.

Contents

Citation Information	vii
Notes on Contributors	ix
Introduction	1
Joanne Pettitt and Vered Weiss	

Section 1: Geographies of the Holocaust

1 Life in space, space in life: Nazi topographies, geographical imaginations, and *Lebensraum*   11
   Paolo Giaccaria and Claudio Minca

2 Controversies surrounding the excavation at Börneplatz, Frankfurt am Main, 1987   32
   Joseph Cronin

Section 2: Remembering and experiencing the concentration camps in the present day

3 "Romantic Auschwitz": examples and perceptions of contemporary visitor photography at the Auschwitz-Birkenau State Museum   45
   Imogen Dalziel

4 The concentration camp brothels in memory   68
   Nicole Bogue

5 The sacred, the profane, and the space in between: site-specific performance at Auschwitz   88
   Samantha Mitschke

CONTENTS

Section 3: Filmic topographies

6 The cinematic city and the destruction of Lublin's Jews 104
Maurizio Cinquegrani

7 Transcultural engagement with Polish memory of the Holocaust while
watching Leszek Wosiewicz's *Kornblumenblau* 116
Victoria Grace Walden

Section 4: Literary topographies

8 Post-witnessing the concentration camps: Paul Auster's and Angela Morgan
Cutler's investigative and imaginative encounters with sites of mass murder 134
Diana I. Popescu

9 Extra-territorial places in W. G. Sebald's *Austerlitz* 149
Melanie Dilly

10 British representations of the camps 163
Sue Vice

Afterword 178
Joanne Pettitt and Vered Weiss

Index 181

Citation Information

The chapters in this book were originally published in *Holocaust Studies*, volume 22, issues 2–3 (April–July 2016). When citing this material, please use the original page numbering for each article, as follows:

Introduction
Joanne Pettitt and Vered Weiss
Holocaust Studies, volume 22, issues 2–3 (April–July 2016) pp. 141–150

Chapter 1
Life in space, space in life: Nazi topographies, geographical imaginations, and Lebensraum
Paolo Giaccaria and Claudio Minca
Holocaust Studies, volume 22, issues 2–3 (April–July 2016) pp. 151–171

Chapter 2
Controversies surrounding the excavation at Börneplatz, Frankfurt am Main, 1987
Joseph Cronin
Holocaust Studies, volume 22, issues 2–3 (April–July 2016) pp. 172–184

Chapter 3
"Romantic Auschwitz": examples and perceptions of contemporary visitor photography at the Auschwitz-Birkenau State Museum
Imogen Dalziel
Holocaust Studies, volume 22, issues 2–3 (April–July 2016) pp. 185–207

Chapter 4
The concentration camp brothels in memory
Nicole Bogue
Holocaust Studies, volume 22, issues 2–3 (April–July 2016) pp. 208–227

Chapter 5
The sacred, the profane, and the space in between: site-specific performance at Auschwitz
Samantha Mitschke
Holocaust Studies, volume 22, issues 2–3 (April–July 2016) pp. 228–243

CITATION INFORMATION

Chapter 6

The cinematic city and the destruction of Lublin's Jews
Maurizio Cinquegrani
Holocaust Studies, volume 22, issues 2–3 (April–July 2016) pp. 244–255

Chapter 7

Transcultural engagement with Polish memory of the Holocaust while watching Leszek Wosiewicz's Kornblumenblau
Victoria Grace Walden
Holocaust Studies, volume 22, issues 2–3 (April–July 2016) pp. 256–273

Chapter 8

Post-witnessing the concentration camps: Paul Auster's and Angela Morgan Cutler's investigative and imaginative encounters with sites of mass murder
Diana I. Popescu
Holocaust Studies, volume 22, issues 2–3 (April–July 2016) pp. 274–288

Chapter 9

Extra-territorial places in W. G. Sebald's Austerlitz
Melanie Dilly
Holocaust Studies, volume 22, issues 2–3 (April–July 2016) pp. 289–302

Chapter 10

British representations of the camps
Sue Vice
Holocaust Studies, volume 22, issues 2–3 (April–July 2016) pp. 303–317

Afterword

Joanne Pettitt and Vered Weiss
Holocaust Studies, volume 22, issues 2–3 (April–July 2016) pp. 318–319

For any permission-related enquiries please visit:
http://www.tandfonline.com/page/help/permissions

Notes on Contributors

Nicole Bogue read History at University of Birmingham, UK, developing an interest in the museological representation of female suffering in the Holocaust and within the concentration camps.

Maurizio Cinquegrani is a Lecturer in Film at the School of Arts, University of Kent, Canterbury, UK.

Joseph Cronin is a Teaching Associate at Queen Mary, University of London, UK. His research interests include modern German-Jewish history, cultural memory studies, and the history of antisemitism.

Imogen Dalziel is a doctoral researcher at Royal Holloway, University of London, UK. She is also Administrator of the College's Holocaust Research Institute.

Melanie Dilly holds a degree in English and German from the Albert-Ludwigs-Universität Freiburg (Staatsexamen), Germany, and a masters degree in Modern German and Comparative Literature from the University of Kent, Canterbury, UK, where she remained to complete her doctoral dissertation. A Teaching Fellowship at the German Department of the University of St Andrews, Scotland, followed. Her research interests lie in the relationship between postcolonial and post-WWII discourses in contemporary expatriate writing.

Paolo Giaccaria is an Assistant Professor of Political and Economic Geography at the Department of Economics, Social Studies, Applied Mathematics and Statistics, University of Turin, Italy.

Claudio Minca is a Professor in the Human Geography Group at the Wageningen University, the Netherlands.

Samantha Mitschke is a theatre historian, specialising in British and American Holocaust theatre. Her research addresses topics ranging from adaptations of Anne Frank's diary and the efficacy of child protagonists to the use of 'Holocaust cabaret' and the concept of the 'Holocaust musical'.

Joanne Pettitt is an Associate Lecturer in Comparative Literature at the University of Kent, Canterbury, UK, and a Postdoctoral Assistant, University of Bern, Switzerland.

NOTES ON CONTRIBUTORS

Her book, *Perpetrators in Holocaust Narratives: Encountering the Nazi Beast*, is forthcoming with Palgrave Macmillan (2017).

Diana I. Popescu is a Research Fellow at Pears Institute for the Study of Antisemitism, Birkbeck, UK. Popescu specialises in the representation and memorialisation of the Holocaust in contemporary culture and public art. She is the co-editor (with Tanja Schult) of *Revisiting Holocaust Representation in the Post-Witness Era* (Palgrave Macmillan, 2015).

Sue Vice is a Professor of English Literature, University of Sheffield, UK. Her recent works include *Representing Perpetrators in Holocaust Literature and Film* (2013), co-edited with Jenni Adams; *Textual Deceptions: False Memoirs and Literary Hoaxes in the Contemporary Era* (2014); and *Barry Hines: 'Kes', 'Threads' and Beyond*, co-written with David Forrest, which is due out in 2017.

Victoria Grace Walden is a Teaching Fellow at the University of Sussex, UK. Her PhD thesis, submitted to Queen Mary, University of London, UK, in 2017 offers a phenomenological reading of Holocaust memory and cinema in contemporary intermedial projects. She has published several articles about Holocaust animation, and is particularly interested in the relationship between cinema and memory spaces, and film archaeology as a way to access suppressed memories.

Vered Weiss is a Lecturer at the Department of Multidisciplinary Studies, Sapir Academic College, Israel. She holds a BA in Comparative and English Literature from Tel Aviv University, Israel, an MA in Comparative and World Literature from San Francisco State University, California, USA, and a PhD in Comparative Literature from the University of Kent, Canterbury, UK. After completing her PhD, she was a Postdoctoral Research Associate in the Program in Jewish Culture and Society, University of Illinois at Urbana-Champaign, USA.

Introduction

Joanne Pettitt[a] and Vered Weiss[b]

[a]Department of Comparative Literature, School of European Culture and Languages, University of Kent, Canterbury, Kent, UK; [b]Program in Jewish Culture and Society; and Comparative and World Literature Department, University of Illinois at Urbana-Champaign, USA

As we mark 70 years since the liberation of Auschwitz, we need to reconsider the commemoration and memory of the Nazi concentration and extermination camps, as well as the Holocaust more broadly. Importantly, the concentration camps are experienced temporally and spatially, physically and theoretically: you can physically go to the camps and you can learn of the camps from the pages of history. Notwithstanding, neither historical nor spatial distancing suffices in order to assuage the horror. Primo Levi suggested that at the moment of the horror, one could not conceive it at its full magnitude; he argued that the victim "felt overwhelmed by an enormous edifice of violence and menace but could not form for himself a representation of it because his eyes were fastened to the ground by every single minute's needs."[1] Levi's concern at the time was that the Lagers did not provide a good "observation post"[2] from which to fully comprehend the true scope of the catastrophe therein. The question now is whether, in addition to the perspective gained from spatial distance, we might have gained perspective through temporal lapse; if so, what kind of new and different perspectives has this distance provided? In order to revisit these historical events, therefore, one has to acknowledge the intricate connection between the spatial and chronological experience of "memory." Space, as Foucault explains, is an active concept, as it takes the form of relations among sites.[3] Space is important in the following discussions precisely as an active participant in the (re)creation of knowledge, identities, and the relations between identities and social conventions. In a Lefebvrian sense, space is socially constructed,[4] and sites of Nazi atrocity are a particularly apt example. One of the central concerns of this volume, then, is the ways in which the implications and connotations of these spaces have changed over time.

In the preface to his influential *The Holocaust and the Literary Imagination* (1975), Lawrence Langer describes the "disparity between expectation and reality" that he perceived during his first visit to Auschwitz in 1964.[5] The children he sees playing near the entrance to the camp illuminate a rupture between the site as a historically significant monument to atrocity and its present day position adjacent to a functioning apartment block. A while later, standing in the Neue Pinakotek art museum in Munich, Langer "once more experienced that uncanny sensation of discontinuity,"[6] when he comes across a painting of an ostensibly peaceful landscape that is provocatively entitled "Dachau." Langer writes, "the disjunction between that tranquil village of an earlier era

1

and the site of the notorious concentration camp in our own age, just a few kilometers from Munich, was so enormous that I was unable to reconcile it by a simple act of the imagination."[7] Space is thus encountered by Langer, both aesthetically and experientially, as a mark of the passage of time: the uncanny effect that the author describes marks the placement of topographical landscapes within a temporal continuum in which the transformation of space – either through physical change or the implications or connotations of its social usage – creates a rupture in experience.

Similarly, in his foreword to *Holocaust Literature: A Handbook of Critical, Historical, and Literary Writings*, Dennis Klein discusses his last visit to Berlin in 1987, two years before the fall of the Berlin Wall. Klein remembers two places "that seemed to freeze the past in time": Potsdamer Platz and a burial ground for Jews further east.[8] On the one hand, Potsdamer Platz, as the former "cultural and political center of Berlin,"[9] precipitates the transportation of the author back in time as he attempts to engage with the past through a process of imagination:

> A flood of like visions filled the vacant spaces of the cemetery as well – not of the particular lives whose names appeared on the tombstones, but of the life of an entire community. Here I could also imagine Jews walking, as I did, down the cemetery's dark and quiet paths, thinking innocently (as I could not) about death as a natural, if unhappy event. It occurred to me that I had come to mourn not a single life, and not only the life of Jews who had once lived and prospered in Berlin.[10]

The cemetery functions as a shared space that connects the past and the present in a kind of post-memorial encounter while, at the same time, the author's acknowledgment that, unlike the liminal figures he imagines, he "could not" consider death "innocently" because of the events of the recent past illustrates the disjuncture between the conception and experience of such sites in different periods of time. Klein continues:

> With the unification of the two Germanys just a few years ago, even memories of the events that predated World War II and the misery and defeat that followed seemed to vanish with the Wall. In that extraordinary year Germans were determined to declare a second *Stunde Null*, a second "zero hour" (the first was in 1945), when nothing before then could possibly count as much as the present and the future. Potsdamer Platz would literally disappear. The Jewish burial ground could easily disappear as well, if not from "urban renewal," which threatens Jewish cemeteries all over Germany, then from persistent local neglect. Although I didn't fully realize it during my visit, an assault on German history was already well under way.[11]

For Klein, then, physical landscapes fulfill a dual function: on the one hand, they are access points to an imagined, collective memory where the past and present exist within the same *spatial* domain; on the other hand, their transformation (or, in the case of Potsdamer Platz, their destruction) establishes a means of erasure of that same past.

What becomes clear, then, is that, as Steven Hoelscher and Derek Alderman point out, there is an "inextricable link between memory and place."[12] Indeed, this is the issue to which Pierre Nora famously alluded in his notion of *lieux de mémoire*, which he describes as sites "where memory crystalizes and secretes itself."[13] Although Nora expands his conception beyond topographical limitations (including in his analysis archives, historical figures, and rituals), he nevertheless uses *les lieux* to discuss what he terms the "eradication of memory by history."[14] That is, "*Lieux de mémoire* originate with the sense that there is no spontaneous memory, that we must deliberately create archives, maintain anniversaries, organize celebrations, present eulogies, and notarize bills, because such activities no longer occur naturally."[15] And, further, "*lieux de mémoire* [are] moments of history torn away from the movement of history, then returned; no longer quite life, not yet death, like shells on the shore when the sea of living memory has receded."[16] In other words, *lieux de mémoire* are liminal spaces in which memory is (re)enacted, (re) created, and (re)solidified in material traces: "The sacred ['real' memory] is invested in the trace that is at the same time its negation."[17] Memory is to be taken as more dynamic than the organizational framework that "history" enables since, according to Nora, this is simply a "representation of the past."[18] *Lieux de mémoire* are thus a connection to a more dynamic past that has been overwritten by static history.

The fixity that is implied by Nora's model is, however, at odds with the ostensible transience of space as it is described by Langer and Klein. Arguing against what they term the "nation-centeredness of Nora's approach," Astrid Erll and Ann Rigney write:

> Initial discussions of cultural memory, especially those inspired by the work of Pierre Nora, tended to focus on those canonical "sites of memory" which provide relatively stable points of reference for individuals and communities recalling a shared past. As the field has advanced, however, one can note a shift towards understanding cultural memory in more dynamic terms: as an ongoing process of remembrance and forgetting in which individuals and groups continue to reconfigure their relationship to the past and hence reposition themselves in relation to established and emergent memory sites.[19]

As modern technology continues to reduce the distance between geographical spaces (and, indeed, between the past and the present, as Andreas Huyssen has noted[20]), our interpretations of particular sites of memory are overlapping, creating what Michael Rothberg has termed "multidirectional" modes of encounter.[21] Continuing in a similar vein, Debarati Sanyal introduces the notion of *Noeuds de Mémoire* as an alternative to the perceived rigidity of Nora's paradigm:

> such knots of memory exceed the borders of Pierre Nora's sites of memory: They are figural knots that migrate across national, ethnocultural, and temporal borders and resist – even reenvision – a memory politics anchored in the nation-state [...].[22]

From this perspective, memorial sites need not be localized within particular national borders, nor must alternative memories continually compete for prominence in the cultural psyche. Instead, different histories converge on a single site, allowing for more dynamic modes of remembrance, which continue to develop over time.

This kind of structure is further developed by Huyssen, whose work on memory as a palimpsest marks an important development in the discourse memory studies. He writes:

> After the waning of modernist fantasies about *creation ex nihilo* and of the desire for the purity of new beginnings, we have come to read cities and buildings as palimpsests of space, monuments as transformable and transitory, and sculpture as subject to the vicissitudes of time. Of course, the majority of buildings are not palimpsests at all. As Freud once remarked, the same space cannot possibly have two different contents. But an urban imaginary in its temporal reach may well put different things in one place: memories of what there was before imagined alternatives to what there is. The strong marks of present space merge in the imaginary with traces of the past, erasures, losses and heterotopias.[23]

Material traces become enmeshed with social, cultural, and political narratives, creating a fluidity of meaning that continually recasts history in different lights. Discussing similar ideas from a postcolonial perspective, Homi Bhabha's concept of "third space" has become imperative in theoretical conceptualizations of identities in relation to space/time. In a 1995 interview Homi Bhabha explains this concept, contextualizing it in relation to Walter Benjamin:

> This is where the influence of Walter Benjamin has been formative for me. His meditations on the disjunctive temporalities of the historical "event" are quite indispensable to thinking the cultural problems of late modernity. His vision of the Angel of History haunts my work as I attempt to grasp, for the purposes of cultural analysis, what he describes as the condition of translation: the "continua of transformation, not abstract ideas of identity and similarity." His work has led me to speculate on differential temporal movements within the process of dialectical thinking and the supplementary or interstitial "conditionality" that opens up alongside the transcendent tendency of dialectical contradiction – I have called this a "third space," or a "time lag." To think of these temporalities in the context of historical events has led me to explore notions of causality that are not expressive of the contradiction "itself," but are contingently effected by it and allow for other translational moves of resistance, and for the establishment of other terms of generality.[24]

This notion of "third space" is productive for our investigation of the topographies of the camps and World War II precisely because these are traceable throughout space/time worldwide, before, during, and after the Holocaust. Moreover, these topographies leave their traces not only in spatial sites, but also in cultural artifacts, books, installations, poems, as well as perpetrators, second- and third-generation victims, and indeed wider socio-historical processes. Imaginary and real spaces can coexist,[25] and the "third space" they occupy is negotiated culturally.

Bhabha's conception of a "third space" connotes spaces in which narratives of authority are challenged and different cultures and perspectives meet. This allows for the construction of hybrid identities. It is our view that sites such as those under consideration in this volume encapsulate this hybrid existence, engaging, as the various contributions show, with different patterns of memory and experience, culminating in the formation of spaces of dynamic interpretation. As Bhabha notes:

> The importance of hybridity is not to be able to trace two original moments from which the third emerges, rather hybridity to [him] is a "third space" which enables other positions to emerge. This third space displaces the histories that constitute it, and sets up new structures of authority, new political initiatives, which are inadequately understood through received wisdom. [...] This process of cultural hybridity gives rise to something different, something new and unrecognizable, a new area of negotiation of meaning and representation.[26]

The overlapping of memories and experiences on a singular site returns us to the observations of Lawrence Langer and Dennis Klein, who, by engaging with these distinct encounters simultaneously, illustrate the multifaceted nature of memorial spaces. What emerges from these initial considerations is a tangible yet complex relationship between geographical sites and memory in what might be considered a quasi-Proustian association between the past and present. More than this, though, these considerations suggest that such sites have the potential to transcend individual memory as they come to form essential components in the collective consciousness that helps different generations to reconnect with what Nora terms "real" memory.[27] This multidisciplinary volume is concerned with this temporal shift and its implications on the cultural construction of space. The following articles consider the ways in which the concentration and extermination camps

TRACING TOPOGRAPHIES

participate in contemporary commemoration of the Holocaust, their role as sites of commemoration, and as sites of memory. Since space and time are intertwined, if not in fact one and the same,[28] an investigation of the spaces, the locations of horror, in relation to the passing of time might provide some manner of comprehension of one of the most troubling moments in human history. It is with this understanding of space, as fluid sites of memory, that the contributors of this volume engage: these are the kinds of shifting topographies that we are seeking to trace.

Accordingly, this volume does not consider topographies merely in relation to geographical analyses but, rather, as markers of allusions and connotations that must be properly eked out. "Auschwitz" is not simply a geographical location on a map but, more fundamentally, it operates as a metonym for suffering, violence, and persecution under the National Socialists during World War II. This understanding of the metonymic function of Auschwitz suggests a hierarchical construction of spaces that we wish to overcome. Although the concentration and extermination camps feature heavily in this volume, owing in large part to their position as exemplars of Nazi power and brutality, this edition also engages with memories of other sites relating to the Holocaust. This follows, loosely, David Rousset's famous conception of *L'Univers Concentrationnaire*, which entails more than simply an allusion to the concentration camp space. Indeed, as Sidra Dekoven Ezrahi asserts,

> The adjective *concentrationary*, used here as in the English version of Rousset's memoire as a rough translation of *concentrationnaire*, is not necessarily limited in its reference to the geographical confines of the camps but may allude to the general condition of the Jew during World War II who, whether incarcerated in a ghetto or a concentration camp, posing as an Aryan, or hiding in a barn, an attic, or a forest, was marked for extermination.[29]

This broader perspective of "concentrationary" spaces allows for a more fruitful engagement with the landscapes of World War II, and it is around this viewpoint that the authors of the following articles coalesce.

The first section is dedicated to spatial analyses of the space and time of horror. Both contributions in this section adopt historical and geographical perspectives to illustrate the developments of space over time. The first article by Paolo Giaccaria and Claudio Minca explores the very basis of Nazi spatiality. In "Nazi Spatialities, Geographical Imaginations, and *Lebensraum*," Giaccaria and Minca expose the significance of spatiality and spatial concepts, and specifically *Lebensraum* in the Nazi worldview, or *Weltanschauung*. The authors offer an important reconsideration of the manner in which "the Holocaust must be contextualized within the Nazi search for territorial expansion," and furthermore claim that space itself was a means for genocide by outlining the various ways in which spatial segregation in the ghettoes and the camps "naturally" increased mortality: transports to the death camps were accurately routinized, camps and ghettoes were planned and managed and often integrated with the surrounding cities and regions, forests were used to perform and hide mass shooting, and forced marches turned into another occasion for torture and murder. Giaccaria and Minca reveal a broad set of spatialities that spanned from the so-called Territorial Solution to the Final Solution. Eventually, the authors outline how the "Third Reich's plans of racial and ethnic reordering of the European space in fact entailed endless classifications of groups and individuals and a series of subsequent (mostly forced) movements in order to fit the population distribution into a

5

stable, hierarchical, racial order that was at the same time biopolitical and geopolitical in nature." By tracing the spatial foundations of Nazi doctrine, this article reveals the fundamentally spatial essence of racism. The in-group/out-group doctrine of the racist is expressed in spatial forms of colonialism and persecution.

Yet, as Giaccaria and Minca note, "these 'geographical imaginations' were at work in German culture decades before the rise of the Third Reich." In "Controversies Surrounding the Excavation at Börneplatz, Frankfurt, 1987," Joseph Cronin leads us through the debates regarding the remains of Frankfurt's medieval Jewish ghetto, which were unearthed by construction workers excavating a car park to make way for a new municipal building in 1987. This article exposes the reality of the meeting points between space and time, history and progress, and the questions of memory and commemoration. The history of racism is here explored through its spatial manifestations, reconsidering in-group/out-group doctrine from the Jewish perspective, as well as from a twentieth-century point of view. Cronin argues that "although this 'Jewish quarter' had disappeared by the late nineteenth century, other, similar Jewish quarters did still exist and *were* destroyed by the Nazis. So Börneplatz became a stand-in for the Jewish communities that disappeared without a trace or whose traces, in any case, lay outside of Germany." Thus, Cronin suggests, Börneplatz represents both the continuation and disruption of Jewish presence upon European soil.

Contemporary Jewish presence upon European soil is evident not only in the flourishing communities of Jews in various European cities, but in the massive presence in sites of commemoration throughout the continent. The second section explores the concentration and extermination camps as sites of commemoration. One of the most disturbing contemporary phenomena regarding the Holocaust is "dark tourism." Formerly locations of abject horror, the concentration camps have arguably been transformed into tourist hotspots, available as part of package deals complete with tour guides, audio-guide headsets, and pertinent photo opportunities. Efraim Sicher, for example, argues that "Auschwitz has become a site of memory with a future, and it has thus become another tourist site with all the required amenities, a 'must' on any itinerary."[30] The concentration camps might have remained stationary in a physical or geographical sense, but their topography has not maintained its horrific essence, and their cultural meaning has shifted substantially. The diachronic shift of the last 70 years has thus – perhaps – facilitated a usurpation of the camps, which have come to be experienced simultaneously as loci of remembrance and profanations against memory. The revisiting of the horror of the Holocaust, evident in the numerous visitors of the various concentration and extermination camps, has been subject to scrutiny. This has reached a level of obsessive engagement that perhaps even misses the point of commemoration and leads to processes of negation of the Holocaust through self-absorption. Contemporary Israeli debate regarding the groups of teenagers sent to Europe every year to witness the horror has been an enduring and controversial discussion. The use of the Holocaust in recent politics has flared the discussion, leading, however, to no conclusive resolution.

In "'Romantic Auschwitz': Examples and Perceptions of Contemporary Visitor Photography at the Auschwitz-Birkenau State Museum," Imogen Dalziel explores visitor photography at the Auschwitz-Birkenau State Museum. Relying on research she conducted, Dalziel argues for diverse rationale for photography in the museum, from commemoration to attempts to create aesthetically valuable photographs. Acknowledging the problematic moral status of the "increasingly popular" "selfie" in Auschwitz, Dalziel suggests that photographic engagement with the site might also lead to its perception "as a global symbol of where prejudice and discrimination can lead if left unchecked." The "selfie" should here be acknowledged as an attempt to (re)construct a sense of "self" in a particular space and time. There is an intricate connection between the spatial and chronological experience of the "self." The visitors in the camp attempt to reconfigure their identities in relation to the space of horror. In a sense, the "selfie" is an attempt to create a "place" in the "space" of horror. Ultimately, as Dalziel attempts to engage with the problematic conflation of sites of horror and sites of tourism, she offers an important reflection upon our contemporary experience of the Holocaust.

Conflating the camps with romantic notions, albeit from a different perspective, in "The Concentration Camp Brothels in History and Memory," Nicole Bogue explores the issue of sex in the camps. The notion of sex and sexualities in the camps appears to offer a cognitive dissonance, as sex is associated with love and reproduction, which are the uttermost antithetical notions to the Nazi concentration and death camps. Yet the particular kinds of sexualities explored by Bogue are, indeed, even more disturbing, as she sheds light upon the brutal employment of "brothels" in the camps. From 1942 until 1945 the Nazis established "brothel" institutions, "euphemistically nicknamed the *Sonderbauten* (special buildings) by the SS, in 10 concentration camps in Germany, Austria, and Poland." These "brothel barracks" held non-Jewish prisoners, who were forced to work as sex laborers for "privileged male prisoners." Ultimately, Bogue notes that "in focusing the lens on the 'ruins' of memory metaphorically and physically on the two museums, this project hopes to prompt further exploration on the geographical and cultural limits on sites of memory in marginal histories from the Nazi period." Thus Bogue strives to centralize lesser-known histories of the Holocaust by re-engaging with memories of gender and sexuality in discourses around concentration camps.

Following the trajectory of this attempt, in "The Sacred, the Profane, and the Space in Between: Site-Specific Performance at Auschwitz," Samantha Mitschke explores moral concerns regarding theatre and performance within Auschwitz, especially as they relate to notions of Holocaust sanctity. Discussing the problem of Holocaust "fatigue," the author argues that "the introduction of innovative and avant-garde ways of examining the Holocaust through theatre, such as the use of balagan, enables practitioners and performers to challenge Holocaust fatigue in their audiences and even themselves." However, as Mitschke observes, site-specific performances run the risk of being gratuitous, thus polluting the sanctity of the site. Nevertheless, the author draws interesting parallels between theatrical performances and tourist trips to concentration camps, contending that "these tours do constitute theatre." Through this process, Mitschke engages with concepts of dark tourism, marking Auschwitz as a site of continued performativity.

Over the years there have been numerous attempts to capture the horror of the Holocaust and engage with it productively via artistic means. The very questions regarding the necessity and moral validity of these artistic representations are known and familiar.[31] For example, there is a linguistic component to Rousset's construction of *L'Univers Concentrationnaire* insofar as the concentration camps, according to Ezrahi, were "a self-contained world which both generated its own vocabulary and invested common language with new, sinister meanings."[32] And, further, "[t]he concentratory idiom informs the literature written by all the prisoners and binds them in a common linguistic universe."[33] Thus

TRACING TOPOGRAPHIES

the question is not only concerned with the implications of space, but also the means by which we can (or cannot) engage with that space through language. Understanding space as a linguistic and semiotic field opens up new avenues of interpretation and understanding and will be important for the articles that make up this volume. Focusing on film and literature, the following two sections offer articles that (re)consider the moral validity of artistic engagement with the Holocaust.

The section dedicated to film offers two articles that approach the subject of Holocaust commemoration from two distinct perspectives: from the point of view of production, and from the point of view of consumption. In "The Cinematic City and the Destruction of Lublin's Jews," Maurizio Cinquegrani focuses on the role Lublin played in the Final Solution by exploring the cinematic depictions of the city and the Majdanek extermination camp, which is located on the outskirts of Lublin. Cinquegrani exposes a diametrically opposed process of cinematic productivity, as whereas Polish filmmakers utilized key locations in Lublin to inscribe the events of 1939–1944 into the context of Polish national martyrdom, Western films re-established the link between the Holocaust and significant locations through "creative cinematic geographies that both failed to reflect the historical topography of the city and often transformed cinematic Lublin and Majdanek into other cities and camps."

While Cinquegrani explores the filmmakers' involvement in the process of Holocaust commemoration, in "Transnational Engagement with Polish Memory of the Holocaust while Watching Leszek Wosiewicz's *Kornblumenblau*," Victoria Grace Walden focuses on the viewers' engagement with cinematic depictions of the Holocaust. Walden argues that "by mimetically engaging with the Polish film *Kornblumenblau* (1989), the spectator, regardless of nationality, is encouraged to confront the complexities of Holocaust memory." While Walden is cautious in suggesting her reading of one film can be indicative of all cinematic encounters with the Holocaust, she proposes this transnational approach as productive in our reconsideration of artistic engagement with this horrific time and place in history.

Fictional accounts also offer significant commentaries on memory and representation. For example, questions of artistic engagement with the Holocaust resonate in the manner by which Angela Morgan Cutler and Paul Auster narrate their visits to concentration camps. In "Post-witnessing the Concentration Camps: Paul Auster's and Angela Morgan Cutler's Investigative and Imaginative Encounters with Sites of Mass Murder," Diana I. Popescu offers a productive analysis of the cognitive dissonance that emerges from the way Cutler and Auster depict their experiences of the concentration camp sites. Moving beyond Marianne Hirsch's celebrated "post-memory," Popescu introduces the alternative concept of post-witnessing, which she uses to facilitate and expose the mechanisms of actively searching for relationships with the past. As the author successfully concludes, the imagination is central to these processes.

In a similar approach to the importance of literary engagement with the Holocaust, in "Extra-territorial Places in W. G. Sebald's *Austerlitz*," Melanie Dilly explores Sebald's narrative technique, arguing that "hybrid constructions of the documentary and the fictional as well as a shift of focus from an objective to a subjective truth put the active reader into the foreground." Over the course of her investigation, Dilly works to reveal the hidden traces that connect Austerlitz's memories with those of World War II, thereby broadening the "scope of the concept of memory, which is no longer to be defined by the simple dichotomy between personal memory and historical fact." Because these historical remnants remain obscured, the reader is challenged to follow the clues that the text lays out, navigating the fragmentary symbols to develop more nuanced interpretations. Thus both Popescu and Dilly focus on the reception of the texts and their productive effect upon the reader. The readers are transported to another space where they experience the past, which is revisited through the engagement in the present.

Finally, in her contribution Sue Vice considers representations of British camps during World War II. As the author suggests, "the topography of these spaces encapsulates British social and imperial history, but is invoked in varied metaphorical and symbolic ways: as a means of exploring differences and similarities between Nazi Germany and Britain." Vice's article offers a distinct shift in perspective, seeking to compare the varying representational strategies that underpin depictions of German and British camp spaces. In her conclusions, Vice exposes a kind of memorial hypocrisy in which Britain's own history is structured in such a (contra-Nazi) way so as to protect its own sense of superiority.

The debates regarding the perception of the Holocaust as a specifically Jewish European trauma, or, conversely, with regard to its worldwide ramifications, continue to be relevant in a world that is witness to horrors of genocide in the twenty-first century. The specificity, however, of the Holocaust, as anchored in its particular time/space singularity, remains to be explored precisely in the context of these unparalleled circumstances of World War II. The discussions this volume offers are relevant to contemporary reconsideration of the place we allot time and history in our hectic, horror-struck, postmodern world.

Notes

1. Primo Levi, *The Drowned and the Saved*, 6.
2. Ibid., 6.
3. Foucault, "Of Other Spaces," 22.
4. Lefebvre, *Introduction to Modernity*.
5. Langer, *The Holocaust*, xi.
6. Ibid., xi.
7. Ibid., xi.
8. Klein, "Foreword," xiii.
9. Ibid., xiii.
10. Ibid., xiv.
11. Ibid., xiv.
12. Hoelscher and Alderman, "Memory and Place," 348.
13. Nora, "Between Memory and History," 7.
14. Ibid., 8.
15. Ibid., 12.
16. Ibid., 12.
17. Ibid., 14.
18. Ibid., 8.
19. Erll and Rigney, *Mediation*, 2.
20. Huyssen, *Present Pasts*, 1.
21. Rothberg, *Multidirectional Memory*, 3.
22. Sanyal, *Memories and Complicity*, 144.
23. Huyssen, *Present Pasts*, 7.
24. Mitchell, "Translator Translated," 83.
25. Soja, *Thirdspace*, 10.
26. Rutherford, "The Third Space," 211.

27. Nora, "Between Memory and History," 8.
28. Schopenhauer, *On the Fourfold Root*.
29. Ezrahi, *By Words Alone*, 10.
30. Sicher, *Breaking Crystal*, 21.
31. Adorno, *Aesthetic Theory*.
32. Ezrahi, *By Words Alone*, 10.
33. Ibid., 11.

Disclosure statement

No potential conflict of interest was reported by the authors.

Bibliography

Adorno, Theodor W. *Aesthetic Theory*. Edited by Gretel Adorno and Rolf Tiedemann. Translated by Robert Hullot-Kentor. London: Continuum, 2004.

Erll, Astrid, and Ann Rigney. *Mediation, Remediation and the Dynamics of Cultural Memory*. New York: Walter de Gruyter, 2009.

Ezrahi, Sidra Dekoven. *By Words Alone: The Holocaust in Literature*. Chicago, IL: University of Chicago Press, 1982.

Foucault, Michel. "Of Other Spaces: Utopias and Heterotopias." *Diacritics* 16, no. 1 (1986): 22–27.

Giaccaria, Paolo, and Claudio Minca. *Hitler's Geographies: The Spatialities of the Third Reich*. Chicago: University of Chicago Press, 2016.

Hoelscher, Steven, and Derek Alderman. "Memory and Place: Geographies of a Critical Relationship." *Social and Cultural Geography* 5, no. 3 (2004): 347–355.

Huyssen, Andreas. *Present Pasts: Urban Palimpsests and the Politics of Memory*. Stanford, CA: Stanford University Press, 2003.

Klein, Dennis. "Foreword: The Fate of Holocaust Literature." In *Holocaust Literature: A Handbook of Critical, Historical, and Literary Writings*, edited by Saul S. Friedman, xiii–xvii. London: Greenwood Press, 1993.

Langer, Lawrence. *The Holocaust and the Literary Imagination*. London: Yale University Press, 1975.

Lefebvre, Henri. *Introduction to Modernity*. Translated by John Moore. London: Verso, (1962) 2011.

Levi, Primo. *The Drowned and the Saved*. Portsmouth: Abacus, 1989.

Mitchell, W. J. T. "Translator Translated: Interview with Cultural Theorist Homi Bhabha." *Artforum* 33, no. 7 (1995): 80–84.

Nora, Pierre. "Between Memory and History: Les Lieux de Mémoire." *Representations* 26 (1989): 7–24.

Rothberg, Michael. *Multidirectional Memory: Remembering the Holocaust in the Age of Decolonisation*. Stanford, CA: Stanford University Press, 2009.

Rutherford, Jonathon. "The Third Space: Interview With Homi Bhaba." *Identity, Community, Culture, Difference*, 207–221. London: Lawrence and Wishart, 1990.

Sanyal, Debarati. *Memories and Complicity: Migrations of Holocaust Remembrance*. New York: Fordham University Press, 2015.

Schopenhauer, Arthur. *On the Fourfold Root of the Principle of Sufficient Reason and Other Writings*. Edited by David E. Cartwright, Edward E. Erdmann, and Christopher Janaway. Cambridge: Cambridge University Press, (1847) 2012.

Sicher, Efraim. *Breaking Crystal: Writing and Memory after Auschwitz*. Urbana, IL and Chicago: University of Illinois Press, 1998.

Soja, Edward W. *Thirdspace: Journeys to Los Angeles and Other Real-and-Imagined Places*. Oxford: Blackwell, 1996.

Life in space, space in life: Nazi topographies, geographical imaginations, and *Lebensraum*

Paolo Giaccaria[a] and Claudio Minca[b]

[a]Department of Economics, Social Studies Applied Mathematics and Statistics, University of Turin, Turin, Italy; [b]Human Geography Group, Wageningen University, Wageningen, The Netherlands

ABSTRACT
This article focuses on the pivotal role the notion of *Lebensraum* played within the Nazi spatial mindscape. Tracing the complex and contradictory genealogies of Lebensraum, we note how geographers' engagement with *Geopolitik* has only made modest reference to the role Lebensraum played in shaping the biopolitical and genocidal machinery implemented by Hitlerism and its followers. Moreover, most of this literature highlights a clear discontinuity between the Lebensraum concept formulated by German academic geographers and the Nazis respectively. Rather than emphasizing the divide between German *Geopolitik* and Nazi biopolitics, we claim that the Third Reich incorporated Lebensraum by merging its duplicitous meaning, as living/vital space and as life-world. Equality important were both Nazi 'functionalist' understandings of Lebensraum as well as its ontological merging of *Lebens* and *Raum* in which the racialised German nation is conceived as a spatial organism whose expansion is the essential expression of life. As such, we approach the Nazi *Lebensraum* grand imagery as a truly geo-bio-political dispositif, in which life and space matched with no gap, no residues. The attempted realisation of this perfect coincidence, we argue, contributed in a crucial way to produce spaces of eviction and displacement and, ultimately, genocide, and annihilation.

The Nazi *Weltanschauung*, the Nazi "worldview," was deeply entangled with spatiality and spatial concepts,[1] among which *Lebensraum* – that is, "living" but also "vital" space – played a particularly significant role. The Third Reich's plans for racial and ethnic reordering of European space in fact entailed endless classifications of groups and individuals and a series of subsequent (mostly forced) movements in order to fit the population distribution into a stable, hierarchical, racial order that was at the same time biopolitical and geopolitical in nature. While the Nazi grand geographies found their key localization and materialization in the Nazi "concentrationary archipelago" of camps, they entailed a broader set of topographies spanning from the territorial to the Final Solution, from early deportation in 1938 to ghettoization, from mass shooting in Ukraine and Belarus during Operation Barbarossa to the Death Marches in the last weeks of war. All these genocidal moments were topographical, not only in the trivial sense that they happened "somewhere";[2] they were intrinsically topographical because space was, at the same time, an objective and a rationale for such practices "to take place." The Holocaust should then be contextualized within the Nazi search for territorial expansion, their quest for land to respond to the needs of a *Volk ohne Raum*, a "people with no space," to recall the title of an influential fiction book penned in 1926 by Völkish author Hans Grimm.[3] Space was also a rationale for genocide: spatial segregation in ghettoes and camps "naturally" increased mortality,[4] they were planned and managed and often integrated with the surrounding cities and regions,[5] the related forced mobilities accurately routinized,[6] and turned into additional occasions for torture and murder,[7] the forests to perform and hide mass shooting.[8]

However, these "topographical imaginations" were at work in German culture decades before the rise of the Third Reich, inside and outside of academic geography, including cognate disciplines[9] and in popular discourse,[10] spreading a geographical culture that spanned from maps to comics, from propaganda to fiction.[11] *Lebensraum*, conceived by the Nazi ideologues as a specialized *Weltanschauung* focused on Eastern Europe, together with its "mindscapes,"[12] its literary and artistic imaginations,[13] and its academic expertise,[14] may thus be a fruitful spatial metaphor to investigate in order to gain new insights into those topographical imaginations that operated as "conditions of possibility" for the genocidal practices implemented by the Third Reich. This article thus focuses on the pivotal role played by the notion of *Lebensraum* within the Nazi spatial mindscape, and aims at repositioning this notion at the very heart of Hitler's geographies of ordering, forced eviction, and, eventually, extermination.

The idea of *Lebensraum* has been often presented by academic geographers[15] and scholars of cognate disciplines[16] as key to understanding the relationship between Nazism and German *Geopolitik*. From Friedrich Ratzel's path-breaking definition, to Adolf Hitler and Heinrich Himmler's popular use of the term, passing through Rudolf Kjellen and Karl Haushofer's different readings of *Geopolitik*, the concept of *Lebensraum* is marked by complex and contradictory genealogies that deserve close investigation.[17] *Lebensraum*, in the context of the German *Geopolitik*, usually referred to the idea of living space vital to the body of the German *Volk*, "the German people" understood in both socio-cultural and racial terms. Here, we suggest to approach the *Lebensraum* concept as a field of tensions between life and space, and to study its Nazi understanding as an ambivalent yet unique field in which a functionalistic geopolitical tradition coexisted with a millennial and ontological understanding of both *life* and *space*. From this perspective, the Nazi *Lebensraum* grand imagery may be read as a geo-bio-political ideology, perhaps even a spatial ontology,[18] according to which life and space should have been made to match.[19] The attempted realization of this perfect coincidence on the part of Nazi ideologues and high ranks, we conclude, contributed in a crucial way to produce spaces of eviction and displacement and, ultimately, genocide and annihilation.

The article is organized into three sections. First, we discuss the genealogy of *Lebensraum* in reference to the discipline of Geography and to German colonial and imperial imaginations and practices. The second section is accordingly dedicated to the "functionalist" understanding of *Lebensraum* that consolidated in the intellectual climate of the Weimar Republic: *Lebensraum* as an actual living/vital space to secure the survival and the prosperity of the German people. In this sense, Hitler's understanding of *Lebensraum* seemed entirely in line with a tradition that, on the one hand, appropriates Ratzel's and Haushofer's geographical thought – although rather problematically – as well as the actual geographies of the Wilhelmine colonial practice together with the main tenets of the longstanding *Ostforschung* (literally, research on the East); on the other hand, this understanding of *Lebensraum* responds to the topographic calculative rationalities of the Nazi state.[20] At the same time, as discussed in the third section, *Lebensraum* was a key expression of Nazi racialized spatial imaginations and the product of an essentially ontological relationship between *life* and *space*.[21]

This is why here we propose to move beyond the more conventional philological and historical accounts that highlight the sharp distinction between early interpretations of *Lebensraum* and its successive "application" by the Nazi regime, pervaded by biological racism.[22] What this article tries to show is that "the functional" and "the ontological" understandings of *Lebensraum* converged in the Third Reich grand geographical imaginations, presenting a rather messy but powerful combination of diverse values, metaphors, meanings, and practices. This makes it difficult if not impossible to operate a distinction between *life* and *space*, between biopolitics and geopolitics, since the Third Reich incorporated *Lebensraum* by merging its duplicitous meaning, as living/vital space *and* as life-world.

Lebensraum, geography, colonialism

It has been fully acknowledged by now that geographers played a role in inspiring Nazi spatial plans and imaginations,[23] within which the emphasis placed on *Lebensraum* by the *Geopolitik* project[24] coexisted with visions of order and geometry based on "central place theory," both part of Hitler's grand imperialist projections.[25] In the English-speaking world, popular and middlebrow policy narratives have traditionally depicted geographer Karl Haushofer as the "evil genius" of Hitlerism.[26] This somewhat exaggerated emphasis on Haushofer's role in the Nazi hierarchy persisted well after the end of the Second World War and projected a stigma of sorts on German *Geopolitik* and, more broadly, on geopolitics.[27] A critical reassessment of German political geography and geopolitics only started in the 1980s thanks to the efforts of a group of German geographers[28] and geographer Mark Bassin.[29] The relationship between geography and Nazism – and accordingly the concept of *Lebensraum* – was at the core of a new important debate about a decade later, with new contributions from both historians[30] and geographers.[31] The "*Geopolitik* debate" of those years was particularly concerned with the presumed affinity (and continuity) between Ratzel's and Haushofer's geographies, and this latter's influence on Rudolf Hess's and Hitler's spatial formulations of politics and policy.

Arguably, most of this literature highlights clear elements of discontinuity in how *Lebensraum* was formulated by German academic geographers and the Nazis respectively, somehow reflecting the fundamental "race contra space" perspective as presented by Bassin in his key 1987 article with the same title.[32] Bassin, in fact, places particular emphasis on Ratzel's environmental determinism and on how this vision of the "man-environment" relationship,"[33] shared also by Haushofer, was irreconcilable with the Nazi obsessions with race:

> … the National Socialists were quite willing to acknowledge the connection of man with the environment, for this was entirely in line with the *völkish* emphasis on the rootedness of the

Volk in the natural landscape. However, the suggestion that this relationship might be subject to inflexible laws, and involves human subjection through dependency on the environment, violated notions of the primacy of racial strength and initiative.[34]

A decade later, historian David Murphy reasserted Bassin's assessment on this discontinuity:

> [...] the greatest discordance between geopolitical thought and Nazi policy lies in the role of race in the two respective worldviews. For geopoliticians race was important, but it always remained subordinated to space. [...] *Raum*, not *Rasse*, was at the core of their understanding of the world. For Hitler and his closest followers [...] race eclipsed all other considerations, including space. The racial restructuring of German society was at the heart of Nazi domestic policies, and race was equally central to their foreign policy.[35]

While Haushofer's influence – and indirectly Ratzel's – appeared less important compared to how it was depicted by the American propaganda machine of the 1940s,[36] clear elements of structural contiguity between academic geography and what Jeffrey Herf has famously named "reactionary modernism"[37] have been delineated, a contiguity that had implications for the shaping of the Third Reich "geographical imaginations."[38] This "rule of experts" is particularly evident in the role that *Geopolitik* and the *Ostforschung* played in connecting previous German colonial imaginations and Nazi Eastern geographical fantasies.[39] Both *Geopolitik* and *Ostforschung* had their roots in nineteenth-century Germany and were not fields exclusive to the Third Reich. However, during the Weimar Republic the leading scholars of these fields (Haushofer and historian Albert Brackmann) repositioned them into the sphere of Völkish revisionism and started "working towards the Fuhrer,"[40] contributing to the Nazi propagandistic jargon and *Weltanschauung*.[41] Geographers, in particular, having given a distinct contribution to the formulation and popularization of both *Geopolitik* and *Ostforschung*, played a key role in the continuity of these spatial imaginations and spatial strategies between the two phases of colonization: from the links between the work of Ratzel, of Ferdinand von Richthofen, and German imperialism in Namibia,[42] to the contribution given by geographers like Albrecht Penck, Wilhelm Volz, and Karl Haushofer[43] in shaping a specifically colonial spatial imagination of the *Ostland*.[44]

The Third Reich expansionism on the Eastern Front was indeed unique in its extremist declinations of modern biopolitics, based on a radical interpretation of racial and biological hierarchies. However, this radicalization did not happen in a void, since both Nazi biopolitics and Nazi geopolitics originated and developed within specific political, professional, and academic circles, all sharing strong concerns about some fundamental issues associated to Germany's place in the world: Versailles' humiliating impositions, the diaspora of the *Volksdeutsche* in Europe, the antagonism of other colonial powers, the relationship with Eastern Europe, and the communist threat. These circles also shared, to some extent, the belief in the potential solutions, often gravitating around ideas of a new German *Lebensraum* to be realized in Eastern Europe, of anti-communist militancy, and of a deeply rooted *Volkskörper* founded on historically remote and mythical origins. As Andrew Zimmerman has clearly demonstrated,[45] an important component of the anthropology practiced under the Wilhelmine regime was marked by an explicit racist form of anti-humanism, something strongly related to the culture driving the colonial project of the day.

Yet the point of this article is not to address the historiographical *vexata quaestio* related to continuities/contiguities between the Third Reich and the various academic, cultural, and popular movements that populated German society in the decades before Hitler's seizure of power. The question of continuity/contiguity, in fact, concerns the *Lebensraum* debate as much as other areas of investigation, such as the relationship with Wilhelmine colonialism[46] or with German ecologism and regionalism.[47] We propose here a different take on *Lebensraum*, and read space and race as mutually constitutive terms in the bio-geopolitical imaginations pervading Nazi spatial ideologies. As noted above, often the notion of *Lebensraum* is presented as if it were subjected to different interpretations by the advocates of traditional *Geopolitik* compared to the *Völkish* interpretation given by the Nazi ideologues. In the abovementioned "race contra space" approaches, *Lebensraum* is discussed as if its two semantic components, "life" and "space," could be considered as separate, and as if, accordingly, it were possible to think of them in a relationship crucial in determining how the term was translated into practice. This presumed separation, therefore, allowed considering *Lebensraum* as a less problematic notion when "the spatial" was the prevailing element in its interpretations; on the contrary, the genocidal practices of the Nazis could be explained by the emergence, in ideas of *Lebensraum*, of a dominant role played by the politics of "the vital," of life, all the more expressed in pure biological racist terms.

Here, we problematize this separation, and claim that *the question of life* should be analyzed *together with the question of space*, the biopolitical together with the geopolitical, since they merged precisely in the notion of *Lebensraum* to become mutually constitutive of the Nazi grand visions of the German nation, and the related realization of a new German Man.[48] With this we do not intend to a-critically support the "continuity" thesis; quite the contrary. We rather suggest to move beyond that very debate and instead focus on the complex geopolitical and biopolitical genealogies that made Nazi understandings of *Lebensraum*, based as they were on a fundamentally racist *Weltanschauung*, part of a broader array of popular and academic discourses and practices that contributed to the formation of (German) modernity. Again, we do not imply here that all German geographers of that period promoted a racial vision of (vital) space, or that Hitler and the Nazi high ranks simply borrowed accounts of *Lebensraum* from Ratzel and Haushofer, or even that geography was the only social science involved in the formulation of this (again, vital) link between race and space.[49] Rather, the broader Nazi "*Lebensraum* ideology" was the result of the intersections and the entanglements of a series of visions, notions, and inspirations, to which the merging of *life and space* in one single term seemed to offer an ambivalent, contradictory, yet powerful set of answers:

> *Lebensraum* was formed from the conjuncture of several limited ideologies of which migrationist colonialism was only the least diffuse and marginally most central to the aggregation that emerged. In the long run, in fact, extensions of migrationist thinking became more important within the overall structure of *Lebensraum* than migrationist colonialism itself. [...] what the formulators of *Lebensraum* did was to attach to the existing migrationist ideology a number of ideological constructions (especially agrarianism), many of which possessed some of the same social and intellectual roots as migrationist colonialism. [...] *Lebensraum*, radical agrarianism, and a number of other new aggregate ideologies were therefore in some senses parallel and related structures with similar histories and political uses, sharing some of

the same intellectual elements and appealing to similar (but not identical) segments of the German public.[50]

In particular, we suggest to approach the *Lebensraum* concept as a field of tensions between life and space, and to study its Nazi interpretations as an ambivalent yet unique topography in which a functionalistic, geopolitical tradition coexisted with a millennial and ontological understanding of both *life* and *space*. From this perspective, the Nazi *Lebensraum* grand imagery may be read as a *geo-bio-political dispositif*, to borrow the term from Foucault, within which life and space were supposed to identify and match with each other.[51] The attempted realization of this coincidence by some key Nazi ideologues, we argue, contributed in a crucial way to produce topographies of eviction and displacement and, ultimately, genocide and annihilation.

The next section is accordingly dedicated to the "functionalist" understandings of *Lebensraum* that consolidated in the intellectual climate of the Weimar Republic: *Lebensraum* as an actual living/vital space to secure the survival and the prosperity of the German people. In this sense, Nazi *Lebensraum* ideology seems entirely in line with a longstanding tradition that responded to the calculative spatial rationalities of the Nazi state[52] and the making of a topographical imagination about Nazi *Raum*. At the same time, as shown in the third section, *Lebensraum* was also a key concept of Hitlerism,[53] an expression of a radically racialized space and the product of an essentially ontological relationship between *life* and *space*.[54] This is why here we propose to move beyond the more conventional philological and historical accounts that highlight the sharp distinction between the early interpretations of *Lebensraum* and its successive "application" by the Nazi regime, pervaded by biological racism. What we argue is that, in the Nazi grand spatial narratives, "the functional" and "the ontological" *Lebensraum* converged, presenting a powerful assemblage of diverse values, metaphors, meanings, and practices. If this is the case, then to operate in Nazi *Lebensraum* conceptualizations, a distinction between *life* and *space*, a "cut" between biopolitics and geopolitics, may prove difficult if not impossible. The Third Reich, we suggest, incorporated *Lebensraum* by merging its duplicitous meaning, as living/vital space *and* as life-world.

Functional space: *Lebensraum* as living space

> But the bread that a people needs in order to live is determined by the *Lebensraum* that is available to it. A healthy people, at least, will always attempt to satisfy its needs from its own territory and land. Every other situation is sick and dangerous, even if it enables the nourishment of a people for centuries. [...] The most secure basis for the existence of a people has always been its own territory and land. [...] The growth in population could only be compensated by growth – expansion – of the *Lebensraum*. Now, however, a people's number is variable, but the land is a constant. [...] The expansion of the land, however, is limited by the general property distribution of the world and [any change in it] is deemed a particularly revolutionary act and an exceptional process; thus, the ease with which a population can be fed stands in opposition to the exceptional difficulty of territorial alteration.[55]

Within so-called "functionalistic" interpretations, *Lebensraum* was read as "living space," as a space necessary to contain and sustain a population – turning a demographic and statistical fact into biopolitical topography. In the Nazi projections, once conquered, colonized, and planned, this living space should have offered the natural and human resources necessary to the reproduction and development of the German *Volkgemeinschaft* (the people's community).[56] The Nazi response to the given condition of history and geography was the expansion of the Germandom "Further East" and, in particular, into Poland,[57] a kind of colonial expansion increasingly based on rural settlers, aiming at both exploiting the conquered territories and occupying them via extensive migration of German colons. These plans were inspired by a specific colonial geographical imagination centered on the idea of the existence of an underdeveloped space available "out there," waiting to be occupied and walked over by German boots. This vision emerged in many parts of Hitler's *Mein Kampf*[58] and eventually found its most passionate and convinced interpreter in Heinrich Himmler.[59]

In his posthumously published *Second Book*,[60] Hitler extensively disserts on the relationship between colonialism and *Lebensraum*. Here he considers the different strategies available to balance the (functional) relationship between population and space.[61] Hitler's favorite solution was clearly the military acquisition of new *Lebensraum*. Colonization, in his vision, was supposed to be realized by means of a bio-geopolitical process of *völkische Flurbereinigung* (racial redistribution), precisely with the aim of realizing a new *Lebensraum* for the elected *Volk ohne Raum*.

Accordingly, *Lebensraum* could only be found in the European East, where a longstanding geography of German settlements secured racial and cultural continuity with the German *Volksgemeinschaft*. To fully appreciate the nature of these geographical imaginations – originated during the closing decades of the previous century and traveled throughout the First World War and the Weimar period to finally feed into Hitler's geopolitical dreams – it is important to recall, as suggested by geographer Kenneth Olwig, the duplicitous meaning of the term *Raum*, which denotes "room or place," as well as "the open absolute space of the map, upon which place is reduced to a locus in space":[62]

> The *Raum* in *Lebensraum* was an enclosed organic room-like area, with clear links to the habitats of organisms in terrestrial nature, but it also demanded the right to expand in the infinite absolute space of the imperial map. […] The theories of *Lebensraum* […] reified the spatial dynamics observed in natural habitats and then extrapolated these abstracted spatial patterns to the level of the nation-state.[63]

This duplicitous meaning also translated into the genealogies of the European "Further East" as the elected *Lebensraum* for the German *Volk*: on the one hand, the East was presented as a sort of topographic, calculable, and somewhat "empty space," available to be colonized and put to (orderly) use; on the other, the East was a space that, within these same narratives, materialized into an almost telluric notion of place, a porous space capable of embracing and valorizing the intrinsic qualities of the German people, of being inhabited and cultivated by, and even identified with, these people's destiny and *Kultur*.

The emergence of Raum

Historian Vejas Liulevicius clearly highlights the role played by geographical concepts such as *Land*, *Raum*, and *Boden* in shaping the geopolitical and colonial agenda of the Third Reich. In particular, he notes that in the process, the notion of "land," traditionally associated to the contingency of state sovereignty, was progressively dismissed and made redundant by Nazi spatial ideology via a reconfiguration of *Raum*, conceptualized as both

TRACING TOPOGRAPHIES

"space" and "soil," this latter intended as empty, measurable, and available space, a frontier open to colonization.

> the East was to be viewed more objectively and coldly, in terms of *Raum*, "space." [...] It now seemed an undifferentiated East, a chaotic and dirty expanse where unmanageable, intrinsically backward, and unclean populations lurked, all part of some vast, threatening presence: the "Ost." A crucial transformation was completed, as the terms of "Land und Leute," "lands and peoples," [...] were overthrown, while new operative terms took their place, another resonant pairing: "*Volk und Raum*," "race and space." "*Volk*," now intoned to stress the term's racial sense, reduced "foreign peoples" to carriers of unchangeable ethnic essences. Their territories, meanwhile, were no longer understood as "lands," areas with history and internal coherence, organization, and meaning all their own. Instead, the category of Land was replaced by a stark, "neutral" concept of *Raum*. Emptied of historical content, *Raum* was triumphantly ahistorical, biological, and "scientific." Empty *Raum* stretched to the eastern horizon, dotted only by scattered races. A decisive conceptual barrier was broken by this formulation of "*Volk und Raum*." Now the lands and peoples were stripped of any legitimate claim to independent existence and stood bare as objects and numbers, resources to be exploited and exhausted.[64]

Raum was thus conjugated by mainstream Nazi spatial ideology according to a dual articulation. On the one hand, *Raum* read as topography, the result of a well-established calculative and cartographic rationality. It was therefore available to and part of the related practices of planning, management, and control. On the other hand, however, when part of Nazi *Lebensraum* projections, *Raum* was often intended as empty space open to German colonization, a space made available to a *Volk ohne Raum*, a people with no (sufficient) space, whose organic expansion was constrained by their insufficient spatial conditions.[65]

The presumed and/or imagined emptiness of (others') space is indeed a trope that has traditionally characterized European colonial geographical imaginations. Robert Nelson, for example, has brought a wealth of evidence on how German colonial imaginations portraying Poland as an empty space were already populating the discourses of *inneren Kolonisation* (inner colonization) and justifying the creation of the Royal Prussian Settlement Commission in the Provinces of West Prussia and Posen in 1886, the Archive for Inner Colonization in 1908, and the Society for the Advancement of Inner Colonization in 1912 – to name three foundational moments of a longstanding process that culminated in the tensions and the malaise of the Weimar years:

> This was of course a colonial fantasy of virgin land, the vacuum domicilium that the colonial gaze always seeks, and a vision constantly spoiled by the restless Poles moving throughout the German colonial landscape. [...] This colonial paradox, the realization that land was both empty and full at the same time, empty for colonizers, but full of "problem" populations, was at the heart of inner colonization.[66]

The embodiment of Raum: Volk, Boden, Kultur

This rather abstract transformation of *Land* into *Raum* was matched by a move toward the materialization of these same imagined geographies. *Raum* was thus also translated into "place," which, in the Weimarian, and eventually Nazi, spatial mythological realm took the form of soil, of German *Boden*.[67] It is in the geographies of the Weimarian *Ostforschung* that this "telluric" connotation of *Raum* first emerged. Already in 1925,

18

geographer Albrecht Penck introduced a clear distinction between terms like *Staatsboden*, *Volksboden*, and *Kulturboden* in his influential essay "*Deutscher Volks-und Kulturboden*,"[68] all categories further developed by another mainstream geographer, Wilhelm Volz.

The theoretical concept of the German *Volks und Kulturboden* (*Boden*, "soil") contained three different "territories": first, the German Reich, in principle within the state borders; second, the German *Volks-Boden* ("ethnic territory"), a wider area mainly settled by German people; and third, the *Kultur-Boden* ("cultural area"), an even wider area, where German cultural influence in the broadest sense was predominant. The latter stood in marked contrast to the actual political frontiers. It was of fundamental importance to geographical research until 1945.[69]

From Penck's standpoint, the German "cultural soil" in Eastern Europe was "characterized by an extremely careful form of cultivation which does not grind to a halt when it encounters difficulties."[70] Moreover, Penck argued that "the German cultural landscape does not result from the interaction of various natural causes, but is the work of people with definite natural abilities, who change nature according to their wills."[71] This statement has important implications for our main argument. The topographical notion of *Raum* is here accompanied and complemented by a cultural notion of *Boden* that goes well beyond the state territory. If this cultural definition makes it particularly difficult to identify the actual German *Boden* in its tripartite articulation, at the same time its ambivalence allows us to think of it as a spatial body constantly remade through a set of variable topographies, a space therefore open to the expansionist projections of the Third Reich. In other words, if the *Volksboden* and the *Kulturboden* were of a different nature compared to the contingent realities of the *Staatsboden*, it was inevitable for the German *Volk* to go beyond the borders of the German state in order to make their *Lebensraum* finally coincide with their *Volksboden* and *Kulturboden*.

Accordingly, *Volksboden* and *Kulturboden* were conceived as spatial "bodies" in relation to the *longue durée* of a people, a trajectory of historical continuity where past and present were supposed to become one and the same. Wilhelm Volz, deliberately drawing from Penck's work, explained that "the soil has been Teutonic-German *Volksboden* for 3000 years" and that "already in the 10th century the German resettlement begins. Higher German *Kultur* triumphed over primitive Slavdom; there Germans wrested massive areas of new settlement land from the primeval forest."[72]

These readings somehow resuscitated the mythical temporalities of the medieval colonization of Eastern Europe on the part of the Teutonic Knights, a temporality explicitly recalled by the Nazi Freikorps fighters first[73] and Himmler later;[74] these temporalities ended up also inspiring the medieval model of colonization of the "Eastern Lands"[75] celebrated in particular by economist and urban planner Gottfried Feder in his influential writings.[76] For the Nazis, this historical continuity based on the idea of *Kulturboden* was essentially racial and vitalistic in nature. Even Hitler, in his critique of past German colonialism, explicitly mentioned the necessary link between the culture and the life of a *Volk*:

> Now, it was noteworthy that especially in the nineteenth century, a general pull toward colonization affected all peoples; the original governing idea, however, had already given way completely. Germany, for example, justified its right to colonize with its competence and its desire to disseminate German culture. This is nonsense. Because one cannot transmit culture, which is a general expression of the life of a certain people, to any other people with a completely different mindset.[77]

The impossibility of "transmitting culture" for Hitler and his closest ideologues was due to the essentially different "racial quality" of the various people, and to the fundamental purity and health of their collective body. In this way, Hitlerism marked a first bifurcation between the Nazi understanding of *Lebensraum* and the context in which this very idea originated and was made popular. Consequently, for Himmler, the Nazi project "in the East is not germanization in the former sense of the term, that is, imposing German language and laws upon the population, but to ensure that only people of pure German blood inhabit the East."[78]

Such a vision then goes well beyond the functionalist interpretation of *Lebensraum* described above that was popular during the previous decades not only in Germany but also in the United States and the rest of Europe.[79] Hitler's *Lebensraum*, while having been somehow prepared by long-term tropes of racial and cultural difference translated into geopolitical projections in the preceding decades, incorporated at the same time something entirely new and different.

Ontological space: *Lebens-Raum* as life-world

> Our demand for strengthening the basic racial principles of our *Volk* […] is also the determining factor in all of the aims of National Socialist domestic and foreign policy. Once we have succeeded in purging and regenerating our *Volk*, foreign countries will very soon realize that they are confronted with a different *Volk* from hitherto. And thus the prerequisites will be given for putting our own land and soil in thorough order and securing the life of the nation on our own for long years to come. […] if the German peasant, the foundation and life source of our *Volk*, is saved, then the entire nation will once again be able to look ahead to the future with confidence.[80]

In the Nazi progression toward total mobilization and war, soil, culture, and race ended up inhabiting, so to speak, the same ontological field, and substantially merged. Therefore, to appreciate the deeply biopolitical foundation of mainstream Nazi *Lebensraum* ideology, it is useful to depart from its most conventional functionalist interpretations, and approach it "ontologically," as a "life-world," as a condition of being (of the Aryan being) projected toward the actual coming together of (German) life and space. As observed, again, by Olwig:

> *Raum* became diabolic in a way that would not have occurred if its use were more clearly understood to be symbolic. A symbol is something that is understood to stand for something else, as when the pattern on the colored material of the flag, or the chorographic pattern outlined on the map, stands for the abstract notion of the nation. This becomes problematic, however, when the symbolic representation becomes confounded with the abstract represented. […] The Second World War was, of course, to a certain extent the outcome of an attempt to make the boundaries of the German state conform to the space of this map, which transcended the complex of places, with varying ethnic identities, that made up the territory within its spatial boundaries.[81]

Life-world

In order to examine the deeper biopolitical nature of the link between space and life as established by Nazi ideology and spatial practice, it is helpful to engage with the distinction introduced by historian Boaz Neumann, between *Lebensraum* intended as "living space" and *Lebens-Raum* as "life-world."[82] This distinction in fact allows us to read the Nazi formulation of *Lebensraum* as the unique coming together of two bio-geopolitical visions: the first, topographical, produced and implemented by German colonialism; the second, driven by a millennial, ontological interpretation of the term/concept. Hitler himself seemed to assume in his writings the need for a necessary coincidence between "the spatial" and "the biological": "[w]hat we desire is […] our freedom, our security, the securing of our *Lebensraum*. It is the securing of our *Volk*'s life itself."[83]

For Neumann, we should therefore engage with the existence of a Nazi biopolitical *Weltanschauung*.[84] The language of Nazism, he argues, did not only translate ideology into symbols and metaphors, but was an eminent manifestation of a *Weltanschauung* directly linked to a related life experience,[85] and in particular to *Anschauung*, the act of seeing: "whereas the activity of mind is based on ideas, *Anschauung* enables one to experience life as a living experience."[86] Accordingly, the *Volkskörper* should not be understood as a mere biopolitical metaphor denoting an organic conceptualization of the state and the nation, but rather:

> the *Volkskörper* in the Nazi *Weltanschauung* should be viewed as the manifestation of an actual, concrete body. […] The Nazi corporeal ontology did not rest on the individual's body, since such a body was vulnerable to biological "whim." The individual body was one that invariably decayed. The Nazi corporeal ontology was based, instead, on a body that did not degenerate. This was the *Volkskörper*, whose existence was autonomous of this or that specific body. The *Volkskörper* was manifested in the Nazi *Weltanschauung* as a result of corporeal catastrophe and trauma.[87]

In other words, life and race stopped being considered as mere biological categories. They became spatio-ontological ones.[88] If the *Volkskörper* was in need of care and prosthesis,[89] its very scars and amputations/mutilations were *in primis* spatial: "Filled with the conviction that the causes of this collapse lie in internal injury to the body of our *Volk*, the government of the national revolution aims to eliminate the afflictions from our national life that would, in future, continue to foil any real recovery."[90]

The illness of the German body politic was indeed mainly expressed as the result of the penetration operated by alien bodies, of border violations of this real-and-imagined German bio-geopolitical space. Sandra Mass describes this identification between the individual body and the people's body, between the individual space and the spaces of the *Volk*:

> The obsession with interracial sexuality and the sexualized language by which acts of rape and non-respectable sexuality were described, were found in the semantic and allegorical analogies appearing in speeches made about the threatened *Volkskörper*. The "humiliation" of the nation was described in anatomical metaphors. The assault on the female body in the texts therefore metonymically stood for the political situation and the generally prevalent idea of crisis and threat. The Versailles Treaty was interpreted as a ripping apart of the community, as a "shameful rape," where the loss of certain German territories was compared to "the foreign powers tearing pieces out of the body of the German Reich." […] With the allegorical representation of the "raped nation" and the reference to the "tearing away of pieces of the national body," the propagandists combined images of individual and collective bodies and connected them with the loss of *Raum* in the West.[91]

According, again, to Neumann, "once space was conceived as a real organic body, the Polish Corridor, established by the Treaty of Versailles to separate East Prussia from the rest of Germany, could be considered a 'bleeding wound,' and the 'Versailles Diktat' a cause of 'bleeding borders'."[92] In this vein, for example, in 1927 Haushofer paralleled the loss of German territory to "unhealed burns in the outer skin of the *Volkskörper*,"[93] while just two years later Goebbels described the Treaty of Versailles as "an open, bleeding, life-threatening wound on the Körper of the German *Volk*."[94] This (spatial) "subjection to injuries" was aggravated by the growing urbanization:

> In the metropolis, the adherents of *Raum* discovered the interface where space clearly displayed a pathology of its own, manifesting itself as an organic force which might be healthy or unhealthy and whose configuration had a drastically damaging biological impact upon its human inhabitants. Exposure to the urban *Raum*, many believed, produced dangerous political effects as well. [...] The conviction that the urban *Raum* constituted a geomedical danger for German political and racial survival was one that its adherents were able to convey to a broad public in a number of venues during the interwar era.[95]

The coincidence between life and space had thus to be conceived as "total," and essentially ontological in nature: Germany was to be thought "not only as an organism in *Raum*, but in a much deeper sense as a spatial organism grown out of *Raum*."[96] Neumann finally claims that the Nazi "notion of *Lebensraum* was not of a living space, but a life-world. Its role was not to provide the resources necessary for maintaining life: it was the expression of life itself."[97] For mainstream Nazi spatial ideology, *Volkskörper* and *Lebensraum* therefore ought to perfectly and immediately coincide, to establish a relationship of identity with no remnants or gaps, a life-world ontologically founded on a specific millennial vision of life.

Blut und Boden

Such an ontological approach to *Lebens-Raum* was also clearly expressed by the Nazis' belief in the need for absolute coincidence between ideology (to be experienced, indeed, as an ontology) and practice,[98] and in the related rhetoric of *Blut und Boden* (literally "blood and soil"), that is, "the idea that a necessary affinity existed between the optimal exploitation of a certain type of natural environment and a certain pure racial type."[99] The ideology of *Blut und Boden* in fact elided the abovementioned threshold between life and space: while blood, understood as a biological and racial fact, materialized life in the body politic of the German nation and in each of its members, the notion of soil turned abstract ideas of space into actual spatial practices.

The ideology of *Blut und Boden*, like that of *Lebensraum*, was also characterized by a complex genealogy that preceded and went beyond its reception by Nazi mainstream propaganda. According to Hau,[100] its origin refers back to the *Lebensreform* movement at the end of the nineteenth century; a movement concerned with the popularization of healthy practices like nudism and vegetarianism, and more in general with an idealized "return" to rural life and its related values, as opposed to urbanization and its cosmopolitan cultures. In particular, *Blut und Boden* values gained full recognition within agrarianist movements like the Artaman League emerging in the 1920s as part of the German Youth Movement, in which both Heinrich Himmler and Walter Darrè were involved.[101] Darrè was indeed a key figure in promoting the symbiotic relationship between blood and soil, between life and space, biopolitics and geopolitics. For Clifford Lovin, "Darré felt that the Nordic race was superior and that one of the chief reasons was its closeness to the soil. And he believed that the race had another principal source of primacy in its biological makeup or, as he put it, in the purity of the blood."[102]

According to David Woodruff Smith, it was precisely with the notion of *Blut und Boden* that the merging of the racial and the spatial into the Nazis' bio-geopolitics was initiated:

> The basic assumptions of *Lebensraum* ideology focused on culture and environment, not race. Both intellectually and in terms of constructing a politically effective argument, the functional link between *Lebensraum* and biological racism was made in the 1920s. [...] In the 1920s, it became customary to argue that both genetic and environmental factors played significant roles in the composition of a *Volk* and that the true German *Volk* could not survive and prosper without a national policy that took account of both. The physical and mental strength of the Germanic race lay in its unusual ability to realize its full potential through interaction with nature in a challenging rural environment. [...] Races such as the Slavs and the Jews, for example, were unsuited to efficient individual peasant farming and could not, even under the best of circumstances, play their proper, biologically determined roles in such a setting.[103]

The contact with and the related rooting in the *Boden* is what produced and allowed for the purity of the German *Volk*. At the same time, the biological elements rooted in the German *Kultur* is what made it capable of transforming uncultivated land into a genuine German *Boden*, infused with the genetic "qualities" of the German people:[104] "it was not state borders but the capacity of a race to etch its culture into the land that provided the decisive justification of ownership."[105] This was, crucially, the cultural context in which the specifically Himmlerian geopolitical imaginary took shape, including the figure of the soldier-peasant (*Wehrbauer*), and the related involvement of SS corps in the colonization of the occupied Eastern European territories.[106]

It is precisely because of this "organic interrelationship of *Blut, Boden* and *Raum*"[107] that biopolitics and geopolitics, in the Nazi context, should not be considered as two separate and distinct phenomena/processes, simply intersecting and overlapping in their spatial practices. They should instead be treated as two fundamentally indistinguishable dimensions of the same bio-spatial ontologies, manifestations of the same life-world in which life and space had to *topographically coincide*, with no gaps, no leftovers. These bio-spatial ontologies, for Hitler and an influential cohort of Nazi racial experts, were deeply rooted into a form of radical immanent worldview, of a true "evolutionary ethics."[108] Accordingly, concepts and ideas did not have their own life, separate and distinct from a specific *Volkskörper* who incorporated them in an equally specific space. As noted by historian Richard Weikart,[109] for Hitler, all human ideas – including ethical ideas – were necessarily tied to human existence. If those humans who uphold a particular idea – whether all of humanity or just one race – perish, their ideas vanish with them: "My Movement, as an expression of will and yearning, encompasses every aspect of the entire *Volk*. It conceives of Germany as a corporate body, as a single organism. There is no such thing as non-responsibility in this organic being, not a single cell which is not responsible, by its very existence, for the welfare and well-being of the whole."[110]

As a consequence, in this life-world ideas and practices were inevitably and biologically determined by race: "as the burgeoning literature on Nazi eugenics has shown [...] Hitler (and many other Nazis) did not draw such a dichotomy between biology and behavior."[111] In the framework of Hitlerism, race, space, *Weltanschauung*, and practice/behavior coincided – or should have coincided – since all the gaps among them ought to be eliminated. In the Nazi imperial projections – driven as they were by the realization of a new German *Lebensraum* – race and space were so tightly entangled, practically and functionally, that they ended up promoting spatial and political conditions in which racism and colonialism, biopolitics and *Geopolitik*, mutually constituted and alimented each other. These entanglements, taken to their extreme consequences by the radical implementation of a set of related policies in the newly colonized Eastern European lands, soon turned *Lebensraum* into a landscape of genocide. What is more, in the Nazi "triumph of *Raum*" – to speak with Liulevicius – of German racialized expansionism, were already present the roots of the collapse and defeat of the Nazi millennial projections – the result of the obsession with space and race that decisively marked the grand visions of the Nazi highest ranks, including Hitler and Himmler:

> The regime used modern techniques for the goal of a terrible future utopia which classical modernity would not recognize, seeking space, rather than development. While the Soviets retreated, "trading space for time," the Nazis gave up time to gain space – seeking an everlasting, timeless present of destructive expansion in their vision of the Ostland. As the tide of events turned in the East, Hitler refused to give up the spaces conquered and forbade withdrawal again and again, producing military disasters. The ideological primacy of *Raum* was fatal in its consequences in the East. At long last, this was brought home to Germans as the Red Army invaded their territory by 1945, turning the utopia of *Raum* into a nightmare of the advancing East.[112]

Coda

In this article we have briefly discussed the debate on the continuities between the original conception of the idea of living/vital space and the Nazi notion of *Lebensraum*, as a way to approach the constellation of conceptual genealogies that made the Nazi colonial ideology possible and largely supported by the German people – an ideology, we have argued, driven by a set of geographical metaphors and spatial theories and practices, and supported by some prominent geographers. Our guiding argument is somehow in line with mainstream interpretations claiming that the Nazi *Lebensraum* was marked by biological racist overtones that were not present in earlier formulations normally attributed to Ratzel and Haushofer. The same may be said for the notion of *Boden* as conceived by the *Blut und Boden* ideology and embraced by, among many others, Darré and Himmler. *Boden* was a far more "biological" notion compared to those of *Volksboden* and the *Kulturboden* proposed by geographers like Penck and Volz. However, at the same time, we resist interpretations that identify a clear and fundamental break between the work of these geographers and the production of Nazi spatial ideologies, that is, in line with the "race contra space" argument as discussed above.

Accordingly, we have suggested that the distinction between *Lebensraum* as a functionalist living space and *Lebens-Raum* as ontological life-world should be read at one time diachronically and synchronically. Diachronically, since the merging of Nazi spatial ideology and practice was the result of a sort of progressive escalation, mainly due to war developments that crucially transformed the meaning of *Lebensraum* in the framework of Hitlerism. Synchronically, because *Lebens-Raum* as a concept was entirely permeated by the actual *Raum* of Eastern Europe, exactly like *Kultur-Boden* always permeated the elaboration of *Blut und Boden* theories and practices. Many populist grand claims from Hitler and other Nazi ideologues reveal a clear tension between functionalist and ontological interpretations of *Lebensraum*, coexisting with and coming across that (often confused and incoherent) coagulation of ideas and practices that made the Nazi spatial ideology and practice as we know them. Indeed, by the moment in which it became a sort of conceptual *passepartout* for a series of rather diverse aspirations, perceptions, and imaginations, the idea of *Lebensraum* could not be contained anymore within the confines of academic discussion of *Geopolitik*. It was in fact incorporated in very popular geopolitical fantasies fueled by the propaganda of the regime, to become part of the genocidal topographical machinery that attempted to produce a perfected millennial *Endreich* – a Reich in which life and space were supposed to fully coincide in the violent materializations of the rather confused but nonetheless powerfully implemented Nazi geo-biopolitical ontologies that we have tried to unravel here.

Notes

1. Giaccaria and Minca, *Hitler's Geographies.*
2. Giaccaria and Minca, "Topographies/Topologies of the Camp."
3. Smith, "Friedrich Ratzel and the Origins of *Lebensraum.*"
4. See Cole, *Holocaust City*; Cole, *Traces of the Holocaust.*
5. Dwork and van Pelt, *Auschwitz.*
6. Sofsky, *The Order of Terror.*
7. Blatman, *The Death Marches.*
8. Giaccaria and Minca, "Nazi Biopolitics."
9. Chiantera-Stutte, "Space, Großraum and Mitteleuropa."
10. Smith, *The Ideological Origins.*
11. Herb, *Under the Map of Germany.*
12. Liulevicius, *War Land on the Eastern Front.*
13. Kopp, *Germany's Wild East.*
14. Burleigh, *Germany Turns Eastwards.*
15. Bassin, "Race Contra Space"; Bassin, "Blood or Soil?"; Heske, "Karl Haushofer"; Herb, "Persuasive Cartography"; Herb, *Under the Map of Germany.*
16. Smith, "Friedrich Ratzel and the Origins of *Lebensraum*"; Smith, *The Ideological Origins*; Murphy, *The Heroic Earth*; Murphy, "'A Sum of the Most Wonderful Things'"; Diner, "Knowledge of Expansion"; Herwig, "Geopolitik."
17. Abrahamsson, "On the Genealogy of *Lebensraum.*"
18. Minca, "Carl Schmitt."
19. Giaccaria and Minca, "Topographies/Topologies of the Camp"; Giaccaria and Minca, "Nazi Biopolitics."
20. Elden, "National Socialism and the Politics of Calculation."
21. Neumann, "The National Socialist Politics of Life."
22. Bassin, "Race Contra Space"; Bassin, "Blood or Soil?"; Murphy, *The Heroic Earth*; Abrahamsson, "On the Genealogy of *Lebensraum.*"
23. Rössler, "Applied Geography and Area Research"; Wolf, "The East as Historical Imagination."
24. Bassin, "Race Contra Space"; Bassin, "Blood or Soil?"
25. Barnes and Minca, "Nazi Spatial Theory"; Barnes and Clayton, "Continental European Geographers."
26. Ó Tuathail, *Critical Geopolitics.*
27. Troll, "Geographic Science in Germany."
28. Mullin, "The Impact of National Socialist Policies"; Heske, "Karl Haushofer"; Fahlbusch, Rössler, and Siegrist, "Conservatism, Ideology and Geography"; Herb, *Under the Map of*

TRACING TOPOGRAPHIES

Germany; Olwig, "The Duplicity of Space"; Kost, "The Conception of Politics"; Rössler, "Applied Geography and Area Research."

29. Bassin, "Race Contra Space"; Bassin, "Imperialism and the Nation State"; Bassin, "Blood or Soil?"
30. Diner, "Knowledge of Expansion"; Kallis, *Fascist Ideology*; Danielsson, "Creating Genocidal Space."
31. Kost, "Anti-Semitism in German Geography"; Wolkersdorfer, "Karl Haushofer and Geopolitics"; Natter, "Geopolitics in Germany"; Natter, "Friedrich Ratzel's Spatial Turn."
32. See also Blackbourn, "The Conquest of Nature."
33. Ibid.
34. Bassin, "Race Contra Space," 126.
35. Murphy, *The Heroic Earth*, 247.
36. Bassin, "Race Contra Space"; Ó Tuathail, *Critical Geopolitics*.
37. Herf, *Reactionary Modernism*.
38. On this see, among others, Fahlbusch, Rössler, and Siegrist, "Conservatism, Ideology and Geography"; Herb, *Under the Map of Germany*; Olwig, "The Duplicity of Space"; Rössler, "Applied Geography and Area Research"; Sandner and Rössler, "Geography and Empire in Germany"; Barnes and Minca, "Nazi Spatial Theory"; Wolf, "The East as Historical Imagination."
39. Liulevicius, *War Land on the Eastern Front*, 253–6.
40. Kershaw, *Hitler 1889–1936*.
41. Burleigh, *Germany Turns Eastwards*.
42. See Danielsson, "Creating Genocidal Space"; also Zimmerer, "In Service of Empire."
43. Hagen, "Mapping the Polish Corridor"; Wolf, "The East as Historical Imagination."
44. Liulevicius, *War Land on the Eastern Front*.
45. Zimmerman, *Anthropology and Antihumanism in Imperial Germany*.
46. Zimmerer, "Colonialism and the Holocaust"; Zimmerer, "The Birth of the Ostland"; Fitzpatrick, "The Pre-history of the Holocaust?"
47. Brüggemeier, Cioc, and Zeller, *How Green Were the Nazis?*
48. Fritzsche, *Life and Death in the Third Reich*.
49. See, for example, Stone, "White Men with Low Moral Standards?"; Penny and Bunzl, *Worldly Provincialism*.
50. Smith, *The Ideological Origins*, 84.
51. Giaccaria and Minca, "Topographies/Topologies of the Camp"; Giaccaria and Minca, "Nazi Biopolitics."
52. Elden, "National Socialism and the Politics of Calculation."
53. Levinas, "Reflections on the Philosophy of Hitlerism."
54. Neumann, "The National Socialist Politics of Life."
55. Hitler, *Hitler's Second Book*, 16.
56. Kühne, *Belonging and Genocide*.
57. Burleigh, *Germany Turns Eastwards*.
58. Musiedlak, "L'espace totalitaire d'Adolf Hitler."
59. Longerich, *Heinrich Himmler*.
60. Hitler, *Hitler's Second Book*.
61. Ibid., 19–27.
62. Olwig, "The Duplicity of Space," 13.
63. Ibid., 3, 14.
64. Liulevicius, *War Land on the Eastern Front*, 252.
65. Bassin, "Race Contra Space"; Bassin, "Imperialism and the Nation State."
66. Nelson, *Germans, Poland, and Colonial Expansion*, 72, 75.
67. Burleigh, *Germany Turns Eastwards*, 25–31; Liulevicius, *War Land on the Eastern Front*, 255.
68. Heske, "Karl Haushofer."
69. Rössler, "Geography and Area Planning," 62.
70. Burleigh, *Germany Turns Eastwards*, 26.

71. Ibid.
72. Volz, 1926, in Burleigh, *Germany Turns Eastwards*, 28.
73. Liulevicius, *War Land on the Eastern Front*, 234–5.
74. Longerich, *Heinrich Himmler*, 273.
75. Mullin, "The Impact of National Socialist Policies."
76. Schenk and Bromley. "Mass-Producing Traditional Small Cities"; Hagen, "Mapping the Polish Corridor."
77. Hitler, *Hitler's Second Book*, 162.
78. Himmler, in Liulevicius, *War Land on the Eastern Front*, 268.
79. Kühl, *The Nazi Connection*; Stone, "White Men with Low Moral Standards?"; Turda and Weindling, *Blood and Homeland*.
80. Hitler, 1933, in Domarus, *The Essential Hitler's Speeches and Commentaries*, 321–2.
81. Olwig, "The Duplicity of Space," 4.
82. Neumann, "The National Socialist Politics of Life," 112, 115.
83. Hitler, in Domarus, *The Essential Hitler's Speeches and Commentaries*, 161.
84. Neumann, "The National Socialist Politics of Life," 109.
85. Koonz, *The Nazi Conscience*.
86. Neumann, "The National Socialist Politics of Life," 117.
87. Neumann, "The Phenomenology of the German People's Body," 154, 156.
88. Neumann, "The National Socialist Politics of Life," 121.
89. Neumann, "Being Prosthetic in the First World War."
90. Hitler, in Domarus, *The Essential Hitler's Speeches and Commentaries*, 225.
91. Mass, "The 'Volkskörper' in Fear," 237–8.
92. Ibid., 167.
93. Ibid., 235.
94. Neumann, "The Phenomenology of the German People's Body," 158.
95. Murphy, "A Sum of the Most Wonderful Things," 126.
96. Maull 1925, in Murphy, "A Sum of the Most Wonderful Things" 124.
97. Neumann, "The National Socialist Politics of Life," 115.
98. Ibid., 109.
99. Smith, *The Ideological Origins*, 243.
100. Hau, "The Holistic Gaze in German Medicine."
101. Bramwell, *Blood and Soil*.
102. Lovin, "*Blut und Boden*."
103. Smith, *The Ideological Origins*, 212–13.
104. Weiss, *The Nazi Symbiosis*.
105. Blackbourn, "The Conquest of Nature," 158.
106. Neumann, "The National Socialist Politics of Life," 112.
107. Pinwinkler, "Volk, Bevölkerung, Rasse, and Raum," 93.
108. Weikart, *Hitler's Ethic*, 2–16.
109. Ibid., 45.
110. Hitler, in Domarus, *The Essential Hitler's Speeches and Commentaries*, 171–2.
111. Weikart, *Hitler's Ethic*, 88.
112. Liulevicius, *War Land on the Eastern Front*, 272.

Disclosure statement

No potential conflict of interest was reported by the authors.

Bibliography

Abrahamsson, Christian. "On the Genealogy of *Lebensraum*." *Geographica Helvetica* 68 (2013): 37–44.

Baranowsky, Shelley. *Nazi Empire*. Cambridge: Cambridge University Press, 2011.

Barnes, Trevor, and Daniel Clayton. "Continental European Geographers and World War II." *Journal of Historical Geography* 47 (2015): 11–15.

Barnes, Trevor, and Claudio Minca. "Nazi Spatial Theory: The Dark Geographies of Carl Schmitt and Walter Christaller." *Annals of the Association of American Geographers* 103, no. 3 (2013): 669–687.

Bassin, Mark. "Race Contra Space: The Conflict between German Geopolitik and National Socialism." *Political Geography* 6, no. 2 (1987): 115–134.

Bassin, Mark. "Imperialism and the Nation State in Friedrich Ratzel's Political Geography." *Progress in Human Geography* 11 (1987): 473–495.

Bassin, Mark. "Blood or Soil? The Völkisch Movement, the Nazis, and the Legacy of Geopolitik." In *How Green Were the Nazis?*, edited by Franz-Josef Bruggemeier, Mark Cioc, and Thomas Zeller, 204–242. Athens: Ohio University Press, 2005.

Blackbourn, David. "The Conquest of Nature and the Mystique of the Eastern Frontier in Nazi Germany." In *Germans, Poland and Colonial Expansion in the East*, edited by Robert L. Nelson, 141–170. New York: Palgrave MacMillan, 2009.

Blatman, Daniel. *The Death Marches*. Harvard: Belknap Press, 2011.

Bramwell, Anna. *Blood and Soil*. London: Kensal Press, 1985.

Brüggemeier, Franz-Josef, Mark Cioc, and Thomas Zeller. *How Green Were the Nazis?*. Athens: Ohio University Press, 2005.

Burleigh, Michael. *Germany Turns Eastwards*. Cambridge: Cambridge University Press, 1988.

Chiantera-Stutte, Pattricia. "Space, Großraum and Mitteleuropa in Some Debates of the Early Twentieth Century." *European Journal of Social Theory* 11, no. 2 (2008): 185–201.

Cole, Tim. *Holocaust City: The Making of a Jewish Ghetto*. New York: Routledge, 2003.

Cole, Tim. *Traces of the Holocaust*. London: Bloomsbury, 2013.

Danielsson, Sarah K. "Creating Genocidal Space: Geographers and the Discourse of Annihilation, 1880–1933." *Space and Polity* 13, no. 1 (2009): 55–68.

Diner, Dan. "Knowledge of Expansion on the Geopolitics of Karl Haushofer." *Geopolitics* 4, no. 3 (1999): 161–188.

Domarus, Max. *The Essential Hitler's Speeches and Commentaries*. Wauconda: Bolchazy-Carducci, 2007.

Dwork, Deborah, and Robert Jan van Pelt. *Auschwitz*. New York: Norton & Company, 2002.

Elden, Stuart. "National Socialism and the Politics of Calculation." *Social and Cultural Geography* 7, no. 5 (2006): 753–769.

Fahlbusch, Michael, Mechtild Rössler, and Dominik Siegrist. "Conservatism, Ideology and Geography in Germany 1920–1950." *Political Geography* 8, no. 4 (1989): 353–367.

Fitzpatrick, Matthew P. "The Pre-history of the Holocaust? The Sonderweg and Historikerstreit Debates and the Abject Colonial Past." *Central European History* 41, no. 3 (2008): 477–503.

Fritzsche, Peter. *Life and Death in the Third Reich*. Cambridge, MA: Belknap Press, 2008.

Giaccaria, Paolo, and Claudio Minca. "For a Tentative Spatial Theory of the Third Reich." In *Hitler's Geographies*, edited by P. Giaccaria and C. Minca, 19–44. Chicago: Chicago University Press, 2016.

Giaccaria, Paolo, and Claudio Minca, eds. *Hitler's Geographies*. Chicago: Chicago University Press, 2016.

Giaccaria, Paolo, and Claudio Minca. "Nazi Biopolitics and the Dark Geographies of the Selva." *Journal of Genocide Research* 13, no. 1–2 (2011): 67–84.

Giaccaria, Paolo, and Claudio Minca. "Topographies/Topologies of the Camp: Auschwitz as a Spatial Threshold." *Political Geography* 30 (2011): 3–12.

Hagen, Joshua. "Mapping the Polish Corridor: Ethnicity, Economics and Geopolitics." *Imago Mundi* 62, no. 1 (2009): 63–82.

Hau, Michael. "The Holistic Gaze in German Medicine, 1890–1930." *Bulletin of the History of Medicine* 74, no. 3 (2003): 495–524.

Herb, Guntram H. "Persuasive Cartography in Geopolitik and National Socialism." *Political Geography* 8, no. 4 (1989): 289–303.

Herb, Guntram H. *Under the Map of Germany*. London: Routledge, 1997.

Herf, Jeffrey. *Reactionary Modernism*. Cambridge: Cambridge University Press, 1984.

Herwig, Holger. "Geopolitik: Haushofer, Hitler and *Lebensraum*." *Journal of Strategic Studies* 22, no. 2–3 (1999): 218–241.

Heske, Henning. "Karl Haushofer: His Role in German Geopolitics and in Nazi Politics." *Political Geography* 6, no. 2 (1987): 135–144.

Hitler, Adolf. *Hitler's Second Book*. New York: Enigma Books, 2006.

Kakel, Carroll. *The Holocaust as Colonial Genocide*. Basingstoke: Palgrave Macmillan, 2013.

Kallis, Aristotle A. *Fascist Ideology*. London: Routledge, 2001.

Kershaw, Ian. *Hitler 1889–1936*. London: Penguin, 2001.

Knowles, Anne, Tim Cole, and Al Giordano. *Geographies of the Holocaust*. Bloomington: Indiana University Press, 2014.

Koonz, Claudia. *The Nazi Conscience*. Cambridge, MA: Harvard University Press, 2003.

Kopp, Kristin. *Germany's Wild East*. Ann Arbor: University of Michigan Press, 2013.

Kost, Klaus. "Anti-Semitism in German Geography 1900–1945." *GeoJournal* 46 (1998): 285–291.

Kost, Klaus. "The Conception of Politics in Political Geography and Geopolitics in Germany until 1945." *Political Geography* 8, no. 4 (1989): 369–385.

Kühl, Stefan. *The Nazi Connection, Eugenics, American Racism, and German National Socialism*. New York: Oxford University Press, 1994.

Kühne, Thomas. *Belonging and Genocide*. New Haven: Yale University Press, 2013.

Kühne, Thomas. "Colonialism and the Holocaust: Continuities, Causations, and Complexities." *Journal of Genocide Research* 15, no. 3 (2013): 339–362.

Levinas, Emmanuel. "Reflections on the Philosophy of Hitlerism." *Critical Inquiry* 17 (1990): 63–71.

Liulevicius, Vejas G. *War Land on the Eastern Front*. Cambridge: Cambridge University Press, 2000.

Longerich, Peter. *Heinrich Himmler*. Oxford: Oxford University Press, 2011.

Lovin, Clifford R. "*Blut und Boden*: The Ideological Basis of the Nazi Agricultural Program." *Journal of the History of Ideas* 28, no. 2 (1967): 279–288.

Lower, Wendy. *Nazi Empire-Building and the Holocaust in Ukraine*. Chapel Hill, NC: University of North Carolina Press, 2005.

Madley, Benjamin. "From Africa to Auschwitz: How German South West Africa Incubated Ideas and Methods Adopted and Developed by the Nazis in Eastern Europe." *European History Quarterly* 35, no. 3 (2005): 429–464.

Malpas, Jeff. *Heidegger's Topology*. Cambridge, MA: MIT Press, 2006.

Mass, Sandra. "The 'Volkskörper' in Fear: Gender, Race and Sexuality in the Weimar Republic." In *New Dangerous Liaisons: Discourses on Europe and Love in the Twentieth Century*, edited by

Liliana Elena, Alexander Geppert, and Luisa Passerini, 233–250. New York: Berghahn Books, 2009.

Mazower, Mark. *Hitler's Empire*. London: Penguin, 2008.

Michael, Robert, and Karen Doerr. *Nazi-Deutsch/Nazi German*. Westport, CT: Greenwood Press, 2002.

Minca, Claudio. "Carl Schmitt and the Question of Spatial Ontology." In *Spatiality, Sovereignty and Carl Schmitt*, edited by Stephen Legg, 163–181. New York: Routledge, 2011.

Minca, Claudio. "Giorgio Agamben and the New Biopolitical Nomos." *Geografiska Annaler B* 88 (2006): 387–403.

Mullin, John R. "The Impact of National Socialist Policies upon Local City Planning in Pre-war Germany (1933–1939). The Rhetoric and the Reality." *Journal of the American Planning Association* 47, no. 1 (1981): 35–47.

Murphy, David T. *The Heroic Earth, 1918–1933*. Kent: Kent State University Press, 1997.

Murphy, David T. "'A Sum of the Most Wonderful Things': Raum, Geopolitics and the German Tradition of Environmental Determinism, 1900–1933." *History of European Ideas* 25 (1999): 121–133.

Musiedlak, Didier. "L'espace totalitaire d'Adolf Hitler." *Vingtième Siècle* 47 (1995): 24–41.

Natter, Wolfgang. "Friedrich Ratzel's Spatial Turn." In *B/ordering Space*, edited by Henk Van Houtum, Olivier Kramsch, and Wolfgang Zierhofer, 171–187. Aldershot: Ashgate, 2005.

Natter, Wolfgang. "Geopolitics in Germany, 1919–45. Karl Haushofer, and the Zeitschrift fur Geopolitik." In *A Companion to Political Geography*, edited by John Agnew, Katharyne Mitchell, and Gerard Toal, 187–203. London: Blackwell, 2003.

Nelson, Robert L. *Germans, Poland, and Colonial Expansion to the East*. New York: Palgrave MacMillan, 2009.

Neumann, Boaz. "Being Prosthetic in the First World War and Weimar Germany." *Body & Society* 16 (2010): 93–126.

Neumann, Boaz. "The National Socialist Politics of Life." *New German Critique* 85 (2002): 107–130.

Neumann, Boaz. "The Phenomenology of the German People's Body (Volkskörper) and the Extermination of the Jewish Body." *New German Critique* 36, no. 1 (2009): 149–181.

Ó Tuathail, Gearóid. *Critical Geopolitics*. London: Routledge, 1996.

Olwig, Kenneth R. "The Duplicity of Space: Germanic 'Raum' and Swedish 'Rum' in English Language Geographical Discourse." *Geografiska Annaler* 84, no. 1 (2002): 1–17.

Olwig, Kenneth R. *Landscape, Nature, and the Body Politic*. Madison: University of Wisconsin Press, 2002.

Penny, H. Glenn, and Matti Bunzl. *Worldly Provincialism*. Ann Arbor: University of Michigan Press, 2003.

Perghera, Roberta, Mark Rosemana, Jürgen Zimmerer, Shelley Baranowskic, Doris L. Bergend, and Zygmunt Bauman. "The Holocaust: A Colonial Genocide? A Scholars' Forum." *Dapim* 27, no. 1 (2013): 40–73.

Pianigiani, Ottorino. *Vocabolario Etimologico Della Lingua Italiana*. Rome: Albrighi & Segati, 1907.

Pinwinkler, Alexander. "Volk, Bevölkerung, Rasse, and Raum: Erich Keyser's Ambiguous Concept of a German History of Population, ca. 1918–1955." In *German Scholars and Ethnic Cleansing 1920–1945*, edited by Ingo Haar and Michael Fahlbusch, 86–99. New York: Berghahn Books, 2005.

Rössler, Mechtild. "Applied Geography and Area Research in Nazi Society: Central Place Theory and Planning, 1933 to 1945." *Environment and Planning D* 7 (1989): 419–431.

Rössler, Mechtild. "Geography and Area Planning under National Socialism." In *Science in the Third Reich*, edited by Margit Szöllösi-Janze, 59–78. New York: Berg, 2001.

Sandner, Gerhard, and Mechtild Rössler. "Geography and Empire in Germany, 1871–1945." In *Geography and Empire*, edited by Anne Godlewska and Neil Smith, 115–127. Oxford: Blackwell, 1994.

Schenk, Tilman A., and Ray Bromley. "Mass-Producing Traditional Small Cities: Gottfried Feder's Vision for a Greater Nazi Germany." *Journal of Planning and History* 2, no. 2 (2003): 107–139.

Smith, Woodruff D. "Friedrich Ratzel and the Origins of *Lebensraum*." *German Studies Review* 3, no. 1 (1980): 51–68.

Smith, Woodruff D. *The Ideological Origins of Nazi Imperialism*. Oxford: Oxford University Press, 1986.

Sofsky, Wolfgang. *The Order of Terror: The Concentration Camp*. Princeton, NJ: Princeton University Press, 1997.

Stone, Dan. "White Men with Low Moral Standards? German Anthropology and the Herero Genocide." *Patterns of Prejudice* 35, no. 2 (2001): 33–45.

Troll, Carl. "Geographic Science in Germany during the Period 1933–1945: A Critique and Justification." *Annals of the Association of American Geographers* 39, no. 2 (1949): 99–137.

Turda, Marius, and Paul Weindling. *Blood and Homeland, Eugenics and Racial Nationalism in Central and Southeast Europe, 1900–1940*. Budapest: Central European University Press, 2007.

Weikart, Richard. *Hitler's Ethic*. London: Palgrave MacMillan, 2009.

Weiss, Sheila F. *The Nazi Symbiosis*. Chicago: University of Chicago Press, 2010.

Wolf, Gerhard. "The East as Historical Imagination and the Germanization Policies of the Third Reich." In *Hitler's Geographies*, edited by Paolo Giaccaria and Claudio Minca. Chicago: Chicago University Press, 2016.

Wolkersdorfer, Gunther. "Karl Haushofer and Geopolitics: The History of a German Mythos." *Geopolitics* 4, no. 3 (1999): 145–160.

Zimmerer, Jürgen. "The Birth of the Ostland out of the Spirit of Colonialism." *Patterns of Prejudice* 39, no. 2 (2005): 197–219.

Zimmerer, Jürgen. "Colonialism and the Holocaust: Towards an Archaeology of Genocide." In *Genocide and Settler Society*, edited by Dirk Moses, 49–76. New York: Berghahn Books, 2004.

Zimmerer, Jürgen. "In Service of Empire: Geographers at Berlin's University between Colonial Studies and Ostforschung." In *Hitler's Geographies*, edited by Paolo Giaccaria and Claudio Minca. Chicago: Chicago University Press, 2016.

Zimmerman, Andrew. *Anthropology and Antihumanism in Imperial Germany*. Chicago: Chicago University Press, 2001.

Controversies surrounding the excavation at Börneplatz, Frankfurt am Main, 1987

Joseph Cronin

School of History, Queen Mary, University of London, UK

ABSTRACT

In summer 1987, the remains of Frankfurt's medieval Jewish ghetto were unearthed by construction workers excavating a car park to make way for a new municipal building. When no effort was made by the city authorities or by Frankfurt's Jewish community to stop the building work, an action group called Rettet den Börneplatz ('Save Börneplatz') occupied the site. This article will investigate, firstly, why Frankfurt's Jewish community failed to do anything to prevent the building work going ahead. Secondly, it will analyse the debates surrounding the excavation which were concerned with whether the Holocaust changed the meaning of this medieval ghetto. The questions raised in these debates included: Is it appropriate to characterize a pre-modern Jewish quarter as a 'ghetto' in light of the Jewish ghettos of the early 1940s? Is there any connection between these two types of ghetto? Does drawing a connection relativize the singularity of the Holocaust? How should we view the oppression of Jews in pre-modern periods in light of the Nazi persecution? Finally, this article will look at why young Frankfurt Jews, in particular, wanted to preserve the ghetto remains.

The word "ghetto" in a Jewish context has two different, but not completely separate, meanings. On the one hand, it is used to refer to the medieval and early modern Jewish quarters in European cities such as Prague, Vienna, Paris, and Frankfurt.[1] This is also the word's original meaning. However, if one thinks about the word ghetto in a Jewish context, the first thing that probably comes to mind is the Nazi ghettos of the early 1940s. These were established in the towns and cities of Nazi-occupied Eastern Europe, including Warsaw, Lodz, Lublin, and Minsk. Jews from the surrounding areas (and later from across Nazi-occupied Europe) were forced into these ghettos, and lived there in appalling conditions, until the ghettos were liquidated and the surviving inhabitants sent to death camps. Both types of ghetto represent forms of anti-Jewish persecution, but of a different character and on a different scale. The question is: to what degree are they connected?

In spring 1987, construction workers excavating a car park in Frankfurt am Main on which the city authorities intended to build a new administrative headquarters for

Frankfurt's municipal gas company discovered the remains of Frankfurt's medieval Jewish ghetto. During the excavation, the remains of several houses and two *mikvahs* (Jewish ritual baths) dating from the late medieval and early modern periods were unearthed. When the city authorities showed no intention of pausing the construction work to discuss what should be done with the remains, the spotlight fell on Frankfurt's Jewish community, which at the time was led by Ignatz Bubis.[2] Two years previously, in October 1985, members of Frankfurt's Jewish community had occupied the stage of a Frankfurt theater-house to protest against the staging of a play by Rainer Werner Fassbinder which they deemed to be antisemitic,[3] and many believed that they would also take action against the destruction of the ghetto remains.

The site was occupied for five days at the end of August and the beginning of September 1987. However, the occupiers were not members of the Jewish community, but of a citizens' action group called *Rettet den Börneplatz* ("Save Börneplatz"), which had formed because, in 1984, the Jewish community had agreed to the building on Börneplatz and was therefore, legally at least, in favor of the construction going ahead. This article is divided into two parts. Part One will investigate the processes that led to the community's incapacitation on this issue and whether its lack of action should be considered a product of indifference or the result of a lack of information combined with political pressure. With regard to this, Part Two will examine broader questions concerning the meaning of Börneplatz and its historical significance. This includes the appropriateness of its characterization as a "ghetto" in light of the Nazi ghettos as well as debates from the period, which sought to determine whether the forms of oppression represented by the Frankfurt ghetto and the persecution and killing of Jews during the Holocaust were connected. These debates attempted, in essence, to delineate the meaning of a ghetto after the Holocaust. The article will conclude by looking at why young Frankfurt Jews would have wanted to save the ghetto remains from destruction.

Part one: why did the Jewish community not oppose the construction plans?

Speaking on a program for *Hessischer Rundfunk* (the public radio service for the German state of Hesse) broadcast in August 1987, Ignatz Bubis said: "If we had known about these findings earlier, if five years ago we had devoted our energies to this site as we do today – and here I assign all of us, the Jewish community included, with a portion of the blame – then I am almost certain that no customer center would be being built there."[4] In 1984, an agreement had been reached between the Jewish community and the city authorities, in which the former had consented to construction on the Börneplatz site. Bubis was in conciliatory mode in this interview, blaming the Jewish community as much as anyone else for the fact that they had put themselves into a position where they could no longer object to the building work going ahead. However, the Frankfurt-based architect and publicist Salomon Korn argued that the Jewish community (of which Korn was a board member) and the Kirchheim'sche Stiftung (an institute for the preservation of Frankfurt's Jewish heritage, of which Korn was director) were both woefully ill-informed about the nature of the Börneplatz development.

In a letter to the *Frankfurter Allgemeine Zeitung* from June 1986, Korn noted that "the Frankfurt city authorities have failed on multiple occasions to consult with the Jewish community and the Kirchheim'sche Stiftung," and that, "now, after all of the crucial decisions have been made without the Jewish community and Kirchheim'sche Stiftung, the city planning department shows willingness to cooperate in the design of the new Börneplatz."[5] Over a year later, in September 1987, Korn elaborated his complaints on *Hessischer Rundfunk*:

> I must first point out that the decision to build on Börneplatz was not agreed either with the Jewish community or with the Kirchheim'sche Stiftung. That is, in the initial phase neither the Jewish community nor the Stiftung was consulted. The nature of the construction was also not discussed with us, and as for the announcement for the architecture competition [for the design of the building – J.C.], neither of the two institutions were asked, consulted or informed. Therefore, the city authorities alone take the responsibility for the customer center.[6]

It took Bubis almost a decade to articulate his feelings on the matter, but when he did, in his 1996 autobiography, he departed starkly from his earlier statements and came to the same conclusions as Korn. He detailed the various ways in which the Jewish community was kept in the dark by the city authorities at crucial stages during the decision-making process. Bubis stated that Hans Küppers, head of the city planning department, had assured the community and the Kirchheim'sche Stiftung that they would be kept updated about future planning developments and also that a member of the community would be included on the panel awarding the prize for the architecture competition. "However," noted Bubis, "none of this happened." After three written requests and several telephone conversations, the community received an excerpt from the competition guidelines (two of its 13 pages) and was invited to participate further in the planning process. However, because the city authorities had "refrained even from keeping us informed, let alone to include our opinion in its plans," the community refused.[7]

The Kirchheim'sche Stiftung eventually sent Salomon Korn to sit at meetings of the panel judging the competition, in order to influence the design of the new Börneplatz building as much as possible. Korn had the right to express his opinion but no voting rights. He argued that none of the seven shortlisted designs met the expectations of the Jewish community in every respect, but agreed with the adjudicators that their selected design – from Zürich architect Ernst Gisel – was the most suitable. After the winner had been chosen, the city authorities promised to coordinate the overall planning for the design with the Jewish community, and to make sure that Gisel remained in close contact with them. "Three months passed," wrote Bubis, "without us having heard anything either from the city authorities or from Gisel."[8] When Korn complained about this, he was sent a copy of the contract between the city authorities and the architect. This detailed the particulars for the design of Börneplatz, which had been drawn up without prior consultation with the community. The memorial for the site had also already been designed, without making use of the Kirchheim'sche Stiftung's submitted proposal. As such, the Jewish community and the Kirchheim'sche Stiftung rejected the design for the memorial when it was finalized in early 1986. The city authorities then withdrew it and in November announced a new design competition, this time for the memorial. Three representatives from the Jewish community were named as judges, while Salomon Korn was appointed specialist adjudicator.

The behavior of the various city authorities involved in the Börneplatz project appears, at best, completely inept, but points more likely to a deliberate attempt to prevent the two

Jewish institutions involved from discovering the true nature of their designs on Börneplatz. One would expect a strong denial from the non-Jewish actors involved, and an insistence that the Jewish community and the Kirchheim'sche Stiftung were kept fully informed about project developments. Yet, when interviewed in the September 1987 edition of the Jewish-issues journal *Tribüne*, Frankfurt mayor Wolfram Brück admitted that the Jewish community was not kept informed. "It is certainly true," he stated, "that in the question of what sort of building should be constructed, the Jewish community was not involved. In the decision regarding whether the property should be sold or whether the municipal building should be constructed there, the Jewish community was not involved."[9] This statement suggests that the city authorities were trying to keep the Jewish community in the dark about their plans for Börneplatz, possibly to prevent its leaders from objecting to them.

If the Jewish community was as badly informed as it appears, why did most of its board members – especially Ignatz Bubis and Michel Friedman (who was the community's cultural spokesman) – insist on upholding their agreement with the city authorities? Writing in 1996, Micha Brumlik, a second-generation, Frankfurt-based scholar and one of the site occupiers, speculated that:

> Had the community leadership … possessed more courage, they would have had no shortage of arguments and allies for a withdrawal of their authorization. After all, they would have had the greater part of public opinion on their side, the Green party and – at any rate outwardly – the Frankfurt SPD,[10] and thus their portion of the city council, behind them. […] In these months the whole city knew that a clear word from the Jewish community and its leadership would have meant a termination of the excavation work and the beginning of a serious, fruitful period of reflection.[11]

With this in mind, the reasons offered by the community for not changing their position seem weak. For example, Bubis raised the prospect of wasting taxpayers' money: "Now, however, there's been three years of planning and – as the mayor has said – 11 million already spent and 53 million accounted for. To simply go back to square one from here isn't simple."[12] Read on its own, this statement suggests that the moral consciences of the community leaders prevented them from changing their stance. But if one looks more closely at statements from the city authorities, it becomes clear that two subtle forms of coercion were being used. The more benign of the two was the threat of wasted taxpayers' money. Brück referred in a speech to the "wasting of over 50 million marks in taxpayers' money" if the plans for the project had to be rethought.[13] Brumlik, assessing more sympathetically the reasons why the community refused to backtrack, wrote that they "had to fear the political liability for several million marks spent for no reason on planning, and the penalties that might entail."[14] Thus it becomes clear that Bubis reiterated this concern because he felt that the Jewish community would bear the brunt of the blame if the construction plans were abandoned.

However, Brück did not confine his threat to financial penalties alone. He argued that the wastage of taxpayers' money would "possibly encourage the antisemitic tendencies of Frankfurt citizens" because they would not be able to understand the reasons for the about-turn and would view it, most likely, as the result of Jewish interference.[15] By implying this, Brück made "the Jews" responsible for any setback to the Börneplatz project – and the wastage of funds deriving therefrom – despite the fact that he himself had admitted that the Jewish community did not participate in the decision-making process that led to the spending of these funds in the first place. Korn, who picked up on Brück's reference to a renewed antisemitism, wrote in 1992 that "in this instance a tragic chapter of German-Jewish history had caught up with him."[16] In other words, Brück was blaming the Jews for instances of antisemitism, just as German politicians of the past had done. Considering Brück's attitude towards those outwardly committed to the building project, it is unsurprising that he was highly critical about the "Save Börneplatz" alliance, especially after they occupied the site. As Brumlik remarked in a speech during the occupation: "You will have heard that the mayor would like to compare those citizens – who since Thursday evening have prevented further vandalism in the area of the former *Judengasse* with their sheer physical presence – to offenders and criminals."[17] Brück's stance here contrasted starkly with that of his mayoral predecessor, Walter Wallmann, who had endorsed the Jewish community's equally "criminal" behavior when they occupied the theater stage against the Fassbinder play two years earlier. The theater occupation, in contrast to the one at Börneplatz, had no potentially damaging economic implications for the city council.

Part two: what does a ghetto mean after Auschwitz?

Walter Wallmann, the former Frankfurt mayor and at that point minister-president for the state of Hesse, delivered a speech on 5 September 1987 before a congress of the Frankfurt Christian Democratic Union, in which he made several points that would prove inflammatory, not only to those trying to save the Börneplatz site, but to the Jewish community in general. Wallmann began:

> My dear friends, it is not right to say that Börneplatz and the Jewish ghetto have anything to do with Auschwitz. And it is therefore also not true that a straight path leads from this ghetto to Auschwitz. [...] It's not medieval Christian antisemitism that's to blame for Auschwitz but ... the false path, which the country went down after the Enlightenment. And it's therefore false and unhistorical – and I say this with emphasis – to draw a connection between Börneplatz and the gas chambers of the Third Reich. We don't need a memorial on this site because the discovered foundations are no cause for shame. On the contrary: if we erect a sophisticated architecture on a place that after 1811 was no longer a Jewish ghetto and where, in 1885, the last remnants of the ghetto were built over in the spirit of the Enlightenment, then we will do more for continuity and memory than has happened so far. [...] We should be careful not to carry out the still necessary mourning at the wrong place with the wrong meaning.[18]

Here, Wallmann attempted to completely separate medieval Christian anti-Judaism from the pseudo-scientific, racist antisemitism that appeared in the nineteenth century. And by making this clear separation he was able to absolve the medieval ghetto from any kind of connection with the Holocaust. Furthermore, by attempting to pin the root causes of the Holocaust on the Enlightenment, he clearly thought of it as an essentially European and not as a specifically German phenomenon.

Twelve days later, his mayoral successor Wolfram Brück, in a speech before the city assembly, not only defended but also extrapolated on the points Wallmann had made: "What the *Judengasse* meant for Frankfurt Jewry has always been misrepresented here. Even at a fundamental level the statement, 'this part of Frankfurt history is a cause for shame,' is not justified." Brück attempted to bolster his argument with historical "facts" he claimed to have gleaned from conversations with the leader of the Frankfurt Jewish

Museum: "The director of the Jewish Museum explained to me a few days ago that the *Judengasse* is now being interpreted in a manner that is contrary to what it was, namely, a refuge for Jews in Germany. For this I can see no justification."[19]

Wallmann and Brück's speeches attracted criticism from various quarters within German society, from the philosopher Jürgen Habermas, who described Wallmann's argument as "naturally false," to ordinary Jewish residents in Frankfurt, one of whom, Barbara Rendtorff, a teacher at a women's school, wrote a letter to *Der Spiegel* in which she declared: "Auschwitz was no brainchild of Hitler and the Nazi party. Without daily and active discrimination, denunciations and finally, destructive antisemitism in the population, there would have been no Auschwitz."[20] This raises the issue of the continuation of antisemitic tendencies "from below" (i.e. antisemitism in the population), which Wallmann and Brück completely avoided, preferring to focus instead on "top down" attitudes (i.e. from the city authorities). The Jewish community took particular offense at Brück's formulation of the ghetto's "protective" function, describing it in a statement on 21 September as "false and contrary to the historical facts. The Frankfurt ghetto served to oppress, disenfranchise, socially exclude and discriminate the Jews."[21] A statement from the "Save Börneplatz" initiative, who unsurprisingly were outspoken critics of both speeches, declared that Brück had made the transition from "neoconservative" to "nationalist" (*völkisch*) with his comment about the ghetto's protective function.[22]

Salomon Korn's riposte to Brück, delivered in a lecture to the German Werkbund (an association of artisans and craftspeople) on 5 December 1987, corrected some of the historical information Brück had cited. Korn began by stating that the ghetto *would* have served a protective function "if the intention of protection stood in the foreground when it was established."[23] In reality, when the Jews first asked if they could build a ghetto within the city walls, so as to protect their houses, the city council refused and set them "defenseless outside the city walls." It was only with the expansion of Frankfurt's city walls, much later, that the Jewish quarter received a tolerable level of protection. Korn concluded: "To single out the 'protective function' of the ghetto, which in reality was an accidental by-product of its otherwise degrading nature, and to bring this to the fore in the hope of justifying it, serves only to disregard and trivialize the history and function of the *Judengasse*."[24]

Korn also isolated the faulty reasoning in Wallmann and Brück's arguments, which "boil down to an attempt to separate the Christian anti-Judaism of the middle ages from modern (racist) antisemitism, in order to avoid historical connections between ghetto and concentration camp." Korn believed that this line of argument was "historically speaking, meaningless," for the simple reason that "a direct causal connection can never be detected between events that are two generations apart."[25] In this light Wallmann's attempt to pin the root causes of the Holocaust on the Enlightenment seem like a convenient excuse not to preserve the Börneplatz findings.

Ignatz Bubis cut through the knot of interpretations with his speech at Frankfurt's Westend synagogue on 9 November 1987, the anniversary of *Kristallnacht*, in which he stated:

> Every kind of ghetto means discrimination and exclusion, and any discrimination or exclusion is a cause for shame. I know also, without wanting to be a historian and, I must confess, without having occupied myself that much with this historical period, how oppressed the

Jews in the Frankfurt ghetto must have been and under what inhumane conditions they must have lived.[26]

Yet Bubis's expression "every kind of ghetto" raises some intriguing questions. What exactly is the meaning of a ghetto after Auschwitz? And how should we view the oppression of Jews in pre-modern periods in light of the Nazi persecution? In a 1992 article for the *Frankfurt Allgemeine Zeitung*, summing up the Börneplatz affair, Salomon Korn acknowledged that, "[h]ad the infernal genocide not been carried out, the remains of the *Judengasse* would appear to us today as mere remnants of a long healed-over historical epoch."[27] Auschwitz had certainly changed the meaning, and potentially the importance, of this medieval ghetto.

In an analytical piece for the Jewish affairs journal *Babylon* in early 1988, the historian Dan Diner interrogated the use of the term "ghetto" for anything predating the Nazi period. He argued that the word had undergone a fundamental semantic shift, and that both definitions now existed side by side in uneasy tension. "The word ghetto," Diner wrote, "is therefore, for Jews *here and now*, charged with the lived experience of *there and then* – Eastern Europe in the early 1940s. This is quite different to those for whom the ruins of this medieval/early modern Jewish ghetto, the '*Judengasse*,' represent a warning-sign and a reminder of an anti-Judaic past, which they understand as humiliating, exclusionary and discriminatory."[28] Brumlik reiterated this point in 1996, stating: "Those members of the Jewish community, who had themselves come to Germany as Displaced Persons, and by extension their children, considered the choice of the term 'ghetto' – in light of the Nazi-established ghettos – to be inappropriate."[29] Speaking in an interview in August 2013, Brumlik gave an example of this: "I will never forget a very curious association, a meeting of the Jewish community where we said: 'Please do something, we have to preserve these very valuable remnants of Jewish life, in this ghetto.' And then an old man said, 'Ah, you all speak about ghettos, we've been under the Nazis in Poland, we know what a ghetto is! Not those medieval houses'."[30]

This problem – how to understand Börneplatz in light of the Holocaust – received a kind of indirect response from two first-generation Jews.[31] Alfred Grosser delivered a speech in Frankfurt's Dominican monastery at the invitation of the "Save Börneplatz" alliance on 4 September, two days after the occupation ended, in which he stated that the ghetto would inevitably remind one of Auschwitz, even though at that time there had been no Auschwitz. Grosser emphasized the singularity of the Holocaust, yet argued that "one cannot establish a singularity merely by asserting it; one can only establish it by way of comparison."[32] One should therefore be able to speak about and remember other crimes and their victims without undermining the Holocaust's uniqueness. Using this approach, Grosser argued, the memorial at Börneplatz could stand, not as a "monopoly of suffering," but rather as an "example of suffering," which would prompt a confrontation with racism and other forms of social exclusion in the present.[33]

The second response came from Ignatz Bubis, who, in his speech on 9 November, argued that to remember the Börneplatz ghetto did not mean that one wished to "reinterpret, belittle, rose-tint or relativize" the National Socialist dictatorship. "That said," continued Bubis, "I do not wish for this ghetto to be understood, in spite of all its discrimination and oppression of Jewish life, as a precursor to the ghettos of the twentieth century." And yet, while Börneplatz was no "precursor" to the Nazi ghettos, Bubis argued that it set a precedent in terms of the spatial concentration of Jews, which enabled the authorities to "access" them more easily. "The creation of ghettos," concluded Bubis, "made access to Jewish people possible at any time, without first having to search for them before they could be rounded up."[34]

Dan Diner found something unnerving about the often voracious support of the non-Jewish supporters of the "Save Börneplatz" alliance. He wrote in *Babylon* that they had "an anxious, artificial and compulsive need to prove" that Börneplatz was somehow linked to the Nazi genocide. The two consequences of this line of thinking that gave Diner particular cause for concern were, firstly, that it presupposed "the idea of an almost ahistorical anti-Judaism," and secondly – paradoxically – it gave "credence to the right to deny the singularity of Auschwitz and to give it ... equal standing with all kinds of horrors in human history." "Therefore," argued Diner, "these efforts to restore a German Jewry in Germany after Auschwitz unwittingly become part of the relativization of the mass destruction."[35] However, Brumlik, who had been an occupier of the site and hence knew the non-Jewish participants well, questioned Diner's logic. He wrote in 1996 that, if Diner's suspicions were correct, this would mean that "the massive and widespread commitment of almost all non-Jewish social powers in the city [to saving Börneplatz] ... was connected to a well-meaning but unconscious effort aiming at the suppression of Auschwitz." Brumlik singled out the efforts of the writer and fellow site-occupier Eva Demski, who, he conceded, "had fought like no other, with all her might, for the preservation and redesign of the Börneplatz site."[36] Could her determination really have emanated from a desire to suppress the memory of the Holocaust? When I interviewed Brumlik in August 2013, he appeared to have made up his mind, stating that, as far as he was concerned, the relativization of the Holocaust was not part of the agenda for any of the actors involved. "But," he added, "for rather trivial reasons it's true. Because in fighting to preserve the site at Börneplatz, for a certain time one did not speak anymore about the shadow of Auschwitz."[37]

However, a closer look at the discourse surrounding the "Save Börneplatz" campaign reveals a couple of terms with more than trivial significance. Eva Demski coined two phrases that became associated with the conflict: "speaking stones" and "open wound." "What once happened to people here," she argued in a speech during the occupation, "what once happened that this site does not want to remember, happens now to the site itself: it is crushed, suppressed and destroyed. [...] But what was once destroyed, comes back. The beautiful words of the 'speaking stones' have come to the surface."[38] Though seemingly innocuous, this statement does contain a problematic element. Demski effectively equated the "suffering" of the site with the suffering of its former inhabitants, and in doing so, overemphasized the importance of material things. She fetishized the stones and implicitly suppressed the memory of those who actually lived there. Similarly, Demski's desire for an "open wound" in the city, by leaving the unearthed remains as they stood, dramatized the significance of the ghetto as a site of suffering, and was too close a comparison to Nazi concentration camps, which were preserved in their exact form to embody such "open wounds."

The Frankfurt-based journalist and museum director Cilly Kugelmann argued that Börneplatz was "surely not an appropriate site at which to leave an architectural-historical 'open wound' as a reminder to future generations of the mass extermination of the Jews" because, as she put it, "the analogy between the *Judengasse* and the Nazi ghetto is not historically accurate."[39] To argue that the non-Jewish participants harbored an intentional desire to downplay the singularity of the Holocaust by overstating the meaning of Börneplatz (and, by extension, other pre-modern Jewish ghettos) is probably going too far. However, by dwelling on the horrors of life in this environment, non-Jewish participants in the "Save Börneplatz" campaign were able to situate the atrocities of the more recent past in an extended historical context, resulting in a partial, perhaps inevitable, relativization of the Holocaust.

There were also two attitudes, held by non-Jews who wished to preserve the findings, that had nothing to do with the significance of these remains for the Jewish community. The first of these attitudes was exemplified by Walter Meier-Arendt of the Frankfurt Museum for Pre- and Early History. Georg Schwinghammer reported Meier-Arendt's argument in *Tribüne*, that all excavated findings at Börneplatz should be preserved, including those which predated the *Judengasse*, because the city's history "did not begin in 1462 with the establishment of the ghetto." In some cases, he argued, the foundations of the Jewish buildings should be swept aside in order to access the more "valuable" early medieval and ancient remains.[40] Some of the non-Jewish site-occupiers also disregarded the Jewish content of the site. As Dieter Bartetzko pointed out, many of them had been involved in the *Frankfurter Häuserkampf* ("Frankfurt housing struggle") a decade earlier – a conflict notorious for its underlying antisemitism, especially with regard to property developer Ignatz Bubis, who at the time was viewed by occupiers as the *Hauptfeind* ("main enemy"),[41] even though his involvement in Frankfurt real estate was no greater than that of his non-Jewish counterparts. Because Bubis was once again in the anti-protest camp (though this time he was there reluctantly), the non-Jewish activists were reminded of the earlier conflict, and presumably ignored the irony of defending a Jewish site of memory in order to act out antisemitic revenge fantasies. Even being generous to them, these activists saw Börneplatz as simply another opportunity to oppose the government and their capitalist designs on the Frankfurt cityscape, not as an opportunity to show solidarity with the Jewish cause.

*

In a piece for the *Allgemeine Jüdische Wochenzeitung* in September 1987, Hermann Alter remarked:

> It's noteworthy that it's mostly representatives of the postwar generation who are working for the preservation of the ghetto remains. It certainly plays a role that the question of continuity falls squarely on the shoulders of the postwar generation; the question of whether continuity can be achieved between the great and tradition-rich history of the Jewish communities in Germany before 1933 and the Jewish communities of today.[42]

Alter was right to argue that the Börneplatz conflict was indicative of the ascendance of later-generation Jews in a way that the Fassbinder conflict two years earlier was not, for that protest was supported and even spearheaded by first-generation Jews. While those in positions of authority in the Jewish institutions in Germany, such as Ignatz Bubis and Werner Nachmann (who was at the time chairman of the Central Council of Jews in Germany), either tacitly or even wholeheartedly supported the construction project, later generations opposed the project and some actively attempted to prevent it from going ahead by occupying the site. Such a clear generational gap requires explanation.

TRACING TOPOGRAPHIES

First-generation Jews had a personal connection to pre-Holocaust Jewish life (they were born into it, whether in Germany or elsewhere in Europe). As such, they did not necessarily view Börneplatz and what it represented as "past" in the same way later generations did. And, as French historian Pierre Nora has emphasized, a "site of memory" cannot exist without its upholders first seeing what it represents as "past."[43] Alter seemed to think that the postwar generation's preoccupation with this remnant of pre-Holocaust Jewish life meant that they were trying to reestablish a continuous form of Jewish life in Germany, that is, that they were attempting to understand it in order to reconnect with and revitalize it. However, this was not the case. Although Börneplatz demonstrated that later generations were clearly interested in pre-Holocaust Jewish life, this was not for the purpose of trying to recreate it. On the contrary, they saw it as irretrievably lost, and as such, an environment that belonged to the past.

When I asked him in August 2013 whether the "Save Börneplatz" group was trying to bridge or reestablish a link with pre-Holocaust Frankfurt Jewish life, Micha Brumlik stated: "I think we were realistic enough to know that this could not be reestablished, but it was an important witness of stone that there was once upon a time such a community."[44] This idea of a "stone witness" belonging to the past certainly did not prevent an emotional or imaginative identification with the site. As Brumlik described in 1996, to occupy the site "was to succumb to a blurring of dreams and reality, to identify in some way with the remnants of late medieval houses and the ruins of Eastern European ghettos, which had to be defended at all costs against a hostile German supremacy."[45] This form of imaginative identification was entirely compatible with the idea that the site belonged essentially to the past as, if the site belonged to the past, imagination would be the only means by which to access it; that is, it could only be experienced within the context of the mind.

Börneplatz had already disappeared by the time Hitler came to power. But because of the Nazi interlude, because of the persecution of the Jews and the Holocaust, Börneplatz had taken on a myriad of symbolic meanings not exclusive to Frankfurt Jews or even to German Jews. Because, although this "Jewish quarter" had disappeared by the late nineteenth century, other, similar Jewish quarters did still exist and *were* destroyed by the Nazis. So Börneplatz became a stand-in for the Jewish communities that disappeared without a trace or whose traces lay outside of Germany. Börneplatz came to represent a whole way of life, a way of life that had suddenly and unnaturally vanished. This helps us to understand why Jews living in Frankfurt in the mid-1980s, who probably had no ancestral connection to the city, or even to Germany, were committed to preserving Börneplatz. The site represented, and as such, bore the weight of, European Jewish life before the Holocaust.

Once the occupation of the Börneplatz site had ended, the construction of the municipal building resumed. However, as a result of the protests, the city council decided to incorporate some of the Judengasse *remains – including the foundations of five houses and the two* mikvahs *– into the building's basement. In November 1992, the Museum Judengasse opened as an annex of the Jewish Museum Frankfurt.*

Notes

1. The word "ghetto" was originally applied to the Jewish quarter in Venice, and was called so probably because a metal foundry, which in Italian is *geto*, had once occupied the same site. See Debenedetti-Stow, "The Etymology of 'Ghetto'," 79–80.

TRACING TOPOGRAPHIES

2. Ignatz Bubis (1937–1999), Jewish leader in the Federal Republic. Bubis moved to Germany after he was liberated from the Nazi labor camp in Częstochowa, Poland. After relocating to Frankfurt in 1956, he established himself in the real estate business and became active in the Jewish community. As a property developer he came into conflict with student activists who occupied his properties on several occasions in the 1970s.
3. See Cronin, "The Impact of the 1985 'Fassbinder Controversy'."
4. "22. August 1987," 66.
5. Korn, "Leserbriefe."
6. "4. September 1987: Diskussion," 86–7.
7. Bubis with Sichrovsky, *Damit bin ich noch längst nicht fertig,* 156.
8. Ibid., 157.
9. Brück, "Es geht um Denkmäler jüdischen Lebens in Frankfurt," 87.
10. The Sozialdemokratische Partei Deutschlands, the main center-left party in Germany.
11. Brumlik, *Kein Weg als Deutscher und Jude,* 167 and 171.
12. "22. August 1987," 66.
13. Bubis with Sichrovsky, *Damit bin ich noch längst nicht fertig,* 159.
14. Brumlik, *Kein Weg als Deutscher und Jude,* 167.
15. Quoted in Korn, "Der Konflikt um den Börneplatz."
16. Ibid.
17. Literally "Jews' alley" or "Jews' lane," *Judengasse* was the term commonly used to refer to the Jewish ghetto in Frankfurt. "29. August 1987: Ansprache von Professor Micha Brumlik," 80.
18. "5. September 1987," 99–100.
19. "17. September 1987," 112–13.
20. Quoted in Scherbaum, "Frankfurts 'Offene Wunde'," 106.
21. "21. September 1987," 119.
22. The signatories of this statement were: Micha Brumlik, Istvan Gzarmati, Miriam Korn, Doron Kiesel, Sammy Speier, Manon Tuckfeld, and Andreas Werle. "21. September 1987," 119.
23. Korn, "Die Moral des Ortes," 158.
24. Ibid., 159.
25. Quoted in Bubis with Sichrovsky, *Damit bin ich noch längst nicht fertig,* 162.
26. "9. November 1987," 124.
27. Korn, "Die Moral des Ortes," 159.
28. Diner, "Schichten der Erinnerung," 20.
29. Brumlik, *Kein Weg als Deutscher und Jude,* 167–8.
30. Interview with Micha Brumlik, 27 August 2013.
31. A first-generation Jew, in this context, is somebody who lived through the Nazi persecution. A second-generation Jew is a child of first-generation Jews.
32. "4. September 1987: Rede," 94.
33. Quoted in "Sieger und Besiegte darf es nicht geben."
34. "9. November 1987," 125.
35. Diner, "Schichten der Erinnerung," 23.
36. Brumlik, *Kein Weg als Deutscher und Jude,* 168.
37. Interview with Micha Brumlik, 27 August 2013.
38. "29. August 1987: Ansprache von Eva Demski," 78.
39. Kugelmann, "Jewish Museums in Germany," 247.
40. Quoted in Schwinghammer, "Deutsches Kaleidoskop," 29.
41. Bartetzko, "Der Frankfurter Börneplatzskandal," 88.
42. Alter, "Prüfstein historischen Bewußtseins."
43. Nora, "Between Memory and History," 7.
44. Interview with Micha Brumlik, 27 August 2013.
45. Brumlik, *Kein Weg als Deutscher und Jude,* 169.

Disclosure statement

No potential conflict of interest was reported by the author.

References

"4. September 1987: Diskussion in der Sendung 'Die Tribüne', Hessischer Rundfunk, 1. Hörfunkprogramm." In *Der Frankfurter Börneplatz: Zur Archäologie eines politischen Konflikts*, edited by Michael Best, 86–90. Frankfurt am Main: Fischer Taschenbuch Verlag, 1988.

"4. September 1987: Rede von Alfred Grosser im Dominikanerkloster auf Einladung des Börneplatz-Bündnisses." In *Der Frankfurter Börneplatz: Zur Archäologie eines politischen Konflikts*, edited by Michael Best, 90–95. Frankfurt am Main: Fischer Taschenbuch Verlag, 1988.

"5. September 1987: Rede des Hessischen Ministerpräsidenten Walter Wallmann vor dem Kreisparteitag der Frankfurter CDU." In *Der Frankfurter Börneplatz: Zur Archäologie eines politischen Konflikts*, edited by Michael Best, 98–101. Frankfurt am Main: Fischer Taschenbuch Verlag, 1988.

"9. November 1987: Rede von Ignatz Bubis in der Westend-Synagoge." In *Der Frankfurter Börneplatz: Zur Archäologie eines politischen Konflikts*, edited by Michael Best, 124–125. Frankfurt am Main: Fischer Taschenbuch Verlag, 1988.

"17. September 1987: Rede von Oberbürgermeister Wolfram Brück vor der Stadtverordnetenversammlung." In *Der Frankfurter Börneplatz: Zur Archäologie eines politischen Konflikts*, edited by Michael Best, 112–118. Frankfurt am Main: Fischer Taschenbuch Verlag, 1988.

"21. September 1987: Erklärung des Vorstands der Jüdischen Gemeinde." In *Der Frankfurter Börneplatz: Zur Archäologie eines politischen Konflikts*, edited by Michael Best, 119. Frankfurt am Main: Fischer Taschenbuch Verlag, 1988.

"22. August 1987: Stellungnahme von Ignatz Bubis, Vorsitzender des Vorstands der Jüdischen Gemeinde, in der Sendung 'Hintergrund' des Hessischen Rundfunks, 1. Hörfunkprogramm." In *Der Frankfurter Börneplatz: Zur Archäologie eines politischen Konflikts*, edited by Michael Best, 66. Frankfurt am Main: Fischer Taschenbuch Verlag, 1988.

"29. August 1987: Ansprache von Eva Demski auf der Kundgebung des Aktionsbündnisses." In *Der Frankfurter Börneplatz: Zur Archäologie eines politischen Konflikts*, edited by Michael Best, 77–78. Frankfurt am Main: Fischer Taschenbuch Verlag, 1988.

"29. August 1987: Ansprache von Professor Micha Brumlik auf der Kundgebung des Aktionsbündnisses." In *Der Frankfurter Börneplatz: Zur Archäologie eines politischen Konflikts*, edited by Michael Best, 79–81. Frankfurt am Main: Fischer Taschenbuch Verlag, 1988.

Alter, Hermann. "Prüfstein historischen Bewußtseins: Die Mauerreste in der Frankfurter Judengasse." *Allgemeine Jüdische Wochenzeitung*, September 18, 1987.

Bartetzko, Dieter. "Der Frankfurter Börneplatzskandal." In *Ignatz Bubis: Ein jüdisches Leben in Deutschland*, edited by Fritz Backhaus, Raphael Gross, and Michael Lenarz, 88–91. Frankfurt am Main: Jüdischer Verlag im Suhrkamp Verlag, 2007.

Brück, Wolfram. "Es geht um Denkmäler jüdischen Lebens in Frankfurt: Gespräch mit den Oberbürgermeister über den Börneplatz." *Tribüne: Zeitschrift zum Verständnis des Judentums*, no. 104 (1987): 86–102.

Brumlik, Micha. *Kein Weg als Deutscher und Jude: Eine bundesrepublikanische Erfahrung*. Munich: Luchterhand, 1996.

Bubis, Ignatz, with Peter Sichrovsky. *"Damit bin ich noch längst nicht fertig": Die Autobiographie*. Frankfurt am Main: Campus Verlag, 1996.

Cronin, Joseph. "The Impact of the 1985 'Fassbinder Controversy' on Jewish Identity in Germany." *Journal of Contemporary Central and Eastern Europe* 23: (forthcoming). doi:10.1080/0965156X.2015.1118850.

Debenedetti-Stow, Sandra. "The Etymology of 'Ghetto': New Evidence from Rome." *Jewish History* 6, no. 1/2 (1992): 79–85. doi:10.1007/BF01695211.

Diner, Dan. "Schichten der Erinnerung: Zum Börneplatz-Konflikt." *Babylon*, no. 3 (1988): 18–26.

Korn, Salomon. 1992. "Der Konflikt um den Börneplatz." *Frankfurter Allgemeine Zeitung*, November 29.

Korn, Salomon. 1986. "Leserbriefe: Börneplatz." *Frankfurter Allgemeine Zeitung*, June 12.

Korn, Salomon. "Die Moral des Ortes: Wider den Versuch Stadtgeschichte zu bereinigen." In *Der Frankfurter Börneplatz: Zur Archäologie eines politischen Konflikts*, edited by Michael Best, 152–161. Frankfurt am Main: Fischer Taschenbuch Verlag, 1988.

Kugelmann, Cilly. "Jewish Museums in Germany: A German-Jewish Problem." In *Speaking Out: Jewish Voices from United Germany*, edited by Susan Stern, 243–256. Berlin: edition q, 1995.

Nora, Pierre. "Between Memory and History: Les Lieux de Mémoire." *Representations*, no. 26 (1989): 7–24. doi:10.2307/2928520.

Scherbaum, Gustav. "Frankfurts 'Offene Wunde': Pressestimmen zu den Auseinandersetzungen um den Börneplatz." *Tribüne: Zeitschrift zum Verständnis des Judentums*, no. 104 (1987): 103–106.

Schwinghammer, Georg. "Deutsches Kaleidoskop '88 (1)." *Tribüne: Zeitschrift zum Verständnis des Judentums*, no. 105 (1988): 23–35.

"Sieger und Besiegte darf es nicht geben: Alfred Grosser spricht sich für Denkpause am Börneplatz aus." 1987. *Frankfurter Allgemeine Zeitung*, September 7.

"Romantic Auschwitz": examples and perceptions of contemporary visitor photography at the Auschwitz-Birkenau State Museum

Imogen Dalziel

Department of History, Royal Holloway, University of London, UK

ABSTRACT
Visitor photography at the Auschwitz-Birkenau State Museum is becoming increasingly popular in the age of the Internet, social media and digitalization. People visit the Auschwitz Museum for a number of reasons, and their motivations for taking photographs at the site also vary. Several of the primary reasons to photograph Auschwitz given by the sixteen participants in this study will be explored in this paper. The ethical dilemma surrounding the taking of 'selfies' will also be considered.

In recent years, photography has increasingly become part of everyday life. The advent of digital photography and smartphones has made the taking of photographs far more widespread than ever before.[1] Devices with internet connection also allow users to upload and share their photographs almost instantly; social networking platforms such as Facebook and Instagram mean that people can receive feedback on their photographs within minutes. As of 2012, around 10 billion photographs had been uploaded to Facebook – with an additional 700 million being added every month.[2]

Nowhere is photography more deeply rooted, however, than in the tourist experience. Indeed, in some ways, photography is now *the* experience, as Susan Sontag wrote even in 1979: "Ultimately, having an experience becomes identical with taking a photograph of it, and participating in a public event comes more and more to be equivalent to looking at it in photographed form."[3] The relatively recent phenomenon of visiting sites connected with "dark tourism," as it has been called by John Lennon and Malcolm Foley, is just one example of what is on the itinerary of many contemporary tourists. Visitors apparently feel compelled to take photographs at these places, too, where death, destruction, and mass suffering have occurred.[4] However, this aspect of the tourist experience has so far been seriously under-researched.

Some of the most visited sites connected to "dark tourism" are those connected to the Holocaust. The Nazi genocide of Europe's Jews remains in living memory, but for only a minority of potential visitors. While relatives of Holocaust survivors may travel to these sites, they are still experiencing a form of post-memory; they will never see the landscape in the same way as someone who was liberated from a camp or site of extermination. The majority of visitors to Holocaust sites, however, have no personal connection to the events, yet continue to visit in their thousands. Questions have been raised, therefore, as to the reasons why so many choose to visit such sites and what actual value these visits offer.

The centerpiece of what Tim Cole calls "the Holocaust heritage industry" – and the focus of this research – is undoubtedly the Auschwitz-Birkenau State Museum (hereafter referred to as "the Auschwitz Museum" or "the Museum"), the largest of the concentration and extermination camps created by the Third Reich.[5] Visitor numbers to the Museum have steadily increased year-on-year: according to the Museum's annual report, a record 1,534,000 people visited in 2014.[6] Holocaust sites are certainly not places of entertainment, and educational visits make up a large part of these figures, but some critics believe the Museum is becoming nothing more than "one of Poland's most important tourist attractions."[7] "Auschwitz-land," as Cole has cynically termed the Museum, is the most widely visited Holocaust site as it has become "the symbol of the murder of all six million Jews and not simply the 900,000 or so who […] died in the place."[8] William F. S. Miles agrees: he suggests that the Museum should be thought of more as "a cemetery without tombstones, a graveyard without graves"; yet it remains "Poland's premier destination," a tourist attraction that is "so 'hit'."[9] One may certainly be inclined to agree with these opinions; a walk around central Krakow reveals a plethora of advertised organized visits to the Auschwitz Museum at so-called bargain prices, often available to purchase as a package deal with a same-day visit to the nearby Wieliczka Salt Mine. In short, a visit to the Museum appears to be part of the itinerary of "must-see" things to do in and around the city. There is also the concern that visits to the Auschwitz Museum only encourage "morbid voyeurism," and that a visit to the Museum "is the ultimate rubbernecker's experience of passing by and gazing at someone else's tragedy."[10]

What can be said, therefore, about the photographs taken by visitors in the Museum? During a period of fieldwork at the Auschwitz Museum, Lennon and Foley observed

Figure 1. Visitors taking photographs at the Museum, April 2015. Copyright: Samantha Mitschke.

"groups of schoolchildren […] taking pictures of each other, parents […] photographing their children at the gates of Birkenau … "[11] I have also witnessed visitors to the Museum taking photographs of each other in places that are instantly recognizable: the barbed wire fencing; the rows of decaying brick chimneys; and the end of the train tracks leading to Crematoria II and III (see Figure 1 for an example).

Indeed, one need only conduct a simple internet search to discover a wide range of photographs taken by the Museum's visitors. Many of these, too, have been posted onto social networking websites, encouraged, at least in part, by the Auschwitz Museum's own Facebook and Instagram pages. As the former is currently "liked" by over 192,000 users, this guarantees wide exposure and the chance for public feedback on these photographs.[12]

Despite the emerging links between post-memory of the Holocaust and the digital age, very little has been written on visitors' photography at Holocaust sites, and even less concerning the rationale behind this interaction and the uses for such photographs. Scholars such as Susan Sontag and Barbie Zelizer have commented specifically on photographs taken directly after the liberation of the camps, but have not referenced modern photography captured at Holocaust sites. In Janina Struk's book *Photographing the Holocaust*, the concept of tourist photography is mentioned but not explored in detail.[13] Furthermore, more critical scholars, including Tim Cole and Norman Finkelstein, have denounced "the Holocaust industry" and its magnetism for tourists without even referring to what could be called the digitalization of Holocaust memory, whether or not they regard this in a positive light.[14] I suggest that investigating visitors' motives for photographing sites such as the Auschwitz Museum is crucial to our understanding of the ways in which the Holocaust is being memorialized and commemorated by younger generations.

The study

Research into digital devices requires a digital approach. I created a research profile on Facebook and Instagram and contacted people whose photographs had either been uploaded to the "Your Gallery" photo album on the Auschwitz Museum's Facebook page[15] or shared by the Museum on its Instagram page. If participants agreed to take part in the research, they were sent a personalized questionnaire. Questions included basic demographic information; questions relating to their visit to the Museum; questions relating to their photograph(s); and their opinions on debates such as people having their photograph taken on-site and "liking" photographs of the former concentration camp on social networking websites. In addition to the photograph(s) they had shared with the Auschwitz Museum, many participants also invited me to select other pictures they had taken at the Museum uploaded to their personal profiles.

Once all completed questionnaires had been gathered, I inserted all respondents' answers into an Excel spreadsheet and searched for specific words or themes that could potentially link them together. For example, answers that included phrases such as "showing they were there," "iconic" and "seen on television" were grouped into the category "Iconic Images," as presented below.

Ethics were a crucial part of this investigation. Participants were given the option of total anonymity in the research paper, and approval was sought for the use of any photographs. Furthermore, if any photograph showed the participant themselves or someone they knew, eyes or faces could be censored according to their preferences. Participants were also assured that their completed questionnaires would not be shared with anyone else, and that they had the right to withdraw from the study or ask for the deletion of their data at any time, without giving a reason.

Sixteen participants took part in this study, ranging from under 21 to 50 years old. Only English-speaking participants could be recruited; although a small majority of participants were British, others identified themselves as Polish, American, Mexican, Slovakian, Canadian, Belgian, Dutch, and Italian. Two participants also revealed direct personal connections to the former camp.[16]

All respondents had visited the Auschwitz Museum at least once since 2011. Some had visited the Museum on their own; others had visited with family, friends, or spouses, or as part of an organized tour group. The initial reasons given for visiting the Museum also varied. Several participants cited their interest in history, particularly relating to World War II and the Holocaust. Others visited for more educational reasons, either in their capacity as a teacher or to confirm what they had read or seen on television. Only one participant gave an answer that could imply visiting Auschwitz for its appeal as a tourist destination: "We were staying in Krakow and we all thought it was something that we would like to see."[17]

Behind the lens

Participants' answers regarding their motivations for taking certain photographs were grouped into six main categories, each revealing the varied – and sometimes surprising – purposes visitors ascribe to the Auschwitz Museum.

1. Iconic images

As the Holocaust has penetrated further into national collective memory, particularly in the Western world, so Auschwitz has become the defining symbol of the deportation and mass murder of Europe's Jews. Although the phrase "*Arbeit Macht Frei*" was emblazoned on gates at several camps, most people instantly associate this slogan with Auschwitz I. Similarly, the large gatehouse and railway tracks at Birkenau are commonly used to accompany articles relating to the Holocaust, and have been used in a plethora of documentaries. Even for people who have not visited Auschwitz or know very little about the Holocaust, these two images have become synonymous with imprisonment, suffering, and genocide.

Almost all of the photographs that participants in this study had taken of either gate were strikingly similar. Most of the pictures taken at Birkenau also showed a portion of the railhead, evoking the famous photograph taken by the camp's liberators in 1945 (Figure 2). According to some of the participants, this was a wholly conscious decision. Sarah Kirton admitted that she would have preferred not to have any people in her photograph of the "*Arbeit Macht Frei*" gate, for example, because, "I think the image would have been striking and more similar to other iconic images of this symbol."[18] It appears, therefore, that some visitors not only take their own photographs of these famous "icons," but wish to *replicate* them almost entirely. Judith Keilbach and Kirsten Wächter believe that this is because certain iconic photographs have become embedded in our "cultural

Figure 2. Reproduced with permission from the Auschwitz-Birkenau State Museum.

memory," and that they now serve as models on which others can attempt to create the same take-home iconic image.[19]

The familiarity of these sights may even provide visitors to the Auschwitz Museum with a sense of reassurance, having seen them so many times before, and grant a form of subconscious permission and compulsion to photograph them. Furthermore, these two infamous structures at Auschwitz may also have become inextricably associated with "part of the ritual behaviour of tourism" of "photographing the photographed."[20] Participants in this study certainly support this idea. "It is a recognisable scene and I wanted to have a picture of it taken by me," stated Debbie S. "[I] found it hard to believe I was standing

Figure 3. Copyright: Martin Carney.

there viewing this, when I had seen it so many times on television."[21] Martin Carney agreed (Figure 3); having initially seen the main gate of Auschwitz-Birkenau in *The World at War*, he admitted, "I was compelled to photograph it in much the same way as a tourist would photograph the Eiffel Tower!"[22]

One interpretation of these photographs confirms Roland Barthes' notion of every photograph providing "a certificate of presence"; people often take photographs to prove that they have visited a place of global recognition or importance – such as, to use Carney's example, the Eiffel Tower – and the Auschwitz Museum is increasingly being ascribed to the same canon of tourist photography.[23] Each visitor, whatever the motivation for their visit, bears witness to the physical ruins that once formed Auschwitz the camp rather than Auschwitz the museum. Photographing the site allows visitors to confirm to themselves, as well as others, what they have seen, reflecting on its dark history and moral value in the modern world.

Alternatively, as Susan Sontag writes, "in a world saturated, no, hyper-saturated with images, those that should matter have a diminishing effect: we become callous."[24] Visitors may take photographs of the most widely recognized aspects of the Auschwitz Museum, therefore, because that is now simply part of the routine of visiting famous places. Buildings in the former camp – especially those that are not directly connected with mass killing – cannot be personified, but what of the exhibits of victims' personal items on display at the Museum? Claude Lanzmann worries that the "worldwide knowledge of some of these exhibits […] can reduce the emotive reaction and harden the visitors."[25] Although many participants in this study did take pictures of personal articles belonging to victims,

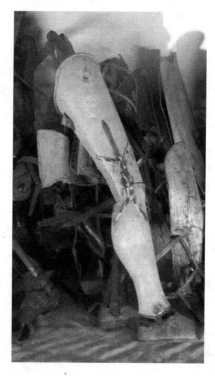

Figure 4. Copyright: Vicky Wasylewsky.

however, all explanations cited feelings of sadness, sympathy, and shock rather than any need to replicate or confirm what they had seen in the media.

2. Aesthetics and "good" photography

Benjamin Walter once wrote, "[Mankind's] self-alienation has reached such a degree that it can experience its own destruction as an aesthetic pleasure of the first order."[26] This would certainly appear true for some of the pictures that Museum visitors have taken, as one reason expressed was that participants were simply trying to take "good" pictures. The content of these photographs varies widely, and the aesthetically pleasing elements of each image are personal to each photographer. Participant Vicky Wasylewsky, for example, explained photographing a victim's prosthetic leg in Auschwitz I (see Figure 4): "At first, it looked [like] a nice picture, in an aesthetical way [...] this leg was almost white. The rest looked grey, darker. To me it was almost illuminated."[27]

Artur Chmielewski photographed a watchtower in between two walls. "I thought that the juxtaposition of the walls and guard towers [would] look good in the picture ... I knew that [this] picture [was] very good. [It's] different [from] all the other pictures."[28] Furthermore, Felipe Bottrel was struck by "the roughness of the brick and stone textures with the softness and colour of the flowers" at the so-called Wall of Death in Auschwitz I.[29] One participant also spoke of his wish that people would "enjoy viewing" his pictures based on their "photographic merit."[30]

In some photographs, therefore, Auschwitz has been transformed from a former concentration and extermination camp to a series of lines, angles and striking objects or landscapes that are appreciated for their aesthetic value. Participants have attempted "to construct idealised images which beautify the object being photographed," even if the object or scene is connected with death and suffering.[31]

According to Sontag, "Photography that bears witness to the calamitous and the reprehensible is much criticised if it seems 'aesthetic'; that is, too much like art," and one can easily denounce photography at a Holocaust site for the simple purpose of creating "good" photographs.[32] Perhaps visitors to the Museum, particularly those with no personal connections to the site, are already so familiar with the imagery of Auschwitz (as shall be seen in the next category) that they view the surroundings on a purely aesthetical basis with less regard for the historical and moral significance of the former camp, in the same way that they may capture photographs of the gates due to their worldwide fame and notoriety.

On the other hand, it can be argued that putting a camera lens between oneself and the object or scene representing atrocity creates a distance that lessens the potentially traumatic effect on the visitor. This is supported by Wasylewsky, who admitted that, after taking a picture of the prosthetic leg, she "couldn't take any more pictures. It just hit me that this belonged to someone. Somebody once wore this, stood on this leg [...] it was too much for me to take."[33]

Franz Kafka stated, "We photograph things in order to drive them out of our minds"; participants may therefore create this distance between themselves and the reality of the Auschwitz Museum so that they can better reflect on what they have witnessed after their experience.[34] The photographs that are captured can be viewed once they have returned from their visit and can be properly processed with the benefit of temporal and spatial distance.

3. Education and visual reminders

Auschwitz, as it is represented today, is first and foremost a site for education. This is delivered in a number of ways: through professional guided tours, available in 18 different languages; the work of the Museum's International Centre for Education about Auschwitz and the Holocaust; and its plethora of publications, many of which are also available in numerous languages.[35]

Photographs are an integral part of these resources. In addition to online lessons, the Museum website includes a dedicated picture gallery containing photographs of the site itself but also of relevant historical documents, prisoners' artwork, the Museum's collections, and preservation work. Furthermore, those who cannot physically visit the Museum can even access an annotated 360-degree panoramic virtual tour of the camp from their computer screen.[36] Images of the camp are crucial in order for those who have not visited to grasp the size and layout of the site, as well as seeing the physical evidence of extermination for themselves.

Participants in this study clearly believe in the importance of photographs as evidence to what they witnessed at the Museum, so they can share the experience with relatives and friends. Sarah Kirton took a photograph of the gas chamber in Auschwitz I; although she worried about appearing "insensitive," she wanted to have a photograph to show her parents upon her return. She also felt that "it would be useful to have a permanent reminder of the site if I were to talk about it in the future."[37] This response is almost identical to a participant's answer in Thurnell-Read's study, who felt that taking photographs was "a problematic but necessary part of her experience."[38]

Figure 5. Copyright: Solange Lalonde.

Similarly, teacher Solange Lalonde photographed the padlock on the gates leading to the courtyard of Block 11 (Figure 5). Although a small detail that many visitors would miss, the padlock, she explained, was symbolic of "unlocking the doors to our collective histories" and made her question, "How can we be the key to reconciliation, how can we contribute to opening gates to understanding and acknowledgment?"[39] Lalonde hoped that she would be able to share these photographs with fellow teachers to use in their lessons about the Holocaust. These examples highlight that, during their visit, at least some participants were already thinking about the educational implications of the Museum, and how they might pass knowledge onto others.

While many visitors' photographs are used as educational tools for others, participants also expressed their use as visual reminders for themselves. In the most extreme example, Julia Nicely-Borland has printed some of her photographs, depicting various aspects of the Museum, onto canvas and displayed them in her home to both share her experiences with her guests and to have continual reflection on her visit.[40]

The category of taking pictures for educational purposes is one of the clearest in demonstrating the deliberate, conscious process behind visitors' photography at the Museum. These are not photographs that visitors have taken mindlessly, to sit in their digital camera's memory or the back of a photo album, but function as educational and reflective resources in their own right. Some visitors are keen to take pictures of even the most horrific aspects of the camp to share with others at home, proving that they were there and personally witnessed their existence, but also to remind themselves at a later time.

4. Commemorating the dead

The notion of the Auschwitz Museum as a tourist attraction and a "must-see" sight in Poland is all the more concerning if we consider it to be "the largest graveyard in the history of the world."[41] Estimates vary regarding the number of people murdered at Auschwitz, but current official statistics usually present the figure at around 1.1 million.[42] Victims' ashes were unceremoniously dumped in various locations around the camp. There is also a little-known mass grave at Auschwitz-Birkenau, the final resting place of approximately 8000 Soviet prisoners of war who died during the construction of the camp between 1941 and 1942. Death occurred around the entire camp on a daily basis, and a visitor may not reflect on the fact that the barrack in which they are standing or a site where roll-call took place also witnessed a form of murder.

Alongside traditional ways of commemorating the dead, photography has become another outlet for remembering and paying respects to those who perished at Auschwitz. Participants highlighted different aspects of the camp at which they felt the need to take pictures in order to honor the camp's victims. For some, this was at the actual killing sites. Artur Chmielewski photographed part of the forest near the crematoria, including one of the Museum's information boards displaying a photograph of people waiting in the same place in 1944, under the impression of waiting their turn for a "shower." He wished to show the peace and stillness of the forest, and the fact that many people would not realize the significance of this area decades later.[43] Both Keila Martinez and Maciej Zabłocki, who took photographs at Crematorium I and Crematorium II respectively, emphasized how emotional they felt at each site and the need for prayer at places where victims were murdered.[44]

Participants also paid tribute to the dead by photographing pictures of victims and their possessions. For instance, Vicky Wasylewsky was overcome by the photographs of prisoners taken upon their arrival into the camp. "I could not believe that the numbers all had a face," she stated. "So many names. So many faces. I wanted to look at each one, to honour them."[45] This personalization of victims is vital; to restore some individualism and humanity to those who perished at Auschwitz is to go directly against what Nazism set out to accomplish.

Finally, participants wanted visual reminders of other forms of commemoration that can be found around both sites, but particularly at Auschwitz-Birkenau. For instance, Julia Nicely-Borland photographed small stones and a rose left on the side of the cattle car that stands on the railway tracks in the former camp (Figure 6). She acknowledges that "when you walk through Auschwitz, especially Birkenau, you are really walking through a mass grave," and has tried to find "beauty" in "the fact that thousands of visitors have laid stones in remembrance of those murdered."[46]

All of these photographs illustrate "a portrait of absence, of death without the dead."[47] Each aspect signifies loss: the loss of individuals, families, memories; the loss of individuality and humanity; the loss of a proper grave for each person who died in Auschwitz. The images of victims' possessions and their photographs especially highlight what can be termed the presence of their absence. The way one remembers victims of mass atrocities such as the Holocaust is a matter of individual choice. Where one visitor may place a rose, another may say a prayer; where one lights a candle, another may take a photograph.

5. Sympathy and empathy

Remembering and commemorating victims of the Holocaust conjures at least some form of sympathy with those who lost their lives. To *empathize* with both Holocaust victims and survivors, on the other hand, is generally agreed upon as impossible.[48]

Figure 6. Copyright: Julia Nicely-Borland.

The difference between sympathy and empathy is relatively subtle but significant. The *Collins English Dictionary* defines sympathy as "the sharing of another's emotions, especially of sorrow or anguish; pity; compassion," whereas empathy is defined as "the power of understanding and *imaginatively entering* into another person's feelings" (emphasis added).[49] The concept of imagining the experiences of someone imprisoned in Auschwitz seems far-fetched, even inappropriate – but this is exactly what several participants admitted to attempting with their photographs.

Feelings of sympathy and sadness were expressed by most respondents across a wide variety of pictures, many of which have already been discussed. Photographs portraying empathy, however, were presented differently. Several images were positioned to show the Museum from the perspective of a prisoner. Martin Carney reflected on the fact that his view of the watchtowers would be the same as the prisoners'.[50] Both Julia Nicely-Borland and Keila Martinez tried to show the iconic gatehouse and railway tracks of Birkenau as though viewing them through the eyes of a new arrival (see Figure 7 for an example).[51] Henk Claassen combined his photograph of the forest near the crematoria with the emotions he believed the victims would be experiencing at that point: "I assume some of them might have looked up to those trees, [anxious] about what would happen next" (Figure 8).[52]

The idea of empathetic photography at the Auschwitz Museum is problematic in two ways: the physical and the mental. Regarding the former, while many of the structures around the site are authentic, many have been reconstructed, replicated, or have undergone a high degree of conservation. Therefore, the Auschwitz that visitors see 70 years after the liberation of the camp is *not* the Auschwitz that prisoners experienced, even from a purely aesthetic point of view. Wooden barracks in Birkenau have been carefully

Figure 7. Copyright: Keila Martinez.

Figure 8. Copyright: Henk Claassen.

disassembled, conserved, and reassembled; only foundations and heaps of rubble remain where four gas chambers and crematoria once stood.[53]

The Museum has, therefore, been somewhat changed and "reordered," meaning that "it cannot do any more than stand for the events which it represents."[54] No visitor who walks through the gates of Auschwitz experiences a concentration camp. What they experience is a museum and memorial, a place of education and remembrance rather than a present place of suffering.

Additionally, it is simply inconceivable for anyone who was not directly affected by the Holocaust to even begin to try and place themselves "in the shoes" of those who were. The average visitor simply has no point of reference with which to compare their life with the suffering endured in places such as Auschwitz. Nevertheless, these photographs are still demonstrative of the engaged cognitive state of many visitors who wish to both sympathize and empathize with the fate of Holocaust victims and survivors.

6. Hope and tolerance

Holocaust sites are certainly not places that one would immediately associate with positive themes such as hope, respect, and tolerance. During their operation, the Nazi concentration camps worked against all such principles, and visitors to Holocaust museums and institutions are taught about Nazi policies of racism, segregation, prejudice, and, ultimately, genocide. The Holocaust, however, is frequently upheld as a warning from which to confront anti-Semitism, hatred, and prejudice, and not to remain a bystander if one is a witness to such persecution.

Some participants in this study did express the belief that visiting Auschwitz would help them "try to make sure that [it] doesn't happen again."[55] While the final category of participants' photographs does emphasize reflections on hope and tolerance, however, these

Figure 9. Copyright: Solange Lalonde.

photographs relate more to physical elements and survivors of the former camp rather than more abstract themes that can be derived from the Holocaust as a general subject. Overwhelmingly, respondents found messages of hope in life's victory over death, through the nature around the site, the legacy of Auschwitz survivors, and the existence of present-day Jewish life and culture.

Trees were a recurring element in this type of picture. Debbie S. captured a photograph of a birch tree in Auschwitz I as she found it "unusual but beautiful"; Keila Martinez photographed the forest in Birkenau because she believed the same trees and their resilience to grow through the hard winters may have inspired "a little faith, a little hope" in the prisoners.[56] Solange Lalonde was also compelled to photograph a tree in the Museum (Figure 9): "In the rubble and the ruins," she explained, "life finds a way to reach up and reach through."[57]

The triumph of survivors over their persecutors was also present in a photograph taken by Vicky Wasylewsky. Visiting Auschwitz was a more personal experience for Wasylewsky than for most visitors, as her grandparents met in the camp just a few days before its liberation in January 1945. Taking a photograph from the ramp in Birkenau, she felt "proud to be able to take the picture. Be able to stand there, where my family history started. And be happy that I am alive."[58]

These examples, therefore, illustrate the ways in which the site has been transformed from a place of murder and inhumanity to a museum and memorial promoting education, tolerance, and a reaffirmation of the value of life.

Figure 10. Copyright: Henk Claassen.

"With my besties in Auschwitz"

This study's participants took many pictures of other people in various locations around the camp. Maciej Zabłocki captured a group of young Israeli Jews, wrapped in Israeli flags,

Figure 11. Copyright: Henk Claassen.

Figure 12. Copyright: Henk Claassen.

gathered around Crematorium II; Ákos Balogh photographed fellow attendees on the March of the Living. Other examples, however, often relate to ideas of sympathy and empathy for prisoners of Auschwitz, as discussed above. Henk Claassen devoted an entire album on his photography website to "Ghosts from the Present," a series of layered pictures of visitors walking around the camp (Figures 10, 11, and 12).[59]

Many of these images, as presented here, focus on sites associated with extermination. Claassen explains that he was overwhelmed by the "vast stream of visitors" around the Museum during his visit, but was also disturbed by the thought of those visitors being

Figure 13. Copyright: Henk Claassen.

59

able to walk in and out freely, compared to those who were forced to enter during the camp's operation. Therefore, Claassen wanted his photographs to carry a double message: not only should they show the numerous visitors around the Museum, but also "let the visitors represent […] a shadow of the prisoners, [and] show the volatility of human life itself." This seems to express the desire to recognize the history of the Museum, as well as form another type of commemoration.[60] In contrast to the portraits of "death without the dead," as termed by Sontag, Claassen pays tribute to Auschwitz's victims almost by attempting to bring them to life in front of the camera, and by highlighting that wherever a visitor walks, thousands of prisoners once made the same journey – often to their deaths.

Additionally, Claassen published an album containing photographs of other people, but with the emphasis on them purely as Museum visitors, as he wished "to record how people react in this specific place i.e. taking posed pictures of themselves as a remembrance or some kind of proof they were there." Figure 13 shows the most extreme example of these, a picture that Claassen says he took because he was "[astonished] by their behaviour."[61]

According to Claassen, these visitors had only just arrived at Birkenau, and one would almost hope they had not yet visited Auschwitz I and seen evidence of the crimes committed at the camp. Such a photograph could certainly support Cole's assertion of the Museum as "Auschwitz-land." It is concerning to see this type of behavior present at a former concentration and extermination camp, but thankfully, what is shown in this photograph remains a small part of visitors' photography at the Auschwitz Museum.

Only two respondents had their photographs taken inside the Museum, both in a respectful manner. Debbie S. was pictured standing in a barracks once designed for prisoners to wash themselves, while Ákos Balogh has a photograph of himself in front of barbed wire and a block in Auschwitz I. I have also observed visitors taking pictures of each other with the gatehouse of Birkenau in the background (see Figure 14 for an example); as well

Figure 14. Copyright: Samantha Mitschke.

as the attempted replication of pictures of "Iconic Images" as previously discussed, many visitors wish to be photographed standing in front of these recognizable landscapes. These examples reiterate Barthes' theory of the photograph as evidence of presence.

Conversely, in addition to the idea of capturing people in front of familiar images, there may also be an aspect of seeking aesthetically pleasing photographs. Urry and Larsen state that part of "tourist photography is to place one's 'loved ones' within an 'attraction' in such a way that both are represented aesthetically."[62] This is undoubtedly problematic when considering the site that has been chosen to capture "good" photographs including people. It is true that photographs may be taken of survivors or their families as a testament to their liberation and life after Auschwitz, but it is safe to assume the majority of visitors have no association with the Museum's history and so their motivations for taking these photographs are somewhat questionable.

By far the most controversial type of photography at the Auschwitz Museum is the relatively recent trend in taking "selfies." With the development of smartphones and GoPro cameras, tourists, especially young people, are now compelled to capture their visit to a particular site or destination with at least one photograph of themselves. A plethora of photographs taken at sites of "dark tourism" have now been shared on the internet, prompting websites such as "Selfies at Serious Places" and Facebook groups like "With My Besties in Auschwitz."[63] The former draws attention to one rather disturbing example of a "selfie" taken at the Auschwitz Museum in July 2013. British teenager John Quirke posed with a mock shock-face inside the gas chamber in Auschwitz I, captioning the photograph "Selfie from the gas chamber in Auschwitz #selfie #respect."[64]

Furthermore, American teenager Breanna Mitchell faced huge backlash from the online community in 2014 after a photograph that she took in Auschwitz I went viral. In the

Figure 15. Copyright: Matt Diamond.

picture that she uploaded to Twitter, Mitchell is seen standing between two rows of brick barracks in the former camp, smiling and with a white headphone in one ear, with the title "Selfie in the Auschwitz concentration camp" followed by a blushing smiley face symbol.

Only one person who has taken a "selfie" at the Museum responded to the invitation to participate in this research; it is likely that other people who have taken these types of photographs at the Museum feared criticism or judgment. Matt Diamond visited the Auschwitz Museum with friends in 2014 and took a picture of himself with the gatehouse of Birkenau in the background (Figure 15). Posting the image on Twitter in the wake of the backlash against Mitchell, Diamond captioned his photograph by tagging Mitchell's account and stating "B**** please. Trying to be me. I'm the original inappropriate selfie taker."

Diamond states that his caption was meant "in complete jest" and he was merely looking for a reaction from Mitchell (although it never prompted one). Regarding his decision to take the photograph itself, however, he explained it as part of a regular process of taking selfies while travelling and uploading them on social media so his friends can see what he is doing. "When I took it," Diamond stated, "I did think of the insensitivity of the selfie, [but] I've been known to 'shock' before, so this was nothing out of the ordinary." When questioned about how he felt taking the photograph, he also admitted:

> I was a little bit hungover when I took the picture, [I'm] not going to lie. I didn't feel bad taking it, a selfie is completely normal in my life. I did try to look sombre, I remember that.[65]

Although this photograph was branded an "offensive selfie" in a *Jewish News* article, Diamond says he has not experienced any hostility on the internet or from friends – in fact, the latter found it "hilarious."[66] He also feels that people who criticize taking "selfies" at Auschwitz "need to get a grip" as it is such a common occurrence "in this day and age."[67]

At first glance, these photographs seem to trivialize the horrific events that took place at Auschwitz, and a site where mass murder was committed is utilized to make a more unusual background for a "selfie." While some participants in this study were of the opinion that photographs including people are acceptable, dependent upon the location of the photograph and displaying respectful behavior, every respondent agreed that taking "selfies" at the Auschwitz Museum is wholly inappropriate and unnecessary. Vicky Wasylewsky summarized general opinion by stating: "This is not a place to look at yourself. It is a place to look at others, who […] suffered."[68]

Conversely, it is not necessarily the case that such pictures are driven by narcissism or a lack of moral understanding. Diamond's answers highlight the normality of taking "selfies" for many young people in the digital age, but motivations other than to shock or to add to regular social media interaction should be explored. Keith Durkin argues, for example, that for "individuals who generally lack first-hand experience with death, the phenomenon of death and dying has become abstract and invisible."[69] Unsure how to respond to the overwhelming statistics and physical evidence of extermination they are presented with, young people may try and shape their experience into a format that they feel more comfortable with. "By rendering death into humour and entertainment," Durkin argues, "we effectively neutralise it; it becomes innocuous, and thus less threatening."[70] Furthermore, Magdalena Hodalska highlights the theme of hope that the Museum presents to some visitors by stating that these "selfies" could be designed "to celebrate life in [...] the most 'creative' way."[71] What seems to be an inappropriate photograph to others, therefore, could be a personal affirmation of the Nazis' defeat and a tribute to survival. Rather than photographing traditional signs of commemoration around the camp, young people turn to the method with which they are familiar and frequently use to show that life can continue, even in the long shadow of a place like Auschwitz. Whether or not this is a suitable commemorative act shall remain a matter of personal opinion.

Conclusion

This research has shown that many of the photographs taken at the Auschwitz-Birkenau State Museum are not taken mindlessly, and that cognitive engagement and reflection are both crucial to the process of capturing images of the former camp. Visitors photograph recognizable sights such as the gates of Auschwitz I and Auschwitz-Birkenau as evidence of their experience, as well as confirming to themselves that they are in physical proximity to a view they have been exposed to many times on television and other media. The idea of taking aesthetically "pleasing" pictures at the Museum may initially appear to be a superficial motivation, but the responses of at least a couple of participants in this study suggest that the camera provides a distance between the photographer and the horrific views or items before them, so that they can better process the experience of bearing witness to the crimes committed at Auschwitz after their visit. Photographs taken by visitors also play an educational role as they are shared with friends and family, as well as providing visual reminders for the visitor so that they can remember their experience and reflect on what they themselves learned while at the Museum.

Moreover, some visitors have decided to commemorate the victims of the Auschwitz concentration and extermination camp by capturing other scenes of remembrance: the placing of stones, as is custom in Jewish tradition; flowers and wreaths left at places such as the Wall of Death; Jewish youth groups adorned with Israeli flags, gathering to pray or celebrate the continuation of Jewish life. Other visitors have also chosen to express the value of life and survival through their pictures, often focusing on nature to show the triumph of those that were not murdered by the Nazis. Furthermore, this stands as testament to the fact that the ruins of Auschwitz still remain as witness to the unendurable suffering that took place and as a warning from history about the capability of mankind to destroy itself. Finally – and slightly more controversially – visitors have attempted to place themselves in the shoes of prisoners and the feelings and emotions they may have experienced. While this type of photography should not be explicitly encouraged, as it is impossible for anyone who did not survive the camp to truly appreciate the horrors of such imprisonment, it serves as yet another example of the ways in which visitors have used photography to shape their own experiences of their visit to the Museum and highlight the aspects of their visit that will stay with them.

The inclusion of people in photographs taken at the Auschwitz Museum continues to be an area of debate, particularly regarding the recent rise in "selfies" captured on-site. The decision to take "selfies" at places connected with dark tourism may not necessarily stem from reasons of vanity, narcissism, or disrespect, and potentially highlights a new trend in commemoration and witnessing that young people are increasingly using. This requires speaking to a much wider range of young people, although, as this study has shown,

TRACING TOPOGRAPHIES

this proves problematic when visitors who have taken "selfies" at the Museum receive so much criticism and negative backlash.

Visitors will take photographs at the Auschwitz-Birkenau State Museum as long it remains open. Therefore, one can only hope that these photographs remain respectful, reflective, and educational as we mark 70 years since the liberation of Auschwitz, the most notorious of the Nazis' network of concentration and extermination camps.

Notes

1. In spring 2014, for example, 129.28 million Americans stated that they lived in a household that owned a digital camera. Furthermore, as of September 2014, 71% of the American population and more than two in three British adults owned at least one smartphone. See "Digital Camera Ownership: Number of People Living in Households that Own a Digital Camera in the United States (USA) from Spring 2008 to Spring 2014 (In Millions)," Statista, http://www.statista.com/statistics/228876/people-living-in-households-that-own-a-digital-camera-usa/ (accessed May 29, 2015); and "Mobile Millennials: Over 85% of Generation Y Owns Smartphones," Nielsen, http://www.nielsen.com/us/en/insights/news/2014/mobile-millennials-over-85-percent-of-generation-y-owns-smartphones.html (accessed May 29, 2015); "Mobile Consumer 2014: The UK Cut, Revolution and Evolution," Deloitte LLP, http://www.deloitte.co.uk/mobileuk/assets/pdf/Deloitte_Mobile_Consumer_2014.pdf (accessed May 28, 2015).
2. Urry and Larsen, *The Tourist Gaze*, 185.
3. Sontag, *On Photography*, 24.
4. Lennon and Foley, *Dark Tourism*, 3.
5. Cole, *Selling the Holocaust*, 110.
6. Auschwitz-Birkenau State Museum, *Report 2014*, 20.
7. See, for example, "The Lessons from Auschwitz Project," Holocaust Educational Trust, http://www.het.org.uk/lessons-from-auschwitz-programme/about-lfa (accessed July 29, 2015); Cole, *Selling the Holocaust*, 105.
8. Cole, *Selling the Holocaust*, 113.
9. Miles, "Auschwitz," 1176–7.
10. Thurnell-Read, "Engaging Auschwitz," 27; Cole, Selling the Holocaust, 114.
11. Lennon and Foley, *Dark Tourism*, 60–61.
12. "Auschwitz Memorial/Muzeum Auschwitz," Facebook, http://www.facebook.com/auschwitzmemorial (figure correct as of 19 August 2015).
13. Struk, *Photographing the Holocaust*, 190.
14. Finkelstein, *The Holocaust Industry*, xi.
15. Facebook, "Your Gallery" on "Auschwitz Memorial/Muzeum Auschwitz" page, https://www.facebook.com/auschwitzmemorial/photos/a.10150532444976097.370321.170493316096/10151084594956097/?type=3&theater (accessed January 4, 2015). "Auschwitz Memorial and Museum," https://www.instagram.com/auschwitzmemorial/ (accessed February 11, 2016).
16. Maciej Zabłocki, Questionnaire, 14 November 2014; Vicky Wasylewsky, Questionnaire, 8 October 2014.
17. Sarah Kirton, Questionnaire, 9 October 2014.
18. Ibid.
19. Keilbach and Wächter, "Photographs, Symbolic Images, and the Holocaust," 55, 73.
20. Osborne, *Travelling Light*, 85.
21. Debbie S., Questionnaire, 19 October 2014.
22. Martin Carney, Questionnaire, 22 October 2014.
23. Barthes, *Camera Lucida*, 87.
24. Sontag, *Regarding the Pain of Others*, 93–4.
25. Lanzmann, "Why Spielberg Has Distorted the Truth," 60.
26. Benjamin, *Illuminations*, 242.

27. Vicky Wasylewsky, Questionnaire, 8 October 2014.
28. Artur Chmielewksi, Questionnaire, 14 November 2014.
29. Felipe Bottrel, Questionnaire, 15 August 2015.
30. Martin Carney, Questionnaire, 22 October 2014.
31. Urry and Larsen, *The Tourist Gaze*, 169.
32. Sontag, *Regarding the Pain of Others*, 68.
33. Vicky Wasylewsky, Questionnaire, 8 October 2014.
34. Barthes, *Camera Lucida*, 53.
35. Auschwitz-Birkenau State Museum, "Bookstore," http://auschwitz.org/en/bookstore/ (accessed August 11, 2015); "Guides," http://auschwitz.org/en/visiting/guides/ (accessed August 11, 2015).
36. Auschwitz-Birkenau State Museum, "Auschwitz-Birkenau Virtual Tour," http://panorama.auschwitz.org/ (accessed August 11, 2015).
37. Sarah Kirton, Questionnaire, 9 October 2014.
38. Thurnell-Read, "Engaging Auschwitz," 37.
39. Solange Lalonde, Questionnaire, 3 November 2014.
40. Julia Nicely-Borland, Questionnaire, 8 October 2014.
41. Rees, *Auschwitz*, 373.
42. While institutions such as the United States Holocaust Memorial Museum and the Auschwitz-Birkenau State Museum cite "over one million people" and "over 1.1 million men, women and children" respectively, others, such as Yad Vashem, state "more than 1,100,000 Jews, 70,000 Poles, 25,000 Sinti and Roma (Gypsies) and some 15,000 prisoners of war from the USSR and other countries were murdered" at Auschwitz. See United States Holocaust Memorial Museum, "Auschwitz," http://www.ushmm.org/outreach/en/article.php?ModuleId=10007718 (accessed August 13, 2015); Auschwitz-Birkenau State Museum, "Home Page", http://auschwitz.org/en/ (accessed August 11, 2015); Yad Vashem, "Holocaust History – Auschwitz-Birkenau Extermination Camp," http://www.yadvashem.org/yv/en/holocaust/about/05/auschwitz_birkenau.asp (accessed August 13, 2015).
43. Artur Chmielewski, Questionnaire, 14 November 2014.
44. Keila Martinez, Questionnaire, 30 November 2014; Maciej Zabłocki, Questionnaire, 14 November 2014.
45. Vicky Wasylewsky, Questionnaire, 8 October 2014.
46. Julia Nicely-Borland, Questionnaire, 3 December 2014.
47. Sontag, *Regarding the Pain of Others*, 45.
48. This point is emphasized in academic study of the Holocaust (for example, Marrus, "'Lessons' of the Holocaust"); in Holocaust education (Short, Supple, and Jinger, *The Holocaust in the School Curriculum*, 46); and by Holocaust survivors themselves (Mala Tribich, personal correspondence with the author, June 2015).
49. *Collins English Dictionary*, 1655, 543.
50. Martin Carney, Questionnaire, 22 October 2014.
51. Julia Nicely-Borland, Questionnaire, 3 December 2014; Keila Martinez, Questionnaire, 30 November 2014.
52. Henk Claassen, Questionnaire, 29 October 2014.
53. Auschwitz-Birkenau State Museum, "To Preserve Authenticity: The Conservation of Five Wooden Barracks at the Former Auschwitz II-Birkenau Extermination Camp," http://www.auschwitz.org/gfx/auschwitz/userfiles/auschwitz/zachowac_autentyzm_pdf/zachowac_autentyzm_2012.pdf (accessed August 13, 2015), 11–16.
54. Keil, "Sightseeing in the Mansions of the Dead."
55. Ilaria Marcia, Questionnaire, 22 December 2014.
56. Debbie S., Questionnaire, 19 October 2014; Keila Martinez, Questionnaire, 30 November 2014.
57. Solange Lalonde, Questionnaire, 3 November 2014.
58. Vicky Wasylewsky, Questionnaire, 8 October 2014.

59. "Ghosts from the Present," In Lumine Vitae, http://www.inluminevitae.nl/gallery2/main.php?g2_itemId=25934 (accessed August 16, 2015). 'Maciej Zabłocki, questionnaire, November 14, 2014; Ákos Balogh, questionnaire, December 2, 2014.
60. Henk Claassen, Questionnaire, 29 October 2014.
61. Ibid.
62. Urry and Larsen, *The Tourist Gaze*, 179.
63. Selfies at Serious Places, http://selfiesatseriousplaces.tumblr.com/ (accessed August 17, 2015).
64. "Wide Eyes for Auschwitz!" Selfies at Serious Places, http://selfiesatseriousplaces.tumblr.com/page/2 (accessed August 17, 2015).
65. Matt Diamond, Questionnaire, 17 August 2015.
66. "Barrage of Abuse for Teen Who Posts Smiling Selfie at Auschwitz," Jewish News Online, http://www.jewishnews.co.uk/barrage-abuse-teen-posts-smiling-selfie-auschwitz/ (accessed July 30, 2015); Matt Diamond, Questionnaire, 17 August 2015.
67. Matt Diamond, Questionnaire, 17 August 2015.
68. Vicky Wasylewsky, Questionnaire, 8 October 2014.
69. Durkin, "Death, Dying and the Dead," 43.
70. Ibid., 47.
71. Hodalska, "Selfies at Horror Sites."

Disclosure statement

No potential conflict of interest was reported by the author.

Bibliography

Auschwitz-Birkenau State Museum. *Report 2014*. Oświęcim: Auschwitz-Birkenau State Museum, 2015.
Barthes, Roland. *Camera Lucida: Reflections on Photography*. London: Vintage, 2000.
Benjamin, Walter. *Illuminations*. New York: Schocken, 1969.
Cole, Tim. *Selling the Holocaust: From Auschwitz to Schindler, How History is Bought, Packaged and Sold*. New York: Routledge, 1999.
Collins English Dictionary. Glasgow: HarperCollins, 2010.
Durkin, Keith F. "Death, Dying and the Dead in Popular Culture." In *Handbook of Death and Dying*, edited by Clifton D. Bryant, 43–49. Thousand Oaks, CA: Sage Publications, 2003.
Finkelstein, Norman G. *The Holocaust Industry: Reflections on the Exploitation of Jewish Suffering*. London: Verso, 2003.
Hodalska, Magdalena. "Selfies at Horror Sites: Dark Tourism, Ghoulish Souvenirs and Digital Narcissism." Paper presented at The Holocaust and the Contemporary World Conference, Krakow, April 23–24, 2015.
Keil, Chris. "Sightseeing in the Mansions of the Dead." *Social & Cultural Geography* 6 (2005): 479–494. doi:10.1080/14649360500200197.
Keilbach, Judith, and Kirsten Wächter. "Photographs, Symbolic Images, and the Holocaust: On the (Im)possibility of Depicting Historical Truth." *History and Theory* 48 (2009): 54–76.

Lanzmann, Claude. 1995. "Why Spielberg Has Distorted the Truth." *The Guardian Weekly*, March 3.

Lennon, John, and Malcolm Foley. *Dark Tourism: The Attraction of Death and Disaster*. London: Thomson Learning, 2007.

Marrus, Michael R. "'Lessons' of the Holocaust and the Ceaseless, Discordant Search for Meaning." In *Holocaust Scholarship: Personal Trajectories and Professional Interpretations*, edited by Christopher R. Browning, Susannah Heschel, Michael R. Marrus, and Milton Shain, 170–186. Basingstoke: Palgrave Macmillan, 2015.

Miles, William F. S. "Auschwitz: Modern Interpretation and Darker Tourism." *Annals of Tourism Research* 29 (2002): 1175–1178.

Osborne, Peter. *Travelling Light: Photography, Travel and Visual Culture*. Manchester: Manchester University Press, 2000.

Rees, Laurence. *Auschwitz: The Nazis and the Final Solution*. London: BBC Books, 2005.

Short, Geoffrey, Carrie Supple, and Katherine Jinger. *The Holocaust in the School Curriculum: A European Perspective, Volume 754*. Strasbourg: Council of Europe Publishing, 1998.

Sontag, Susan. *On Photography*. London: Penguin, 1979.

Sontag, Susan. *Regarding the Pain of Others*. London: Penguin, 2003.

Struk, Janina. *Photographing the Holocaust: Interpretations of the Evidence*. London: I. B. Tauris, 2005.

Thurnell-Read, Thomas P. "Engaging Auschwitz: An Analysis of Young Travellers' Experience of Holocaust Tourism." *Journal of Tourism Consumption and Practice* 1 (2009): 26–52.

Urry, John, and Jonas Larsen. *The Tourist Gaze 3.0*. London: Sage Publications, 2012.

The concentration camp brothels in memory

Nicole Bogue

Independent Scholar

ABSTRACT

This paper examines the differing representations of the history of concentration camp brothels. It examines how two specific sites of memory, Ravensbrück Gedenkstätte and Auschwitz-Birkenau State Museum have taken dichotomous approaches in whether to explore this difficult and marginal experiences of around two hundred women who were forced to serve in prisoner camp brothels. Building on research visits to both sites in 2013, it evaluates and argues that differing national sensitivities, roles the topographies play in memory and history and the pressures of visitor numbers to the sites are fundamental in these juxtaposing representations.

We were now in a prisoner brothel … as long as we submitted then nothing would happen to us. (Frau W.)[1]

The *Sonderbauten*

The Nazi regime, and its methods of terror within concentration camps, is one of the most comprehensively documented, memorialized, and infamous historical periods. Yet it is a largely unknown fact that from 1942 until 1945 the Nazis established 10 "brothel" institutions euphemistically nicknamed the *Sonderbauten* (special buildings) by the SS, in 10 concentration camps in Germany, Austria, and Poland.[2] Brothel barracks were used to house female non-Jewish prisoners forced to work as sex laborers for privileged male prisoners.[3] Prisoner brothels were established at Neuengamme, Dachau, Auschwitz-Monowitz, Auschwitz-Stammlager (main camp), Sachsenhausen, Mittelbau-Dora, Mauthausen, Gusen (a Mauthausen sub-camp), Buchenwald, and Flossenbürg.[4] In regards to the inmates who served in the *Sonderbau*, Ravensbrück survivor Herbermann noted: "I will leave it up to others to report of this in more detail."[5] Yet most of the women never did "report" back and the sites in which they were incarcerated as sex slaves have not been fully used as a starting point for historical discussion of this sensitive history.[6]

This is not to argue that the suffering of women in the *Sonderbauten* has not been discussed or examined at all. In Germany, Sommer's *Das KZ-Bordell*, published in 2009 (building upon Paul's foundational *Zwangsprostitution*) brought forced prostitution within the camps and the archival evidence and first-hand testimony to German historical attention. Unfortunately, in British scholarship the topic has only been dealt with cursorily, if at all. Overwhelmingly, the camp brothels are rarely mentioned in historical monographs of the camps. Steinbacher's comprehensive book on Auschwitz does not once mention the existence of prisoner brothels at either Auschwitz I or Auschwitz-Monowitz.[7] The issue has, occasionally, been tentatively discussed in British academic works around sexual violence and gender during the Holocaust and within Nazi Germany. Yet, in these examples, the discussion is a largely fragmentary one made to fit into a broader framework and in a confused manner. A key example is Gertjejanssen's *Victims, Heroes and Survivors* (a detailed analysis of sexual violence in Eastern Europe under the Nazis).[8] It introduced the topic of camp brothels, but used primary material from Wehrmacht (German army) military brothels and examples of sexual violence against Jews to substantiate the discussion of brothels that was neither for the Wehrmacht nor involved Jewish men or women.[9] Likewise, Sommer's article on the camp brothel is published in *Sexual Violence against Jewish Women during the Holocaust* despite the fact that camp brothels were not part of the experience of mass annihilation in the Holocaust.[10] These two examples highlight how academic discourse on the camp brothels has been carried out within studies of larger topics, which has often led to a misrepresentation of this history.

However, these academic works highlight how there has been a scholarly movement to explore the history of the *Sonderbauten*, especially in Germany, within historiography. On the other hand, this has meant discussions have focused primarily on the history of these institutions, while the discussion of their representation at "sites of memory" has been neglected. The buildings and sites of memory have been marginalized in the wider discussion of the brothel's role in the daily and gendered history of these female prisoners. As part of the larger research project conducted, the history of the brothels and how they functioned within Nazi ideology was explored in detail.[11] Nevertheless, while historians may consider the daily life and administrative aspects of concentration camp brothels, one should not ignore how the identity of this sensitive history has been adapted, or in cases ignored in the places where it could be represented or disseminated to the public. This article will endeavor to explore "the interaction between the history of the camp brothels" (the past) and the spatial areas of the former concentration camps (the present) in which they could be discussed.[12]

This article will examine the memorialization of the prisoner brothels at Ravensbrück *Gedenkstätte* (memorial site) and Auschwitz-Birkenau State Museum. Although not discussed in detail within this article, it is important to note that in 2014, the Jüdisches Museum (Berlin) hosted an exhibition on the *Sonderbau* of which catalogues are readily available. This representation was fully possible away from the sites of the Holocaust or Nora's notion of the "lieux de mémoire."[13] This highlighted how important it was to address how the actual sites of former concentration camps deal with this history. It draws on recent extensive fieldwork conducted in 2013, to demonstrate how these sites represent the camp brothels. Thus, these research trips provided the opportunity for detailed notes of exhibitions for which there is no published catalogue, and limited awareness outside Germany. From this research, it has been critical to compare and examine the reasons and motivations for these museums' differing depictions of the *Sonderbauten*. It will raise the issue of how the cultural, political, and geographical roles and inheritances of each site mediate the history that is represented or considered "worthwhile" by the curators who formulate the memory transmitted at such "topographies of terror."

Figure 1. Auschwitz camp entrance (photo by the author, 16 September 2013).

Figure 2. Camp brothels exhibition, Ravensbrück (photo by the author, 16 July 2013).

TRACING TOPOGRAPHIES

The question of representation and the *Sonderbauten*

The fieldwork carried out for this project made it evident that there were factors which have led to the resisting or facilitating of open public discourse and museological representations on the topic of forced prostitution under the Nazi regime. To put it simply, Auschwitz-Birkenau State Museum does not provide any indication in its museum format of the existence of prisoner camp brothels at Auschwitz I or Auschwitz-Monowitz. In contrast, Ravensbrück *Gedenkstätte* has held the exhibition "Camp Brothels" in its Cell Building since 2007.[14] Thus, the topic was omitted from the representations of the history of Auschwitz, yet simultaneously it was openly discussed at the German former women's camp, Ravensbrück. The use of personal correspondence with Dr Setkiewicz of the Auschwitz museum, photographic material from site visits, and museum pamphlets held in the Wiener Library will facilitate this comparative discussion. This section will firstly establish the helpfulness of memorialization as part of historical enquiry, and then set out the dichotomous representations of the museums. It will subsequently survey how the symbolism of the sites, the demands of visitor numbers, and national sensitivities are crucial in determining the divergent positions taken by these sites.

Initially, however, this discussion may prompt the question: is analysis of representation and memorialization a historical exercise? The recently burgeoning area of scholarship around history and memory strongly refutes this claim. The value of pioneering studies by James Young and Sybil Milton has highlighted that memorialization and museological representations are important in illustrating the ways in which difficult historical topics, like the Nazi regime, have been portrayed to the public.[15] Additionally, Auschwitz-Birkenau State Museum and Ravensbrück *Gedenkstätte* are not immune from history. On the contrary, they both have their own histories following 1945 and, today, are the result of interaction between historians, history, and the public.[16] Ludmilla Jordanova, historian and philosopher, discusses the role of museums (like those at the sites of former concentration camps) as transmitters of "public history."[17] This "public history," she argues, is neither detached nor irrelevant to the discipline of "academic history."[18] This section will follow this line of argument, by revealing how these two museums and memorial sites operate within a network of sensitivities and constraints in relaying their own pre-1945 histories, specifically the development of concentration camp brothels. By examining the portrayal of the *Sonderbauten*, this research will display a self-awareness around the topic and its historical representation. It will also highlight the memorialization and representation of Ravensbrück, which scholars of historical memory, like Young, have neglected.[19]

The Auschwitz-Birkenau State Museum does not identify, nor represent, that there were prisoner camp brothels at either Auschwitz-Stammlager or Auschwitz-Monowitz. In the case of the Auschwitz's main camp, Block 24a, the former brothel building, survives. This provides ample opportunity for its role to be explored, or at least noted within the museum. In spite of this, the fieldwork revealed that Block 24a, according to museum maps, tour guides and guidebook, was represented according to its historical use as a former barrack and its current role as home to the archive and administration of the State Museum.[20] The map, which is used throughout the site of the museum, states: "[Barracks] ... 22–24 blocks [were] used for a temporary work camp of Soviet Prisoners of War."[21] This may be a truth, but it is not the full historical truth. Soviet

POWs were held in the aforementioned blocks from 7 October 1941 until March 1942 when they were either "liquidated" or moved to Auschwitz-Birkenau; from this time until 1943 Block 24 held protective prisoners.[22] Yet, from October 1943 up until January 1945, a substantial period of the camp's four-year existence, the upper floor of Block 24a was used as the camp brothel and barracks for the forced prostitutes.[23] Despite this evidence, Setkiewicz strongly asserts that the Auschwitz museum does "not ignore the issue of brothels in Auschwitz," by discussing it in scholarly publications, but this answer distorts the reality.[24] As a museum, its exhibition space does not reveal that there were camp brothels; scholarly work by the museum is not part of the experience gleaned by the majority of visitors to the site. Hence, all museological methods employed by the museum to discuss the history of the camp do not draw attention to the subject of forced sexual labor in the camp.

In comparison, the Ravensbrück *Gedenkstätte*, which was the concentration camp from which the majority of forced sex workers were selected, represents the issue comprehensively. Ravensbrück holds a detailed exhibition dedicated to addressing the topic in its special exhibition space, "Forced Sex Labor. Nazi Concentration Camp Brothels."[25] It has also incorporated the topic into part of its permanent exhibition, placed within the former commandant's house. Additionally, correspondence with the museum staff has suggested that the special exhibition has become a permanent part of the Cell Building exhibition. Both these efforts are presented in English translations. In this way, the *Gedenkstätte* does not just represent an effort to acknowledge the existence of camp brothels, but seeks to contextualize their history by showcasing the official directives by Himmler, testimonies of forced sex workers and visitors, and background discussions of the attitudes toward prostitution, in general, within the Third Reich.[26] Thus, the Ravensbrück memorial site and Auschwitz Museum offer juxtaposing representations of the *Sonderbauten*, the reasons for which will now be discussed.

The differing symbolic roles of the current sites play a key role in determining the matters discussed within the museum exhibitions. The Auschwitz Museum functions as a "symbol" of the Nazis' murder of six million Jews.[27] This is detached from its own recorded, scholarly history. Historiography has shown it was the place of the murder of one million Jews in the Auschwitz-Birkenau camp, but Auschwitz's three sites were also the place of murder or persecution of non-Jewish victims, including Sinti and Roma, Polish-political, "criminals" or asocials, Soviet POWs, and homosexual prisoners.[28] Critics such as Tim Cole have been vehement in identifying Auschwitz's attained symbolic role, which, he argues, from the late 1960s has become synonymous with the "Holocaust."[29] Isabel Wollaston echoes this claim, stating that the Auschwitz complex's historically multifaceted roles are contemporarily ignored in the face of the "Auschwitz" of today which is an "undifferentiated mass."[30] In line with this, particular images of the camp, particularly the irony of the *Arbeit Macht Frei* gate, have become metonymies for the Holocaust. This symbolism, markedly, creates difficulties for representing the camp brothel in Block 24a in Auschwitz due to its topographical location. The former brothel block stands behind what Dwork and Van Pelt have labeled a "fixed point in our collective memory" (Figure 1); it is situated to the left of the *Arbeit Macht Frei* gate.[31] These two juxtaposing narratives of the history of Auschwitz, which are far removed in the experiences they represent, have a geographical proximity, presenting an uneasy friction. Although this friction essentially mirrors the complexity of the camp's role, its symbolism is rooted from a fundamental part of the site's history. However, its role in a key place of the "Judeocide"[32] was a result of the complex hierarchical racial and gendered ideology of the Nazis. It was such ideologies, explored further in other works, that meant that the camp brothels were run along racial lines and women's bodies were exploited by the state. This highlights that despite the small number of women forced to work in these institutions, the history of brothels was a marginal history, but this does not mean, as Setkiewicz dismissively says, that they were of "minor importance."[33] The camp brothels do present an uneasy friction, but when explored throughout the framework of ideology, they do not contradict the symbolism of the site. However, the overwhelming symbolism of Auschwitz (as the "undifferentiated mass"[34]) as a site and the location of iconic images of Jewish suffering, is emblematic as the site of Jewish extermination, opposing the seemingly dichotomous representation of it as the site of camp brothels.

Ravensbrück's symbolic role is not just distinct from that of Auschwitz; it is also a less strongly symbolic role. Regrettably, scholarship on sites of Nazi persecution memorialization has largely overlooked the former women's camp at Ravensbrück.[35] Nevertheless, the scarcity of historiographical studies on the camp reflects the non-central position Ravensbrück *Gedenkstätte* plays in symbolism and memorialization of the Holocaust. Ravensbrück's prisoner population was made up of largely "asocial" and "criminal" German inmates. Saidel estimates that only around 13.7% of the female inmates were Jewish.[36] Hence, its place in historical memory has been of a site of Nazi atrocities and crimes, rather than the "Judeocide."[37] This is in sharp contrast to the aforementioned identity of the Auschwitz-Birkenau State Museum. Additionally, Ravensbrück was the sole camp created by the Nazis exclusively for female inmates. Thus, the site has focused its memorialization around women's gendered experiences under the Nazis. The sculptures and memorial art around the museum echo this female-specific focus; Will Lambert's sculpture of two women suffering is a specific example of this focus.[38] This specificity of Ravensbrück's role in relation to Nazi crimes prevents it being emblematic of the extermination of the Jews in the same way as Auschwitz. This, coupled with its gendered symbolism due to its role as a female only camp, enables the extensive portrayals of the camp brothels.

A further crucial concern of the Auschwitz-Birkenau State Museum is its recently attained role as a site of mass tourism. The 2012 Museum Report indicates increasing visitor numbers from 2001 to 2012, and since 2007 numbers have peaked well above one million annually.[39] A consequence of this development, as the director of the museum Dr Cywinski has articulated, is that the Auschwitz museum has had a "fearful obligation" placed upon it.[40] This burden, caused by diverse and quantifiably large visitor numbers, means that a key aim of the museum has become one of education and influencing "what future generations will know."[41] This is all the more pertinent as the last survivors of the camp pass away, and the role of the site as one of mourning and spiritual reflection recedes. Academics such as Engelhardt have observed this trend of museums as historical educators. Engelhardt has stated: "'Education' now serves as the argument for justifying different kinds of representation."[42] This statement points to the fact that educating effectively about the Holocaust can only be done within certain parameters, and alludes to Bhabha's theory of how history is "reconstituted" for the present; the present here is the need of a young generation to be educated.[43] Thus, what is focused upon is of note: it is most definitely *not* the history of the brothel at Auschwitz I. The master narrative of Auschwitz that is discussed is of the genocide of one million Jews within the Auschwitz camp complex.[44] Indeed, the rhetoric of this "museum education" is focused specifically on the mass annihilation of camp inmates, rather than a wider discussion of various forms of persecution within the different camp institutions. This lesson is delivered through the form of tour guides or information boards around the former KZ-Auschwitz I. A visitor commented on the "million pieces of information" her guide gave them in just explaining the master narrative of Auschwitz.[45] Thus, the complex and difficult history of the brothels is set aside in favor of what is deemed to be the more important master narrative that the museum has a moral obligation to try and impart on the large number of people who visit the site. However, this poses an ethical question in museum representation. The museum must consider the complexity of the camp brothels, and other marginal histories, for they reveal the multifaceted, highly ideological, and economic realities of the Nazi regime. In disseminating a simple master narrative, the Auschwitz museum is not allowing its visitors to engage with the multifaceted and often what Rees termed the *seemingly* "bizarre" elements of Nazi ideology.[46]

This stands dichotomous to Ravensbrück *Gedenkstätte*'s number of visitors. Problematically, Ravensbrück's official website or publications do not display the number of annual visitors, unlike Auschwitz, which produces annual reports on the difficulties and successes of its museum. However, the demographic of the visitors to Ravensbrück camp is very different to that of Auschwitz. As Jacobs notes, Ravensbrück is a place "where the Jewish tour groups rarely go"; its visitors are predominantly Germans.[47] Furthermore, there is not the "tourist" culture that packages and organizes day trips to Ravensbrück. The day trips to Auschwitz place time burdens on educating a mass audience, which therefore has resulted in it relying on a simple narrative that does not discuss the *Sonderbauten*. Due to these differences, the museological focus at Ravensbrück is different to that at Auschwitz. The lower numbers of visitors and their predominantly German nationality allows Ravensbrück a wider freedom of representation. It enables the *Gedenkstätte* to examine the variety of persecuting methods against women of all nationalities and races at Ravensbrück KZ, including the forced sex laborers.

National sensitivities of the countries where these memorial sites are based are decisive in whether the issue of camp brothels is represented or not. Both sites, prior to 1990, were part of the Eastern Bloc. Communist domination had meant Ravensbrück and Auschwitz memorials and museums were part of an anti-fascist historical dialogue, as were Buchenwald and Sachsenhausen. Museum publications show this political agenda with statements that the sites were proof of the "anti-fascist struggle."[48] Thus, with the fall of the iron curtain in 1990, formulation of new and stronger national identities occurred.

In the case of Poland, a part of its national identity remains "rooted in the moral values of Catholicism and the institutions of the Catholic Church".[49] The supremacy of the Catholic religion for its population is evident; in 2005 the BBC recorded that 95% of the population self-identified as Roman Catholics.[50] This acts in a way that challenges open discussion of a topic that is focused on non-marital sexual activity. Yet the application of national sensitivities to the museum is hard to quantifiably pin down. Nevertheless, controversies like the field of crosses, where between 1998 and 1999 hundreds of crosses had been erected by Auschwitz, showed Polish Catholicism claiming a stake in memory at the Auschwitz Museum.[51] However, historians have pointed out that from the late 1990s the centrality of Auschwitz's role in the murder of Jews has been accepted.[52] Yet this is not to say that in admitting the importance of the site in Jewish persecution, Catholicism has fully removed its stakehold in memory formulation. In Polish law and policy, it still plays a fundamental role. In a 2013 foreign policy address, Catholic goals were still discussed.[53] Similarly, in legal frameworks its role is still identifiable; abortions are considered illegal, apart from in "severely limited" circumstances.[54] Thus, Catholicism still plays a key role in the Polish state and nation, and the museum of Auschwitz is self-admittedly a "state institution," with a museum staff that is largely composed of Polish nationals.[55] Catholic dogma or sensitivities in Poland, to some extent, bar discussion of camp brothels.

With the fall of the Berlin Wall and reunification of Germany in 1989, a new national circumstance was initiated for East and West Germany to wholeheartedly address its Nazi past. The German word *Vergangenheitsbewältigung* was formulated in the 1950s to represent the West German "coming to terms" with the genocide and other crimes perpetrated during Hitler's regime.[56] In the 1990s, the proliferation of gendered historiography coincided with this reinvigorated *Vergangenheitsbewältigung*. In fact, Paul's founding study, *Zwangsprositution*, was part of a political effort to gain compensation for the forced prostitutes who had not been classified as victims.[57] Thus, the German pursuit of a thorough examination of their past actively facilitates discussion of the topic. The documentary *System Sonderbau* ("Special Constructions"), shown on German television in 2013, displayed the continued willingness to combat even minor historical occurrences, in their full complexity.[58] In addition, the six former camp brothels based in Germany are marked at each museum.[59] This is indicative of the national trend to deal with this difficult history at the sites of suffering.

The representation of the history of camp brothels is constrained by a variety of factors: nationally distinct factors, differing emblematic roles, and the effects of visitor numbers. This illustrates the complexity of competing historical discourses and master narratives that operate around histories of the Nazi regime at the memorial and museum sites of former concentration camps. The concentration camp brothels were a microelement, but were nonetheless a difficult part of the Nazis' persecuting measures between 1942 and 1945.

Conclusion

This article has illuminated the differing museological representations of the concentration camp brothels. It has examined, analyzed, and brought new material into British academia without invading the privacy of the many women who did not want to discuss their experiences. It has explored how the sites of memory at Ravensbrück *Gedenkstätte* and Auschwitz-Birkenau State Museum reveal how a variety of factors resist or facilitate the discussion of camp brothels. It has examined and considered Auschwitz's special role in relation to mass tourism and symbolism, and how curators see this as a limiting factor for its maneuverability to portray a complex historical portrait of concentration camp life and extermination camp death. This, indeed, leads to complex and difficult issues in the ethics of memorialization and how far institutions are obligated to one narrative over a full and complex "semblance" of history as far as possible. In contrast, Ravensbrück has much lower visitor numbers and a rather different post-war symbolism that allows space for portrayal of this difficult history. As previously discussed, this leads to a welcome, detailed, and complex representation of the sensitive history in a scholarly and in-depth way.

TRACING TOPOGRAPHIES

In history, the brothels were complex institutions, created and run for complex reasons and ideological influences. Yet, equally pertinently, the ideology of the present interacts and affects these sites; Auschwitz State Museum and Ravensbrück *Gedenkstätte* are subject to multifaceted concerns in their historiographical representation in museology. History of trauma and the suffering within the camps is not something that makes itself simply known in the site and its physical topography; the memory to be passed on to visitors to such sites is formulated and not apart from the acting forces of the present. As this article has explored, the present is what is opposing or enabling whether sites even acknowledge the existence of brothels and their historical role and narratives. The national sensitivities or attitudes, the role of tourism, or the symbolism of Auschwitz State Museum and Ravensbrück *Gedenkstätte* and other former concentration camp sites is the product of a time, and one that is quite separate and distinct from the past which these sites are left to represent.

This article is the starting point of a topic that deserves more scholarly attention in British academia. The need for detailed discussion, and the length constraints of this project, have meant that discussion of various other elements has not been possible and prior research on the establishment of these brothels and their central roots in Nazi financial policy and ideology has had to be omitted for this publication. However, in focusing the lens on the "ruins" of memory metaphorically, and physically on the two museums, this project hopes to prompt further exploration of the geographical and cultural limits on sites of memory in marginal histories from the Nazi period.

Notes

1. Paul, *Zwangsprostitution*, 53.
2. Sonderbauten meant "Special Construction," but referred to camp brothels.
3. Sommer, "Camp Brothels," 176.
4. Sommer, "Sexual Exploitation of Women," 47.
5. Herbermann, *The Blessed Abyss*, 132.
6. Ibid., 132.
7. Steinbacher, *Auschwitz. A History*.
8. Gertjejanssen, *Victims, Heroes and Survivors*, 225–51.
9. Ibid., 251–2.
10. Sommer, "Camp Brothels," 173.
11. See Bogue, *The History of Camp Brothels in History and Memory*, for full discussion of camp brothels' contextual history.
12. Ibid., 211.
13. Nora, "Between Memory and History: Les Lieux de Mémoire," 7.
14. Jacobs, *Memorializing the Holocaust*, 59.
15. Milton, *In Fitting Memory*; Young, *Texture of Memory*.
16. See Huener, *Auschwitz, Poland*.
17. Jordanova, *History in Practice*, 141.
18. Ibid., 142.
19. Young, *Texture of Memory*.
20. Auschwitz-Birkenau State Museum, *Auschwitz-Birkenau Guide Book*.
21. See Appendix 2 for photographs from fieldwork.
22. Piper and Strzelecka, "Construction and Development," 76–8.
23. Sommer, "Sexual Exploitation," 47; Sommer, *Das KZ-Bordell*, 284.
24. Setkiewicz, email exchange, 20 January 2014.
25. Jacobs, *Memorializing the Holocaust*, 59–62.

26. See Appendix 1 for the structure of the exhibition.
27. USHMM, "Introduction to the Holocaust," http://www.ushmm.org/wlc/en/article.php?ModuleId=10005143 (accessed March 10, 2014).
28. Rees, *Auschwitz: The Nazis*, 374.
29. Cole, *Images of the Holocaust*, 98.
30. Wollaston, "Sharing Sacred Space?" 22.
31. Dwork and Van Pelt, *Auschwitz*, 359.
32. Mayer, *Why Did the Heavens Not Darken?*, 3.
33. Setkiewicz, personal correspondence, Appendix 3.
34. Wollaston, "Sharing Sacred Space?" 22.
35. See Helm, *If This Is a Woman*, as a very recent and welcome addition to scholarship on Ravensbrück's history.
36. Saidel, *Jewish Women of Ravensbrück*, 24.
37. Mayer, *Why Did the Heavens Not Darken?*, 3.
38. See Appendix 2 for photographs from fieldwork.
39. Auschwitz-Birkenau Museum, *Auschwitz Report 2012*, 20.
40. *Ibid.*, 5.
41. *Ibid.*, 5.
42. Engelhardt, *Topography of Memory*, 213.
43. Bhabha, "On Global Memory."
44. Rees, *Auschwitz*, 374.
45. Bittner, "Dark Tourism," 153.
46. Rees, *Auschwitz*, 5.
47. Jacobs, *Memorializing the Holocaust*, 154.
48. Litschke, *National Memorial of Ravensbrück*.
49. Kurczewska, "National Identities," 329.
50. "World Factfile: Roman Catholicism," http://news.bbc.co.uk/1/hi/in_depth/4243727.stm (accessed March 2, 2014).
51. Zubrzycki, *The Crosses of Auschwitz*, 2.
52. Kucia, Dutch-Dyngosz, and Magierowski, "Collective Memory of Auschwitz," 137.
53. "Address – Minister of Foreign Affairs" (20 March 2013), http://msz.gov.pl/en/news/address_by_the_minister_of_foreign_affairs_on_the_goals_of_polish_foreign_policy_in2013_ (accessed March 8, 2014).
54. World Health Organization, "Abortion in the European Region," http://www.euro.who.int/en/health-topics/Life-stages/sexual-and-reproductive-health/activities/abortion/facts-and-figures-about-abortion-in-the-european-region (accessed March 10, 2014).
55. Auschwitz-Birkenau Museum, *Auschwitz Report 2013*, 58, 54–7.
56. Mayerhofer, "Coming to Terms."
57. Paul, *Zwangsprostitution*.
58. ZDF, "System Sonderbau: Haftlingsbordell im KZ" [Special Building System: Prisoner Brothels in Concentration Camps] (ZDF Info, 18 July 2013).
59. See Appendix 2 for Sachsenhausen example.

Disclosure statement

No potential conflict of interest was reported by the author

Bibliography

Primary sources

Camp Brothels. Forced Sex Labor in Nazi Concentration Camps, Ravensbrück Gedenkstätte (Curator: Robert Sommer):
"Addendum to the Service Regulation, 14 February 1944."
"Edgar Kupfer-Koberwitz Diary Extract, 19 May 1944."
"Interrogation of Franz Dobermann, 10 October 1946."
"Interrogation of Karl Gärtig, 16 October 1946."
"Interrogation of Max Pawel, 12 October 1946."
"Interrogation of Walter Bartel, 19 October 1946."
"Letter from Himmler to Pohl, 23 March 1942."
"Letter from Himmler to Pohl, 5 March 1943."
"Mr. J's Account, October 1993."
"Ms. B's Account, February 1991."
"Service Regulation for the granting of Benefits to prisoners, 'Bonus Order' 15 May 1943."
"Testimony of Albert Tiefenbacher."
"Walter Bartel – Question of the Sonderbau Letter, 3 February 1977."
International Tracing Service Digital Archive Collection: Wiener Library for the Study of the Holocaust and Genocide, London:
"Buchenwald Camp: The Report of a Parliamentary Delegation," April 1945, as in *List Material Buchenwald*, Wiener Library, ITS, 1.1.5.0/82087662.
"Concentration Camp Inmates Questionnaire," 19 May 1945, as in *Individual Documents Regarding Female Detainees Buchenwald*, Wiener Library, ITS, 1.1.5.4/7551509.
"Neuzugänge – Weibliche Haftlinge von KL. Ravensbrück nach KL. Buchenwald," 7 September 1944, as in *List Material Buchenwald*, Wiener Library, ITS, 1.1.5.1/5289809.
"Statement of E.H," No date given, as in *General Information Dachau*, Wiener Library, ITS, 1.1.6.0/8104785.
"Weibliche Häftlinge (Sonderbau)," 12 December 1944, as in *List Material Dachau*, Wiener Library, ITS, 1.1.6.1/9943698.

Other primary materials

Auschwitz-Birkenau State Museum. *Auschwitz-Birkenau Guide Book*. Oświęcim: Wroclaw, 2013.
Berler, Willy. *Journey through Darkness: Monowitz, Auschwitz, Gross-Rosen and Buchenwald*. London: Vallentine & Mitchell, 2004.
Borowski, Tadeusz. *This Way for the Gas Ladies and Gentlemen*. London: Penguin, 1976.
Buber-Neumann, Margarete. *Under Two Dictators: Prisoner of Stalin and Hitler*. London: Victor Gollancz, 2008.
Frankl, Viktor. *Man's Search for Meaning*. London: Rider, 2008.
Gärtig, Carl. "The Special Building." In *The Buchenwald Report*, ed. David Hackett, 235–237. Oxford: Basic Books, 1995.
Herbermann, Nanda. *The Blessed Abyss: Inmate #5682 in Ravensbrück Concentration Camp for Women*. Detroit: Wayne State University Press, 2000.

TRACING TOPOGRAPHIES

Langbein, Hermann. *People in Auschwitz*. Chapel Hill: The University of North Carolina Press, 2004.

Litschke, E. *National Memorial of Ravensbrück Museum* (Furstenberg, 1989).

Secondary sources

Alakus, Baris, Katherina Kniefacz, and Robert Vorberg. *Sex-Zwangsarbeit im Nationalsozialismus Konzentrationslagern [Forced Sexual Labor in National Socialist Concentration Camps]*. Vienna: Mandelbaum, 2007.

Auschwitz-Birkenau State Museum. *Auschwitz-Birkenau Museum Report 2012*. Oświęcim, 2012. http://en.auschwitz.org/m/index.php?option=com_content&task=view&id=620&Itemid=49.

Auschwitz-Birkenau State Museum. *Auschwitz-Birkenau Museum Report 2013*. Oświęcim, 2013. http://en.auschwitz.org/m/index.php?option=com_content&task=view&id=620&Itemid=49.

Barkai, Avaraham. *Nazi Economics: Ideology, Theory and Policy*. Oxford: Berg, 1990.

BBC. "Corruption." Episode Three: Auschwitz: The Nazis and the Final Solution (BBC2, 1 February 2005).

Bhabha, Homi. "On Global Memory: Reflections on Barbaric Transmission". In *Crossing Cultures: Conflict, Migration, and Convergence: The Proceedings of the 32nd International Congress in the History of Art*, edited by Jaynie Anderson, 46–56. Australia: Miegunyah Press, 2009.

Bittner, Marijana. "'Dark Tourism' – Evaluation of Visitors' Experience after Visiting Thanatological Tourist Attractions." *Turizam* 15, no. 4 (2011): 148–158.

Bogue, Nicole. "The Concentration Camp Brothels in History and Memory." BA thesis, University of Birmingham, (2014).

Cesarani, David. *Holocaust: Critical Concepts in Historical Studies*. London: Routledge, 2004.

Cole, Tim. *Images of the Holocaust: The Myth of the Shoah Business*. London: Duckworth, 1999.

Dwork, Debórah, and Jan Van Pelt, Robert. *Auschwitz*. New York: W. W. Norton and Company, 2002.

Engelhardt, Isabelle. *Topography of Memory: Representations of the Holocaust at Dachau and Buchenwald in Comparison with Auschwitz, Yad Vashem and Washington, DC*. Oxford: European Inter-University Press, 2002.

Gertjejanssen, Wendy Jo. "Victims, Heroes and Survivors: Sexual Violence on the Eastern Front during World War Two." PhD thesis, University of Minnesota, 2004.

Grossmann, Anita. "Continuities and Ruptures. Sexuality in Twentieth Century Germany: Historiography and Its Discontents." In *Gendering Modern German History: Rewriting Historiography*, edited by Karen Hagemann and Jean Quataert, 208–227. Oxford: Berghahn Books, 2007.

Halbmayr, Bridgette. "Sexualized Violence against Women during the Nazi 'Racial' Persecution." In *Sexual Violence against Jewish Women during the Holocaust*, edited by Sonja Hedgepeth and Rochelle Saidel, 29–44. London: Brandeis University Press, 2010.

Helm, Sarah. *If this is a Woman: Inside Ravensbrück: Hitler's Concentration Camp for Women*. London: Little, Brown Company, 2015.

Huener, Jonathan. *Auschwitz, Poland, and the Politics of Commemoration: 1945–1979*. Ohio: Ohio University Press, 2003.

Jacobs, Janet. *Memorializing the Holocaust: Gender, Genocide and Collective Memory*. London: IB Tauris and Co Ltd., 2010.

Jordanova, Ludmilla. *History in Practice*. London: Bloomsbury Academic, 2000.

Kershaw, Ian. *The Nazi Dictatorship: Problems and Perspectives of Interpretation*. London: Bloomsbury Academic, 2010.

Kucia, Marek, Marta Dutch-Dyngosz, and Mateusz Magierowski. "The Collective Memory of Auschwitz and World War II among Catholics in Poland: A Quantitative Study of Three Communities." *History and Memory* 25, no. 2 (2013): 132–173.

Kurczewska, Joanna. "National Identities vis-à-vis Democracy and Catholicism (The Polish Case after 1989)." *Polish Sociological Review* 152 (2005): 329–347.

TRACING TOPOGRAPHIES

Mayer, Arno. *Why Did the Heavens Not Darken? The "Final Solution" in History*. London: Verso, 1990.

Mayerhofer, Bernd. "'Coming to Terms' with the Nazi Past" (September 2009). http://www.goethe.de/ges/pok/ein/en5023188.htm.

Milton, Syil. *In Fitting Memory: The Art and Politics of Holocaust Memorials*. Berkeley: Wayne University Press, 1991.

Nora, Pierre. "Between History and Memory: Les Lieux de Mémoire." *Representations* 26, (1989): 7–24.

Paul, Christa. *Zwangsprostitution: Staatlich Errichtete Bordelle im Nationalsozialismus [Forced Prostitution: Brothels Established by the Nazi German State]*. Berlin: Hentrich, 1994.

Piper, Franciszek, and Teresa Swiebocka. *Auschwitz: Nazi Death Camp*. Oświęcim: Auschwitz-Birkenau State Museum, 1996.

Piper, Franciszek, and Irena Strzelecka. "The Construction and Development of the Camp and its Branches." In *Auschwitz 1940–1945: Central Issues in the History of the Camp, Vol. 1*, edited by Franciszek Piper and Waclaw Dlugoborski. Oświęcim: Auschwitz State Museum, 2000.

Rees, Laurence. *Auschwitz: The Nazis and the "Final Solution"*. London: BBC Books, 2005.

Saidel, Rochelle. *The Jewish Women of Ravensbrück Concentration Camp*. Wisconsin: University of Wisconsin Press, 2004.

Schikorra, Christa. "Forced Prostitution in the Nazi Concentration Camps." In *Lessons and Legacies Volume VII*, edited by D. Herzog, 169–178. Evanston, IL: North Western University Press, 2006.

Setkiewicz, Piotr. *The Histories of Auschwitz IG Farben Werk Camps, 1941–1945*. Oświęcim: Auschwitz State Museum, 2001.

Shik, Na'ama. "Sexual Abuse of Jewish Women in Auschwitz-Birkenau." In *Brutality and Desire: War and Sexuality in Europe's Twentieth Century*, edited by Dagmar Herzog, 221–246. London: Palgrave Macmillan, 2011.

Snyder, David. *Sex Crimes under the Wehrmacht*. Nebraska: University of Nebraska, 2007.

Sommer, Robert. "Camp Brothels: Forced Sex Labor in Nazi Concentration Camps." In *Brutality and Desire: War and Sexuality in Europe's Twentieth Century*, edited by Dagmar Herzog, 168–196. London: Palgrave Macmillan, 2011.

Sommer, Robert. *Das KZ-Bordell: Sexuelle Zwangsarbeit in nationalsozialistischen Konzentrationslagern [The Camp Brothel: Forced Sexual Labor in National Socialist Concentration Camps]*. Munich, Schoeningh Ferdinand Gmbh, 2009.

Sommer, Robert. "Sexual Exploitation of Women in Nazi Concentration Camp Brothels." In *Sexual Violence against Jewish Women during the Holocaust*, edited by Sonja Hedgepeth and Rochelle Saidel, 45–60. London: Brandeis University Press, 2010.

Steinbacher, Sybil. *Auschwitz. A History*. London: Ecoo, 2005.

Stephenson, Jill. *Women in Nazi Germany*. Harlow: Routledge, 2001.

United States Holocaust Memorial Museum (USHMM). "Introduction to the Holocaust." *Holocaust Encyclopaedia*. Accessed March 10, 2014. http://www.ushmm.org/wlc/en/article.php?ModuleId=10005143.

United States Holocaust Memorial Museum (USHMM). "Invasion of the Soviet Union, June 1941." *Holocaust Encyclopaedia*. Accessed March 3, 2014. http://www.ushmm.org/wlc/en/article.php?ModuleId=10005164.

Wiener Library. "International Tracing Service Archive." Accessed February 6, 2014. http://www.wienerlibrary.co.uk/International-Tracing-Service.

Wollaston, Isabel. "Sharing Sacred Space? The Carmelite Controversy and the Politics of Commemoration." *Patterns of Prejudice* 28, no. 3/4 (1994): 19–27.

Wollheim Memorial. "Camp Brothel." Accessed March 6, 2014. http://www.wollheim-memorial.de/en/lagerbordell_en.

Young, James. *The Texture of Memory: Holocaust Memorials and Meaning*. London: Yale University Press, 1993.

Zubrzycki, Genevieve. *The Crosses of Auschwitz: Nationalism and Religion in Post-communist Poland*. Chicago: University of Chicago Press, 2006.

Appendix 1

"Camp Brothels. Forced Sex Labor in Nazi Concentration Camps" (R. Sommer) Ravensbrück *Gedenkstätte* – Special Exhibition Structure
Background Information:

    i. Prostitution in Nazi Germany, 1939–1942.
    ii. Brothels for Ethnic Foreign Workers, 1941–1945.
    iii. German Military Brothels, 1943–1945.

The Establishment of Camp Brothels:

    i. Official Correspondence of the SS-WVHA on the Brothels.
    ii. Unrealized Architectural Plans for a *Sonderbau* at Auschwitz I.
    iii. Extract from the Architectural Drawing for the Flossenbürg *Sonderbau*.

The Organization of Camp Brothels:

    i. Example 'Häftlingskarte' (Prisoner Card) of a Forced Sex Laborer.
    ii. Saving Prisoner Data on Punch Cards.
    iii. The Medical Supervision of Brothels.
    iv. Accounting the Earnings of Forced Sex Labor.

The Continuities of Exclusion:

    i. Mr. J.'s Account about Meeting a Former Sex Slave Worker.
    ii. A Former Sex Slave Worker's Account of Her Life after the War.
    iii. Compensation Claims of a Former Sex Worker.

The Brothel Visitors and Reactions of Male Prisoners:

  i. Accounts of Brothel Visitors.
  ii. Resistance to Camp Brothels (Buchenwald and Dachau).

Recruitment of Forced Sex Workers:

  i. Recruitment Document Testimonies of SS Men.
  ii. Women's Account about their Selection for Camp Brothels
  iii. Headphones Playing Audio Testimony on Everyday Life in the Brothel for these Women.

Extra Side Pieces and Wall Text of Exhibition:

  i. The History of the Ten Camp Brothels: Images and Documents.
  ii. Photographs of How Camp Brothels are Marked or Not at Current Memorial Sites.
  iii. Sexual Violence and War.

Information taken from: "Camp Brothels. Forced Sex Labor in Nazi Concentration Camps," Ravensbrück *Gedenkstätte* (Fürstenberg, 16 July 2013).

Appendix 2

Photographs from Fieldwork

Auschwitz-Birkenau State Museum

Auschwitz-I Museum Map (author's photo, 16 September 2013).

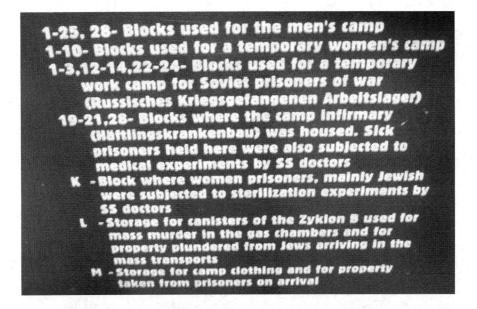

Auschwitz-I Museum Map Text (author's photo, 16 September 2013).

Auschwitz Block 24a (author's photo, 16 September 2013).

Ravensbrück Gedenkstätte

Auschwitz, Side of Block 24a (author's photo, 16 September 2013).

Sachsenhausen Gedenkstätte

Will Lambert Statue at Ravensbrück (author's photo, 16 July 2013).

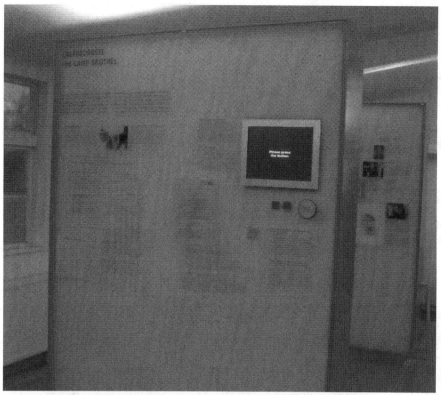

Lagerbordell – The Camp Brothel at Sachsenhausen (author's photo, 13 December 2013).

Sonderbau Building Foundations Marked at Sachsenhausen (author's photo, 13 December 2013).

Appendix 3

Email Correspondence with Dr. Piotr Setkiewicz, Head of the Research Department of the Auschwitz-Birkenau State Museum, 20 January 2014

Q: Is there a particular reason this particular former use of Block 24a is not marked, when the seemingly similar anomaly of the Camp Orchestra is signposted and pointed out by guides?

A: Block 24 was also, for example, the library (although in practice it was not used by prisoners), the orchestra rehearsal room and the "museum" where the SS gathered all sorts of curiosities - objects from the luggage of murdered Jews. It was also the room for artists (painters, sculptors), the main Schreibstube of the camp director's department (Abteilung Schutzhaftlagerführung), a room in which Jewish watchmakers were repairing watches, the room for two Jews who translated Talmud into German and the room where in 1941 the Gestapo officers condemned to death Soviet prisoners of war.

Q: In the design of the new permanent exhibition is this topic to now be included?

A: No. Visitors to the exhibition will have only a little over an hour to learn about some fundamental facts related to the history of the Holocaust and Auschwitz.To sum up: we do not ignore the issue of brothels in Auschwitz, the information about it can be found in our publications, including my own work. But it is nevertheless the subject of a minor importance. We also want to avoid a situation when young people after a visit to Auschwitz would remember it particularly (for obvious reasons) rather than a story of the gas chambers.

Sincerely yours,

Piotr Setkiewicz

The sacred, the profane, and the space in between: site-specific performance at Auschwitz

Samantha Mitschke

Department of Drama and Theatre Arts, University of Birmingham, UK

ABSTRACT

The concept of performance in the concentration camps is not a new one. Rovit and Goldfarb (1999) have chronicled a range of inmate performances from the cabarets of Theresienstadt to the variety shows at Auschwitz-Birkenau, created for many diverse reasons. Yet since the liberation of the camps there has been virtually no theatrical performance in these sites of memory. The very notion is generally seen as taboo, but the reasons for this are somewhat vague and appear to centre around the widespread idea of performance as 'frivolous'; to perform within a concentration camp would be to somehow deface Holocaust memory and mock the suffering of those imprisoned there. Such 'profane' performance can be located within the 'selfie' photographs of tourists visiting the camps. But what of the daily shows that take place in the guise of guided tours – 'sacred' performances? What makes these performances acceptable to the public and the camp authorities, when theatrical performances are not? Can there ever be an acceptable theatrical performance within a concentration camp?

Taking Auschwitz-Birkenau as a case study, this article seeks to address these questions through a considered discussion of 'sacred' and 'profane' performances in the camp. It begins by outlining the components of the guided tour, from the learned script of the guide to the 'promenade performance' nature of the space, and what makes this a 'sacred' performance. It defines the 'profane' performance hypothesis through a reflection upon several examples of tourist photographs taken within Auschwitz. It questions where site-specific theatrical performance would fall within these parameters through an interrogation of aspects including its purpose, the identity of the performers, the (intended) audience, and the short- and long-term ramifications for the performance and the camp. Ultimately, this article probes whether site-specific performance at Auschwitz could ever be efficacious and anything but profane.

Introduction

My consideration of the concept of site-specific performance within a concentration camp arose quite by accident during the initial stages of my research as a PhD student. I attended a meeting with my then-supervisor to discuss my work on Martin Sherman's 1979 play

Bent, which chronicles the queer Holocaust experience. The second act of the play is set in the concentration camp of Dachau and during the conversation my supervisor asked what appeared to be a simple question: "Do you think there will ever be a site-specific performance of *Bent* at Dachau?" I was both amused and skeptical, and answered in the negative. However, when she questioned me as to the reasons why, I discovered that I could not give a definitive answer. I mumbled something about the ethics of representation and respect for the dead, and we left it at that. But further questions had been ignited within me. Why *was* I so sure that the museum authorities at Dachau – or at any former concentration camp, for that matter – would automatically refuse a performance of a play about the Holocaust? Theatre and performance have already existed in the camps and this was recorded as early as 1941, when former prisoner Curt Daniel wrote an article describing performances that took place at Buchenwald and – ironically, given my reaction to the suggestion of performance there – Dachau.[1] Poet Charlotte Delbo performed in Auschwitz and subsequently used theatre as a means of ensuring that Auschwitz did not disappear from the landscape of public memory,[2] using it as both a means of survival and a defense for the survival of memory. Rebecca Rovit and Alvin Goldfarb have documented a wide variety of plays, cabarets, concerts, and revues that were staged by inmates, often for their SS captors, in locations ranging from Bergen-Belsen and Westerbork to Theresienstadt and Auschwitz.[3] But in spite of this, could wider reservations about site-specific performance in the camps have something to do with a perception of theatre as somehow being frivolous, especially in the context of the Nazi genocide, and therefore a sense of its being "profane" in terms of the inherent sanctity of Holocaust memory? As Chris Keil observes, "Visitors bring to Auschwitz, and perhaps expect it to confer on them, a certain solemnity."[4] Would telling the stories of those who died in the camps really be detrimental to respect for their memory? Can theatre in the concentration camps be an efficacious tool toward education about the Holocaust? For example, would it attract more school groups and further enable a new generation to engage, or would it be another facet of the apparent increase in so-called "dark tourism?"[5] It is not my intention – nor would it be possible – for me to attempt to give any exhaustive answers to these questions within this article. Instead, I will offer a series of provocations that I hope will lead to further engagement with the concept of site-specific performance within the physical sites of former concentration camps; in this instance, Auschwitz-Birkenau.

It is worth pausing briefly to define "site-specific performance" within the context of this article. The term remains a source of critique and debate within scholarly realms, particularly in terms of what Mike Pearson refers to as "the search for a practicable, encompassing definition."[6] The most popular conception of site-specific performance follows that laid down by Patrice Pavis:

> […] a staging and performance conceived on the basis of a place in the real world (ergo, outside the established theatre). A large part of the work has to do with researching a place, often an unusual one that is imbued with history or permeated with atmosphere: [such as] an airplane hangar, [or] unused factory […].[7]

In instances of site-specific performance it is not always a case of simply transporting an otherwise ordinary play to an outside or non-theatrical location. Instead, what makes site-specific performance uniquely engaging is that the performance itself is both inspired by and responsive to the environment in which it takes place.[8] Moreover, such performances are "inseparable from their sites, the only contexts within which they are 'readable'."[9] The guided tours of Auschwitz are a highly illustrative example: the spoken words of the tour would not be "readable" if they were to be given in a stately home or a school, for instance.

I will now begin by drawing upon the dictums of "Holocaust etiquette" as outlined by Terrence Des Pres[10] to define what I term "profane" Holocaust performance, including reflecting upon the use of comedy, cabaret, and the musical as ways of representing the Holocaust. I will examine the concept of what Gad Kaynar refers to as "balagan,"[11] the breaking of Holocaust taboos, in conventional theatre and the perceived profanity of the "performance" of the so-called "Auschwitz selfie." I will interrogate the notion of "sacred" performance through a close discussion of the museum-run guided tours given at Auschwitz, and posit that these constitute a theatre event through aspects that they can be seen to have in common with conventional theatre performances, including: the presence of performers and spectators; the structure of the tour; the utilization of a "script"; and the fulfillment of an "ideological transaction" between the guide (as performer) and the visitor (as spectator).[12] Finally, I will outline a number of provocations in relation to site-specific performance at Auschwitz, namely: its potential function as a means of engaging the "Auschwitz selfie" generation; its use as a means of furthering knowledge in the context of re-enactments of historical performances; and the representation of different victim groups.

"Profane" Holocaust performance defined: "Auschwitz selfies" and "balagan"

The concept of "profane" performance in a concentration camp is best encapsulated by the notorious "Auschwitz selfie," in which subjects take photographs of themselves within the camp. The most well-known example of this is the case of Breanna Mitchell, an American teenager who posted a smiling photo of herself at Auschwitz I on Twitter (*Daily Mail*, 21 July 2014). The image went viral on the internet and, in response to the subsequent uproar, Mitchell claimed that the photograph had been taken in memory of her father, who had taught her about the Holocaust before his death (*Huffington Post*, 24 July 2014). However, when posited alongside other Auschwitz selfies it is possible to see that a pattern has emerged which enables a definition of "profane" performance. The images, which are frequently posted on social media forums, usually feature smiling facial expressions and exaggerated and/or overtly posed body language. Such photographs are often taken at sites such as the crematoria in Auschwitz I or on the railway tracks at Birkenau, with these sites seemingly providing little more than an interesting backdrop for the subject. The performance is "frivolous" and geared toward entertainment rather than engagement with the history of Auschwitz or reflection upon its legacy; all of the "actors" are smiling. The performer of the profane thus chooses to focus upon the self as an end result, rather than cast a reflection or question back at society. What occurs in such instances is an inversion of what Chris Keil refers to as the "psychic topography" of Auschwitz – specifically the way in which it is mapped in collective imagination.[13] In discussing the repositioning of the notional entry point into Auschwitz I (from the original block that new prisoners entered in the 1940s to the "Arbeit Macht Frei" gate) Keil discerns that the behavioral norms of visitors are influenced by their perception of whether they have "truly" entered Auschwitz[14] – that is, if they have passed through the gate. In the block, which now houses the museum reception and other public facilities, visitors converse with their friends; according to a museum guide, people consume drinks and food, have children with them, and in summer Auschwitz I resembles "a park and a picnic place."[15] The performers of Auschwitz selfies can be seen to more forcefully transgress the psychic topography of the camp by bringing "outside" behaviors within its boundaries – "the violation of memory by current concerns"[16] through foregrounding the present self in place of historical memory.

It must be noted, however, that Auschwitz selfies do bring about discussions of the Holocaust through reactions to the photographs, as well as raising questions about societal values. The inherent "entertainment" factor and the focus upon the self violate what Terrence Des Pres refers to as the "sanctity" of the Holocaust.[17] In the form of three "prescriptions," Des Pres outlines the previously unwritten and deeply entrenched conventions by which the Holocaust is approached socially, culturally, and politically:

1. The Holocaust shall be represented, in its totality, as a unique event, as a special case and kingdom of its own, above or below or apart from history.
2. Representations of the Holocaust shall be as accurate and faithful as possible to the facts and conditions of the event, without change or manipulation for any reason – artistic reasons included.
3. The Holocaust shall be approached as a solemn or even a sacred event, with a seriousness admitting no response that might obscure its enormity or dishonor its dead.[18]

Des Pres states that such rules are not "tyrannical" but concedes that they "foster strong restrictions," insightfully referring to them as "Holocaust etiquette."[19] I contend that these rules are indeed "tyrannical," and impose seemingly insurmountable obstacles when it comes to representing and exploring the Holocaust through different theatrical mediums[20] (and other art forms) – especially in terms of combatting "Holocaust fatigue," which I will discuss shortly. For instance, the dictum that Holocaust representations shall be "accurate and faithful" insists upon the implementation of set conventions when portraying the Holocaust in the theatre, namely: the portrayal of victims as martyrs, innocent sacrifices, or long-suffering tragic figures; sympathy for the victims; the portrayal of perpetrators as "evil"; and the overall representation of the Holocaust in the "tragic" mode.[21] I posit that the influence of Des Pres' third "prescription" provides a necessary framework for wider treatment of the Holocaust. It is worth pointing out that society initiated these dictums; Des Pres simply codified them. However, these dictums have developed from "Holocaust etiquette" into what Gillian Rose terms "Holocaust piety."[22] A key aspect of this is that performers and audiences alike are often frustratingly reluctant to engage with "Holocaust performances" as there is either a perceived danger that to do so would "domesticate [trivialise] the horrific experiences of millions";[23] or a fear that the Holocaust, as an event which is deemed "ineffable" and beyond human comprehension, may actually "'be all too understandable, all too continuous with what we are – human, all too human'."[24] When performers and spectators do engage with Holocaust-related performances, they are likewise unwilling to engage with those that could either be seen as straying outside the boundaries of Holocaust etiquette (in terms of its use as a guiding framework) or violating it outright ("profane" theatre). Examples of this include comedy, such as Peter Barnes' 1978 one-act play *Auschwitz*, which revolves around a trio of petty Nazi bureaucrats caught up in red tape and office rivalry in the midst of supplying orders for building materials and such like to Auschwitz; cabaret, such as Eugene Lion's 2003 play *Sammy's Follies: A Criminal Comedy*, in which a bar owner and his troupe carry out the trial of a concentration camp commandant for the crime of "indifference"; and musicals, such as Shuki Levy and David Goldsmith's *Imagine This* (2007), centering around a group of Jewish actors in the Warsaw ghetto. The latter was intended to show that musicals can have an "emotional impact" and "the ability to deal with meaningful subject matter in a powerful and sensitive manner" (*Playbill*, 8 December 2008) while the comedy of *Auschwitz* and *Sammy's Follies* is designed to reflect the playwrights' rage at the world's apathy toward genocide and persecution. At the conclusion of each play, "our comic enjoyment has implicated us in the atrocity."[25] Nevertheless, the intended long-term transfer of *Auschwitz* was canceled by Barnes himself when he realized that audiences were generally missing his intended message and believed that he was being contemptuous of the Holocaust; *Sammy's Follies* has yet to receive a professional production; and *Imagine This* closed after a run of just four weeks in London's West End following scathing critical reviews.

The reasons for the perceived "profanity" of each piece are varied and bound up with Holocaust etiquette and/or Holocaust piety. There is a seeming incongruity in the very concept of *Imagine This* through utilizing the genre of a musical to represent the Holocaust – that is, the use of a theatrical genre that is conventionally perceived as a means of commercially popular entertainment or escapism to tell a story of mass persecution and genocide – and this dichotomy contributed to varying extents toward the critical derision of the show (examples include Michael Billington's "Imagine This" [*Guardian*, 20 November 2008]; Michael Coveney's "Imagine This, New London Theatre, London" [*Independent*, 24 November 2008]; and Matt Wolf's "Why the Holocaust Musical Was Right to Close" [*Guardian*, 8 December 2008]). The use of "sight gags, one-liners, farcical business, witty reversals of identity, and a general refusal to take life or art too seriously for too long"[26] in *Auschwitz* is provocative, especially as the play is set in an office and – for the majority of the action – is far removed from the horrors of the camps. The play focuses on "the banal exactitude of the Third Reich bureaucracy,"[27] featuring three protagonists – Else, Cranach, and Stroop – whose complicity and guilt is only realized by themselves near the end of the play; as Robert Skloot observes, they are "ordinary German bureaucrats who, on a daily basis and with little knowledge and less concern, make the extermination of the Jews possible."[28] The audience finally hears the voices of the victims at the play's conclusion in the form of a music hall routine by two Jewish comedians imprisoned in Auschwitz, who are then gassed and die onstage. In *Sammy's Follies*, a concentration camp inmate re-enacts his own hanging, culminating in a popular dance routine performed at the end of the rope;[29] a parody of a medical experiment is performed, using everyday household items as surgical equipment and removing foodstuffs from the hysterically laughing "victim," apparently to be fed to the cast and audience;[30] and a female prisoner describes her arrival at Auschwitz and subsequent stripping and shaving, simultaneously performing a striptease to the erotic pleasure of the male chorus.[31] As I have argued elsewhere, this deliberate violation of the sanctity of the Holocaust constitutes what Israeli scholar Gad Kaynar refers to as "balagan."[32]

In his essay "The Holocaust experience through theatrical profanation," Kaynar examines the notion of the breach, and thus the re-canonization, of iconic codes in Holocaust representation to be found in Israeli theatre.[33] This begins with the identification of acknowledged Holocaust symbols that function on an internationally recognized semiotic level, including the guard tower, the gas chambers, the tattooed arm, and so on.[34] These symbols are so deeply engrained on the public consciousness, Kaynar asserts, that this causes them to "deteriorate to the level of ready-made and mechanically applicable semiotic vehicles [...] losing with each manipulation a little more of the authentic horror originally imbued in them."[35] It is precisely because of the fact that these symbols have become so widely associated with and representative of the Holocaust that their original power and dreadfulness has diminished. In order to re-implement their full horror, Kaynar argues, the "holiest taboos" of the Holocaust must be breached,[36] and this refers back to Des Pres' prescription regarding the Holocaust as a sacred event. By toppling these semiotic signifiers before an audience in a way that violates Holocaust etiquette, the question can ultimately be raised in the minds of the spectators as to what it is that makes those symbols "holy" in the first place, leading back directly to the Nazi genocide and its associated atrocities. As Kaynar observes, it is a way of "reactivating its memory by defaming it,"[37] and as the voices of the survivors are gradually lost, it is a way of re-introducing the horror of which, one day, no eyewitnesses will be left to tell.[38] However, the majority of people who visit a concentration camp have a need and/or desire for doing so, from familial connections to research or educational purposes, and there is little cause to instill a sense of shock in them – although I must admit to a desire to "shock" the Auschwitz selfie enthusiasts of the world.

In the context of theatre about the Holocaust, the notion of "profane" performance manifests in other ways. At the most basic level, aspects such as incorrect costuming, forgetting of lines, or a contrived and/or factually incorrect plot can be deemed embarrassing at best and disrespect and/or incomprehension at worst, tying back in with the concept of the "profane" in relation to Auschwitz selfies. The ethics of representation mean that even the most earnest efforts to present an appropriate performance within a concentration camp could lead to the profane. How, for example, are well-fed actors supposed to play starving prisoners? To attempt to portray the inherent violence of the camp environment would require either extreme skill in stage combat or literal mutilation of the actors. Mutilation in performance – or rather, mutilation *as* performance – is exhibited by performance artists such as Kira O'Reilly and Franco B, who in their respective works have undergone self-mutilation by cutting with a scalpel – *Untitled (Syncope)* (2007)[39] – and partial exsanguination via intravenous cannulas – *Still Life* (2003).[40] In terms of Holocaust theatre, such action risks harm to actors and audience alike, and is a profanity considering the very real suffering already inflicted within the Auschwitz complex. My first provocation, then, is this: can there ever really be a place for the "profane" in Holocaust theatre? My simple answer is yes: but not within a concentration camp. I argue that within *conventional* theatre, and with the ever-encroaching existence of "Holocaust fatigue," there is a growing need to "shake" audiences and encourage a deeper consideration of the Holocaust on their part.

Precise definitions of the term "Holocaust fatigue" vary. For instance, in "Holocaust Fatigue and the Lure of Normality," blogger Arlene Stein (2013) centers her argument around the overpowering nature of the Holocaust in terms of defining Jewish identity, affirming that "[g]rowing numbers of Jewish Americans yearn to be an ethnic and religious group [...] defined by distinctive foods and ritual customs, rather than by the legacy of pain and suffering." From this perspective Holocaust fatigue has arisen from a desire to celebrate what it means to be Jewish, rather than dwell upon persecution. As early as 1981, questions were raised over "How much 'Holocaust' is healthy […]?" and concerns were voiced that "overemphasis on the Holocaust overshadows other important dimensions of Jewish education, history, thought, culture, and literature."[41] In an article for the *Jewish Chronicle* on 13 December 2013, journalist Miriam Shaviv wrote: "About 10 years ago […] I felt myself getting Holocaust fatigue. […] I had reached saturation point. I had been surrounded by Holocaust stories and history for so long, I did not feel the need to know any more." In his review of *The Fragility of Empathy after the Holocaust* (2004) by Carolyn J. Dean, Holocaust scholar Berel Lang asserts that such an output of Holocaust-related material negates Dean's claim of a loss of empathy in the wake of the Holocaust.[42] However, I argue that this output, further to Shaviv's discussion, actually contributes to Holocaust fatigue by "saturating" audiences in Holocaust accounts and narratives that rarely differ. Interviewed by Barry Gewen for the *New York Times* on 15 June 2003, Holocaust survivor Aviva Slesin stated that "'[…] Even I roll my eyes when I hear about another Holocaust documentary […]'."[43] The term "Holocaust fatigue" therefore encompasses the reluctance of many people to engage further with the Holocaust beyond a basic comprehension, primarily due to a perceived saturation of Holocaust films, television programs, and literature that can consequently cause spectators to feel that exposure to just one of these constitutes an adequate encounter – for instance, watching *Schindler's List* or reading Anne Frank's *Diary of a Young Girl*. From both Jewish and non-Jewish perspectives, Holocaust fatigue also comprises an unwillingness to dwell upon the legacy of persecution and suffering.[44] I posit that the introduction of innovative and avant-garde ways of examining the Holocaust through theatre, such as the use of balagan, enables practitioners and performers to challenge Holocaust fatigue in their audiences and even themselves (assuming that Holocaust piety has been overcome). However, the literal and figurative sanctity of Auschwitz as a site of memory (in its (first space) status as the mass gravesite of over one million people and the (second space) place most commonly associated with, and representative of, the Nazi genocide), coupled with the pre-existing awareness of the majority of those who visit the camp, means that the use of outright "profane" theatre here is rendered unnecessary and gratuitous. Emma Willis observes how the objects and architecture of the site represent the dead, especially in view of the fact that archival objects are positioned as "surrogate witnesses who testify to the past."[45] These include the dense rows of prisoner photographs inside the barracks of Auschwitz I; the displays of human hair; the execution wall of the infamous Block 11; and the ruins of barracks at Auschwitz-Birkenau. According to Willis, Auschwitz thus stages its history and asks visitors to "participate as attentive audience members who are willing to listen" – a "reverential" act.[46]

"Sacred" Holocaust theatre: the Auschwitz-Birkenau guided tour

If Auschwitz selfies and balagan are examples of "profane" Holocaust performance, then, what constitutes "sacred?" I suggest that the majority of people who visit Auschwitz and undertake one of the guided tours will most likely not consider themselves as having participated in a theatre event. Yet I submit that these tours do constitute theatre, and in the following ways.

TRACING TOPOGRAPHIES

While many theatre events are free and open to the public (Auschwitz *is* free and open to the public during certain hours, while Birkenau is continually accessible), those who undertake a tour at Auschwitz must purchase tickets, establishing the beginning of what Bruce McConachie calls a "social contract"[47] by founding their expectation of witnessing – of becoming spectators. From my own experiences of visiting the camp, and in line with those described by Chris Keil, upon arrival outside the main reception building at Auschwitz I one finds a bustling car park and large groups of people of all ages, some of whom indulge in a quick cigarette before heading in to begin their visit. Inside the reception building there are queues of people buying or collecting tickets, and this is immediately comparable to a theatre box office in that visitors choose the specified time at which they want to undertake their tour (depending on which language their preferred tour is in). Also within the reception building is a shop selling hot and cold drinks, snacks, and postcards, much like the bar or equivalent facilities usually provided at theatre venues (although alcohol is prohibited at Auschwitz). A small bookshop adjacent sells a variety of books about Auschwitz and the Holocaust, including memoirs, biographies, historical accounts, non-fiction, illustrated books for children, and so on; posters depicting photographs of the camp, as well as artistic responses to it, are for sale, and British visitors can recognize the parallel between this shop and those of the National Theatre and the Royal Court. The consumption of food and drink and the use of photography and mobile phones is restricted within the Auschwitz complex. This is designated by a multilingual sign on the way into Auschwitz I from the reception building, in much the same way that an announcement is usually made prior to the start of a performance, reminding patrons to switch off or silence their mobile devices, while signs in theatre foyers frequently state that drinks must be consumed from plastic "glasses."

Visitors undertaking an Auschwitz tour are issued with audio headsets to enable them to hear their guide speak as they move through the camp, and tour groups usually comprise around 20 people following a single guide. The first part of the tour, which takes place in Auschwitz I, includes stops at the camp gate; multiple barracks containing displays of the history of Auschwitz as well as sizeable displays of artefacts (shoes, hair, glasses, suitcases, etc.); Block 11; and the public gallows. At each stopping point the guide relates information about that particular site and its context within the history and day-to-day life of the camp. At the conclusion of the first part of the tour, visitors are given the opportunity for a short break before boarding a shuttle bus to Birkenau; akin to a theatre interval, the group can purchase drinks, snacks, and merchandise, and go to the toilet, before undertaking the second part of the tour. At Birkenau the tour concentrates on the front part of the camp (up to the ruins of the crematoria), and the stopping points include a cattle car on the railway tracks inside the camp; a barracks in the men's camp; several barracks and a public latrine in the women's camp; the ruins of the crematoria; and the watchtower in "Hell's Gate." Tour groups are able to go up inside the watchtower to see out across the expanse of the camp, entering via an electronic turnstile. At the conclusion of the tour in Birkenau, and during the walk between stopping points both at Auschwitz and Birkenau, visitors are able to put questions to the guide. Like its equivalent at Auschwitz I, a tiny shop at Birkenau sells postcards and related memorabilia, and in recent years a small refreshment room with vending machines has been installed along from the toilets – all housed within the watchtower building.

Apart from the somewhat materialistic elements that can reasonably be found in virtually any space designed to accommodate large numbers of visitors – from zoos and cathedrals to museums and theatres – what makes the guided tour at Auschwitz constitute theatre, and "sacred" theatre at that? The overarching factor is that the tours are ordained by the museum authorities. The word "ordained" – meaning both given permission and invested with religious authority – is especially pertinent in this case, given that the museum authorities are seen as an omniscient presence with infallible authority regarding what is permissible on the site and what is not. The very existence of the tours, ordained by the museum authorities, immediately invests them with an implied sanctity. The sense of sanctity is heightened by way of further omnipotent involvement by those authorities, such as the opening of specific buildings (and not others) to the public, and the allowance and prevention of certain behaviors. It is interesting to note at this point that theatre as we know it today arose from the Ancient Greek festivals surrounding religious observances and ceremonies – and, as I will shortly discuss, some of that which takes place on the Auschwitz guided tours might be regarded more as profane theatre than sacred.

In its most basic form, theatre consists of one person carrying out an action while another person watches – the actor and the spectator. As renowned director Peter Brook has declared, "I can take any empty space and call it a bare stage. A man walks across this empty space whilst someone else is watching him, and this is all that is needed for an act of theatre to be engaged."[48] The guide of an Auschwitz tour thus becomes the "actor," and the tour group are his/her "spectators." Rather than the proscenium arch and clearly delineated spaces of the actor and the spectator to be found in the conventional theatre, Auschwitz itself becomes a gigantic auditorium, in which the visitor-spectators follow the guide-actor around the space of the camp in a form of promenade performance. The guide him/herself is a performer: s/he knows a "script," which is broken down into scenes depending on the specific location within the space, and even his/her movements through the space have been pre-determined or, in theatrical terms, "blocked" by the "director" – a role fulfilled in this case by the museum authorities. While the museum authorities have overall control over which direction the tours will take both literally and figuratively, the guides themselves have an input into the spoken word of the performance while carrying it out, and in such a sense they become actor-directors. Just as theatre directors will have different interpretations of the same text, the "script" that the Auschwitz guide "performs" varies in focus depending on the perspective and beliefs of each particular individual. During my first visit to Auschwitz in 2008, the guide emphasized the camp as the site of the mass murder of predominantly Jewish victims, and this view is consistently held in wider public consciousness. Yet during my second visit in 2011, the guide referred to Auschwitz throughout as "the site of the martyrdom of the Polish people," and stressed the origins of the camp as a place of incarceration and suffering for Polish prisoners. Both guides relayed a similar history of the camp in terms of its function as a Nazi labor and extermination camp, yet their personal ideologies influenced which group of victims they identified with and so the emphasis that was subsequently placed during the tour.[49] While the differences in the "script" potentially could be seen as a breach of Des Pres' second dictum – "Representations of the Holocaust shall be as accurate and faithful as possible to the facts and conditions [...] *without change or manipulation for any reason*"[50] – each one represents a different facet of the prisoner experience at Auschwitz across nationalities, religious beliefs, and other factors that, according to the Nazis, determined the "undesirability" of an individual. The "script" that each guide-actor performs is still "accurate and faithful" to the events that took place within Auschwitz; the "facts and conditions" remain the same. It is only the point of view of the victim that is different.

The notion of the Auschwitz guided tour as "sacred" performance is maintained in the manifestation of Des Pres' third dictum – "The Holocaust shall be approached as a solemn or even a sacred event, with a seriousness admitting no response that might obscure its enormity or dishonor its dead"[51] – in the social contract or "ideological transaction" completed and maintained by the guide-actor and the visitor-spectators. Baz Kershaw describes an ideological transaction as taking place between performers and the "community of their audience":

> Ideology is the source of the collective ability of performers and audience to make more or less common sense of the signs used in performance, the means by which the aims and intentions of theatre companies connect with the responses and interpretations of their audiences. Thus, ideology provides the framework within which companies encode and audiences decode the signifiers of performance. I view performance as a transaction because, evidently, communication in performance is not simply uni-directional, from actors to audience. […] [A]s any actor will tell you, the reactions of audiences influence the nature of a performance. It is not simply that the audience affects emotional tone or stylistic nuance: the spectator is engaged fundamentally in the active construction of meaning as a performance event proceeds. In this sense performance is "about" the transaction of meaning.[52]

Simply put, both the actor and the spectator bring their own senses of what the performance will mean to that performance event. The actor places their "aims and intentions" before the spectator through the performance, and the spectator will "respond and interpret" accordingly. If the aims and intentions of the actor and/or performance are not explicitly clear, then multiple interpretations will occur and none of these may correspond with the original intention(s) of the actor. However, in the case of Auschwitz both the actor-guide and visitor-spectator bring with them pre-conceptions of what the performance event of the tour aims and intends to do: the guide-actor will educate/inform/engage the visitor-spectators by taking them around the site and outlining its history. In addition these pre-conceptions are informed by the conventions of Holocaust etiquette on both the part of the guide-actor and visitor-spectator, and the ideological transaction is continually informed by one or both as the tour progresses.

Before the performance begins, the guide-actor establishes the rules of conduct expected from the visitor-spectators, for instance asking them to refrain from using flash photography (in order to help preserve displays) or even to avoid photographs altogether in certain areas such as the gas chamber (to ensure that what essentially is a crime scene remains a place of respect for the dead), and to switch off or silence mobile devices (to maintain respect for the dead, and also to avoid interruption to the tour), reflecting the typical instructions given to audiences of conventional theatre. In this way the ground rules of the ideological transaction, and the experience as a whole, are made clear: this is a site of memory, and all involved will behave and treat it as such. During the performance the guide-actor maintains the role that the visitor-spectators and the director subsequently expect from him/her, such as sustaining a calm and solemn demeanor, mindful of the need for respect for the dead and appropriate composure of behavior, and endeavoring to keep the audience engaged. In turn, the ideological transaction is completed by the visitor-spectators in fulfilling their expected role through following the guide-actor, obeying their instructions, reflecting his/her demeanor (which for both guide-actor and visitor-spectators is determined by the space in which they find themselves), and manifesting expressions of sorrow, pity, anger, disbelief, and so on in reaction to what the guide-actor is saying. They experience affective and emotional responses that vary between and within spectators, with it being fully anticipated that each individual will undergo, in very general terms, a different response with each scene presented.

There is an additional heightened sense of the dramatic when moving through certain areas of the space. For example, during my visit to Auschwitz in 2008 the guide took us through the gas chamber and crematorium in Auschwitz I and then to stand outside. Having outlined when and how the crematorium was used, he asked us what we thought the SS had done with the ashes of their victims from this particular site. After several guesses by his audience, ranging from throwing them into the river to burying them, the guide took a moment to make eye contact with us all and quietly, if intensely, replied: "You're standing on them." As one the group looked down at their feet with expressions of horror, re-surveying the white chalky substance beneath them, before quickly relocating – a perhaps unwelcome manifestation of audience participation. This notion of the guided tour as theatre event continues with the equivalent of scene changes, with pauses in which the guide-actor and visitor-spectators move to the next scene or the visitor-spectators are encouraged to further explore their surroundings. As outlined above, there is even an interval: between the end of the first part of the tour at Auschwitz and its resumption at Birkenau, spectators are able to purchase drinks and snacks and go to the toilet before taking the shuttle bus. Just as conventional plays often permit the audience to perceive, however briefly, the perspective of the antagonist, at Birkenau the visitor-spectators are afforded the chance to glimpse the perspective of the SS by ascending the stairs of the main watchtower to see the camp from above. During the tour, and especially at the end, the guide is called upon to enact a well-known aspect of actor training and performance in the form of improvisation via answering questions from the spectators, although he can still rely on the script (and his training and knowledge) to furnish answers.

I have described the Auschwitz guided tour as "sacred," and yet within this framework of sanctity there exist elements of the profane. These are couched in terms of Chris Keil's reference to "the violation of memory by current concerns," outlined above. The concept of "current concerns" runs the gamut of "foregrounding the present self in place of historical memory" – allowing one's own needs and desires to overtake the sense of historical place. To illustrate: when the guide-actor does not forbid photography outright, for example, the visitor-spectator is able to place their current concern – in this case a desire to take a photograph – ahead of the historical memory of the space around them, whether they are photographing a glass display case or a barbed wire fence. While they may engage with the space and its historical memory while walking through it, and thus trace their own psychic topography of the camp, a glimpse of a particular archival object, coupled with the desire to photograph it *and* awareness that such a photograph is allowed, means that the historical memory of the site is briefly forgotten as the visitor-spectator moves to take a picture in accordance with that "current concern" – even if the intention is for the photo to ultimately document the visitor-spectator's remembrance of the historical memory. Elements of current concern will always interfere when it comes to encountering memory in the context of a site like Auschwitz – the necessity of a refreshment and toilet break between Auschwitz I and Birkenau is a basic example. The willful or protracted placement of the self's current concerns is the real cause for disquiet. Note the manner in which the guide alerted us that we were walking on ashes; while having an impact upon the group and ensuring that we would remember the experience, it placed our own reactions – disgust, horror, and so on – above the memory of what – and who – those ashes represented. In such a sense the visitor-spectator's experience shimmers between historical memory and current concerns; between their own comfort and desires, and an awareness of what the physical space of Auschwitz stands for.

The guided tour as a whole fits across a variety of theatrical forms. It is immersive theatre, in that the audience are completely surrounded by an experience encompassing sight, smell, movement, and touch, through all of which they are able to create and maintain meaning, and which is more closely aligned to an outright experience than a simple "play." It is participatory theatre, in which the audience has a role in determining the action and outcome according to explicit or implicit guidelines, such as the asking of questions. It is site-specific theatre, in that it is readable only within Auschwitz and created solely for its topography. In fundamental terms it is, quite simply, theatre, in that a person speaks or carries out an action in front of others who watch.

My next provocation thus becomes: would those undertaking the tour be "happy" to consider themselves as having paid for, and undertaken, a theatrical performance – a "play?" Does the double meaning of the word "play" – both an act of performance and a game – potentially affect this consideration, especially in relation to the Holocaust? Does the application of the word "theatre" diminish the embodied sanctity of the tour or increase its value, in whatever ideological currency that value may be seen as being worth? Does the perceived value of the piece increase if the audience see themselves as having actually contributed to it, rather than having been passive witnesses?

Conclusion: the "space between": a case for site-specific performance at Auschwitz?

There are varying arguments for and against the use of theatre and performance within Auschwitz. It can be perceived how the notion of a theatre event at Auschwitz could be deemed unnecessary, particularly as it is so well known and its place in public consciousness is secured through its being the site of mass industrialized murder and the final resting place of most of its victims. However, *is* there a case for site-specific performance at Auschwitz? What are the ramifications? Popular concepts of the theatre as being somehow "frivolous" and a form of "entertainment" and/or "escapism" place immediate ideological obstacles in terms of a perception that a site-specific theatre performance at Auschwitz would consequently be inappropriate given the unspoken rule that "[t]he Holocaust shall be approached […] with a seriousness admitting no response that might obscure its enormity or dishonor its dead."[53] In this instance there is an automatic assumption that, somehow, this will be violated and this is directly linked to Holocaust etiquette/Holocaust piety. The "narrative of authority" and the somewhat fixed notions of the first and second spaces in relation to Auschwitz-Birkenau mean that to attempt to populate the third space with new meaning would most likely not be seen as an effort to engage visitors with the Holocaust but, as described, a desecration.

There are further considerations to be borne in mind and the most immediate of these centers upon the perception of the Holocaust as, foremost, the Nazi genocide of the Jewish people. But does this mean that the Jewish perspective should be emphasized over that of other victim groups, such as the Roma and Sinti, Jehovah's Witnesses, homosexuals, members of the resistance, and prisoners of war? How is the point of view of the protagonist in a performance at Auschwitz, and the very protagonist themselves, to be decided? As I have already described above in the case of my personal experiences with different guides, even the tours at Auschwitz offer different victim perspectives to visitors. Whose perspective should visitor-spectators leave with? As I have stated, many visitors to Auschwitz have a familial or educational reason for going to the camp. Yet if we take such visitors out of our considerations and note the observation of Hank Greenspan that we need Holocaust theatre due to the fact that we do not listen properly to survivors,[54] site-specific performance in Auschwitz could prove to be a way of engaging those who might otherwise belong to the Auschwitz selfie generation. Auschwitz is advertised as a tourist destination in Krakow; tourists are offered a visit to the camp followed by lunch and a trip to the Wieliczka salt mine. Does the promise of "theatre at Auschwitz" not sound just as attractive to those who are drawn in by the idea of a jaunt to Auschwitz as part of a novelty day out? And by playing upon the pre-conceptions of those drawn to such an "attraction," could theatre in Auschwitz adhere to the essence of good drama by setting up the expectations of such an audience (to be entertained, for example), only to break or turn away from those expectations by presenting a challenging, provocative, and thought-provoking performance event?

On the other side of this argument, and turning away from the concept of dark tourism and Auschwitz selfies, site-specific performance at Auschwitz could be used as a tool for academics, educators, and historians. Throughout this article I have referred in broad terms to performance at Auschwitz drawn from *after* the Holocaust, but I suggest that it would be of great interest to scholars and non-scholars alike to see re-enactments of the performances that were staged by inmates themselves during their imprisonment at Auschwitz. "Underground" performances that were staged without the knowledge or consent of the SS guards included comic poetry, recitations, and songs drawn from Jewish tradition.[55] Alvin Goldfarb notes that many performances, such as those that satirized the SS in the form of cabaret, were frequently used as a tacit form of resistance.[56] On other occasions SS guards at Auschwitz rewarded performers for entertaining them.[57] I suggest that re-enactments of such performances could deepen the knowledge of academics, practitioners, and more "involved" spectators (such as those with a familial connection to the Holocaust) while potentially offering further opportunities for engagement to others without a connection or with a lesser degree of knowledge/involvement.

There are numerous social, political, and cultural barriers in the way of site-specific performance at Auschwitz, including the deeply entrenched conventions of Holocaust etiquette. For instance, given that Poland is a deeply Catholic country, would a theatre event featuring a homosexual man as a protagonist be well received? Jehovah's Witnesses and the Roma and Sinti are still widely perceived as "undesirables" throughout Europe; how could their stories be portrayed? Once the social, political, cultural, and even historical barriers have been removed, then perhaps there will be the potential for theatre at Auschwitz. However, I submit that the eradication of these barriers would mean that theatre at Auschwitz would no longer be necessary, as the lessons of the Holocaust would finally have been learned – and even Auschwitz itself would be rendered obsolete. Perhaps site-specific performance is not suited for major sites of memory such as Auschwitz, but rather as a way of gaining attention and increasing interest in the network of lesser known, even forgotten camps throughout Poland and Europe, and putting them back on the map: undeserving of and disallowing the "profane," not elevated enough to be deemed as "sacred," but occupying the space in between.

Notes

1. Daniel, "The Freest Theatre," 150–55.
2. Schumacher, *Charlotte Delbo*.
3. Rovit and Goldfarb, *Theatrical Performance*.
4. Keil, "Mansions of the Dead," 483.
5. See, for example, Lennon and Foley, *Dark Tourism*; and Sharpley and Stone, *The Darker Side of Travel*.
6. Pearson, *Site-Specific Performance*, 7.
7. Pavis, *Dictionary of the Theatre*, 337.
8. Pearson, *Site-Specific Performance*, 3.
9. Ibid., 4.
10. Des Pres, "Holocaust *Laughter?*" 217.
11. Kaynar, "The Holocaust Experience," 57.
12. Kershaw, *The Politics of Performance*, 16.
13. Keil, "Mansions of the Dead," 484.
14. Ibid., 484.
15. Ibid., 484.
16. Ibid., 485.
17. Des Pres, "Holocaust *Laughter?*" 217.
18. Ibid., 217.
19. Ibid., 218.
20. Mitschke, "Empathy Effects," 169.
21. Isser, *Stages of Annihilation*, 14; Mitschke, "Empathy Effects," 169.
22. Schick, *Gillian Rose*, 74.
23. Ibid., 74.
24. Ibid., 74.
25. Fuchs, *Plays of the Holocaust*, xvi.
26. Skloot, *The Darkness We Carry*, 63.
27. Fuchs, *Plays of the Holocaust*, xvi.
28. Skloot, *The Darkness We Carry*, 63.
29. Lion, "Sammy's Follies," 377–82.
30. Ibid., 407–14.
31. Ibid., 422–31.
32. Kaynar, "The Holocaust Experience," 57; Mitschke, "Empathy Effects," 176.
33. Kaynar, "The Holocaust Experience," 56.
34. Ibid., 57.
35. Ibid., 57.
36. Ibid., 56.
37. Ibid., 59.
38. Mitschke, "Against the 'Holocaust Fairytale'"; Mitschke, "Empathy Effects," 176–7.
39. Duggan, *Trauma-Tragedy*, 142–4.

TRACING TOPOGRAPHIES

40. Ibid., 76.
41. Magid, "The Holocaust and Jewish Identity," 120–21.
42. Dean, *The Fragility of Empathy*, as cited in Mitschke, "Empathy Effects," 8.
43. Ibid., 8.
44. Ibid., 8.
45. Willis, *Theatricality*, 10.
46. Ibid., 10.
47. McConachie, "Introduction," 188.
48. Brook, *The Empty Space*, 9.
49. It is interesting to note Keil's observation, following a personal interview with an Auschwitz tour guide, that the "Museum authorities" – including tour guides – "do not feel that they are involved in […] providing religious or philosophical aspects of interpretation […]. Their job is to present the history of the place." Keil, "Mansions of the Dead," 484.
50. Des Pres, "Holocaust *Laughter?*" 217 (italics added).
51. Ibid., 217.
52. Kershaw, *The Politics of Performance*, 16.
53. Des Pres, "Holocaust *Laughter?*" 217.
54. Greenspan, "The Power and Limits."
55. Turkov, "Latvia and Auschwitz," 115–16.
56. Goldfarb, "Theatrical Activities," 120.
57. Ibid., 120.

Disclosure statement

No potential conflict of interest was reported by the author.

References

Barnes, Peter. "Auschwitz." In *Plays of the Holocaust: An International Anthology*, edited by Elinor Fuchs, 105–145. New York: Theatre Communications Group, 1987.

Brook, Peter. *The Empty Space*. New York: Touchstone, 1968.

Daniel, Curt. "'The Freest Theatre in the Reich': In the German Concentration Camps." In *Theatrical Performance during the Holocaust*, edited by Rebecca Rovit and Alvin Goldfarb, 150–155. Baltimore, MD: The John Hopkins University Press, 1999.

Dean, Carolyn J. *The Fragility of Empathy After the Holocaust*. Ithaca, NY: Cornell University Press, 2004.

Des Pres, Terrence. "Holocaust Laughter?" In *Writing and the Holocaust*, edited by Berel Lang, 216–233. London and New York: Holmes & Meier Publishers, 1988.

Duggan, Patrick. *Trauma-Tragedy: Symptoms of Contemporary Performance*. Manchester: Manchester University Press, 2012.

Fuchs, Elinor, ed. *Plays of the Holocaust: An International Anthology*. New York: Theatre Communications Group, 1987.

TRACING TOPOGRAPHIES

Goldfarb, Alvin. "Theatrical Activities in Nazi Concentration Camps." In *Theatrical Performance during the Holocaust*, edited by Rebecca Rovit and Alvin Goldfarb, 117–124. Baltimore, MD: The John Hopkins University Press, 1999.

Greenspan, Hank. "The Power and Limits of the Metaphor of Survivors' Testimony." In *Staging the Holocaust: The Shoah in Drama and Performance*, edited by Claude Schumacher, 27–39. Cambridge: Cambridge University Press, 1998.

Isser, Edward R. *Stages of Annihilation: Theatrical Representations of the Holocaust*. London: Associated University Presses, 1997.

Kaynar, Gad. "The Holocaust Experience through Theatrical Profanation." In *Staging the Holocaust: The Shoah in Drama and Performance*, edited by Claude Schumacher, 53–69. Cambridge: Cambridge University Press, 1998.

Kershaw, Baz. *The Politics of Performance: Radical Theatre as Cultural Intervention*. London: Routledge, 1992.

Keil, Chris. "Sightseeing in the Mansions of the Dead." *Social & Cultural Geography* 6, no. 4 (2005): 479–494.

Lennon, John, and Malcolm Foley. *Dark Tourism: The Attraction of Death and Disaster*. London and Boston, MA: Cengage Learning, 2010.

Lion, Eugene. "Sammy's Follies: A Criminal Comedy." In *A Terrible Truth: Anthology of Holocaust Drama, Vol 1*, edited by Irene N. Watts, 359–467. Toronto: Playwrights Canada Press, 2003.

Magid, Shaul. "The Holocaust and Jewish Identity in America: Memory, the Unique, and the Universal." *Jewish Social Studies* 18, no. 2 (2012): 100–135.

McConachie, Bruce. "Introduction: Spectating as Sandbox Play." In *Affective Performance and Cognitive Science: Body, Brain and Being*, edited by Nicola Shaughnessy, 183–197. London: Bloomsbury, 2013.

Mitschke, Samantha. "Against the 'Holocaust Fairytale': Balagan and Child Protagonists." Paper presented at Global Perspectives on the Holocaust, Murfreesboro, October 15–18, 2013.

Mitschke, Samantha. "Empathy Effects: Towards an Understanding of Empathy in British and American Holocaust Theatre." PhD diss., University of Birmingham, 2014.

Pavis, Patrice. *Dictionary of the Theatre: Terms, Concepts, and Analysis*. Translated by Christine Shantz. Toronto: University of Toronto Press, 1998.

Pearson, Mike. *Site-Specific Performance*. Basingstoke: Palgrave Macmillan, 2010.

Rovit, Rebecca, and Alvin Goldfarb, eds. *Theatrical Performance during the Holocaust: Texts, Documents, Memoirs*. Baltimore, MD: The John Hopkins University Press, 1999.

Schick, Kate. *Gillian Rose: A Good Enough Justice*. Edinburgh: Edinburgh University Press, 2012.

Schumacher, Claude. "Charlotte Delbo: Theatre as a Means of Survival." In *Staging the Holocaust: The Shoah in Drama and Performance*, edited by Claude Schumacher, 216–228. Cambridge: Cambridge University Press, 1998.

Sharpley, Richard, and Philip Stone. *The Darker Side of Travel: The Theory and Practice of Dark Tourism*. Bristol: Channel View Publications.

Skloot, Robert. *The Darkness We Carry: The Drama of the Holocaust*. Madison: The University of Wisconsin Press, 1988.

Striff, Erin, ed. *Performance Studies*. Basingstoke: Palgrave Macmillan, 2003.

Turkov, Yonas. "Latvia and Auschwitz." In *Theatrical Performance during the Holocaust*, edited by Rebecca Rovit and Alvin Goldfarb, 113–116. Baltimore, MD: The John Hopkins University Press, 1999.

Willis, Emma. *Theatricality, Dark Tourism and Ethical Spectatorship: Absent Others*. Basingstoke: Palgrave Macmillan, 2014.

The cinematic city and the destruction of Lublin's Jews

Maurizio Cinquegrani

School of Arts, University of Kent, Canterbury, UK

ABSTRACT

> They took me up, up. Very far, maybe 300 miles, until we came to Lublin. (Art Speigelman, *Maus*[1])

> With the words cited above, in Art Spiegelman's graphic novel *Maus* (1980-1991), Holocaust survivor Vladek Spiegelman remembers his journey from Częstochowa to Lublin as a Jewish prisoner of war in 1941. The name of the city of Lublin resounds as a distant place on map of Europe during the Second World War and, insofar as the study of film and the Holocaust is concerned, Lublin has entirely slipped under the radar as an understudied subject of investigation. This article aims at filling this gap and discusses the role of this city in the Final Solution by means of a study of its cinematic image and that of the concentration and extermination camp of Majdanek, at the outskirts of Lublin.

In the context of the interdisciplinary study of cinema and urban space, James Hay has argued that "films serve as maps within (and thus territorialize) the places where they are engaged" and that "the 'cinematic' is defined by a relation among sites and flows."[2] François Penz and Andong Lu have reflected upon this framework of analysis in their own theorization of "urban cinematics," which they define as the moving image's ability "to reveal a new spatial and narrative structure, to challenge the traditional organization of the city as new geographies and new thematic connections may emerge."[3] According to Penz and Lu, these geographies can be unwrapped by means of what they call "cinematic urban archaeology," a retrospective longitudinal way of making visible filmic spaces of the past and the present by means of digging through chronological layers of filmic representations of a particular space.[4] Building on Lev Kuleshov's theorization of the construction of imaginary places that exist only on film, Penz and Lu have discussed the relationship between the real site and its cinematic image in terms of *creative geography* and *topographical coherence*, two distinct ways of reading cinematic urban geographies:

> Cinema may use cities in creative ways to reorganize the city spaces into narrative geographies where urban fragments are collaged into spatial episodes. The alternative to creative geographies is cinematic topographical coherence. Both approaches – used in montage as

well as in continuity editing traditions – may give different readings of the city and have a different impact on our spatial perception. The use of creative geographies is one of the key principles of city symphonies, creating imaginary, artificial landscapes that exist only on the screen and where disparate physical locations construct a composite cinematic space through montage manipulation of the urban terrain.[5]

The present investigation aims at exploring the ways in which the city of Lublin has been used as a film location both in a geographically creative way, based on loose connections to the real identity and function of the sites, and in a topographically coherent manner, where the use of streets and buildings is historically accurate. In particular, this article addresses for the first time spatial issues and cinematics in relation to the ways in which the annihilation of Lublin's Jewry during the Holocaust has been portrayed on the screen. In his recent book, Marek Haltof has demonstrated how an in-depth study of Polish cinema and the Holocaust can contribute to providing answers to a series of key historical questions regarding the persecution of the Jews and the memorialization of their annihilation.[6] However, while a significant part of Haltof's work focuses on the ghetto of Warsaw, Lublin, the city that was at the heart of Nazi plans of expansion to the east, is absent from this book and from all other studies of Holocaust cinema. Lublin has indeed been under-represented in Holocaust cinema and yet, as we shall see, there are several significant films set during the war that use this city as a location. The films discussed here were all shot in Lublin in different languages and by filmmakers from Poland and other countries, including Britain, Israel, and Belgium. This heterogeneous group of films will be used to address spatial issues in film and to investigate the relationship between film and urban space according to James Hay's theorization of the process of "considering the places(s) of film practices within an environment and their relation to other ways of organizing this environment, of organizing social relations into an environment."[7]

In his study of the relationship between Poles and Jews, Michael C. Steinlauf has argued that the struggle to integrate the image of the murdered Jews into Polish national memory is crucial to an understanding of the history and culture of post-war Poland.[8] Haltof has articulated the dynamics of this struggle as they are revealed in Polish cinema from the immediate post-war period, in the years of the so-called "organized forgetting" (1965–1980) and in relation to the more recent and reluctant re-emergence of what had been repressed.[9] As we shall see, the urban cinematics of Lublin revealed in most Polish films discussed in this article reflect the ways in which the Holocaust was incorporated in the broader idea of the martyrdom of the Polish nation. War-time Lublin and Majdanek are here filmed with a selective gaze that emphasizes the Polish suffering and neglects the specificity of the destruction of the Jews. More recent Western films, on the contrary, re-appropriate the spaces of Lublin in relation to the Holocaust and yet, as we shall see, they do so by employing a largely creative approach to a cinematic city deprived of topographical coherence.

In May 1924, a formal ceremony marked the laying of the cornerstone at 85 Lubartowska Street of what would have become one of the most important Talmudic academies in Eastern Europe. Chachmei Lublin Yeshiva opened in 1930. Ten years later the Nazis ransacked the building, burnt the library and established there the headquarters of the military police. In the months and years that followed, the entire Jewish community of Lublin was annihilated. In 2005, two years after the building had been returned to the Jewish community of Poland, Leszek Wiśniewski visited the former yeshiva and filmed

TRACING TOPOGRAPHIES

Uczniowie Widzącego z Lublina (*Students of the Seer of Lublin*), a documentary on the history of Polish Hasidism which focuses on the figure of Hassidic Rabbi Jacob Isaac Horovitz-Sternfed (1745–1815), the seer or visionary of Lublin. This film records a tradition and anticipates the re-opening of the synagogue in Lubartowska Street in 2007. And yet this documentary ultimately bears witness to an absence, to a void impossible to fill, to the catastrophe of Lublin's Jews. Before the Nazi invasion of Poland, the city had a number of Jewish-owned factories, free-loan societies and savings-and-loan associations, Jewish trade unions, charitable and welfare associations, a Jewish hostel and summer camp, clinics, a hospital, an orphanage, religious schools, and cells of Jewish parties such as the Bund and Agudath Israel.[10] This world ceased to exist with the Holocaust. After the liquidation of the Lublin ghetto in November 1942, 4000 Jews were deported to the concentration and extermination camp of Majdanek, only three miles south-east of the city center, and another 30,000 were gassed in the death camp of Bełżec, situated between Lublin and Lwów. The 34,000 Jews persecuted by the Nazis had amounted to one third of the overall population of Lublin in the 1930s and only 200 of them survived the war. The streets of Lublin are pervaded by traces of the Final Solution. In particular, it was from a building at 1 Spokojna Street that Odilo Globocnik ran the death camps at Treblinka, Sobibor, and Bełżec.[11] The city of Lublin was central to the plans of the Nazis both in relation to the extermination of the Jews and to the conquest of a "living space" (*Lebensraum*) in the east, with long-term plans to Germanize the city and the entire district.[12] Litewski Square was at the heart of Nazi Lublin, with the German Head Field Command at number 3 and the headquarters in Spokojna Street at less than 500 yards from the square.[13] On the other side of Lublin and around its castle, the Jews, who had lived there for centuries, were trapped in the ghetto and lived on the brink of their annihilation.[14] The specific cinematics of this space, as they emerge from a number of key films, will be investigated in what follows in relation to three locations: Zamek Lubelski (Lublin Castle), Stare Miasto (Old Town), and the Nazi camp at Majdanek.

A comparison between the ways in which the Zamek Lubelski has been portrayed in Pathé's war-time newsreel *The Tragic City of Lublin* (1944), Soviet television production *Żołnierze Wolności* (*Soldiers of Freedom*, Jurij Ozierov, 1977), and British-American production *The Aryan Couple* (John Daly, 2004) can reveal an interesting paradox. Pathé's and Ozierov's films make a topographically coherent use of this location: the films are made and set in Lublin and portray events which took place in 1944. However, they neglect the role played by the castle in the broader context of the persecution of the Jews. On the contrary, Daly's film presents a creative geography of the city where Lublin is called to play the role of an unnamed Hungarian city. The events portrayed here are fictional and only loosely based on the life of Jewish industrialist Manfred Weiss, and yet this film finally associates the castle with the Holocaust while *The Tragic City of Lublin* and *Soldiers of Freedom* re-appropriated the building, under whose shadow the Jews of Lublin lived and were killed, as a site of Polish martyrdom.

On 23 July 1944, the Nazis massacred 300 Polish prisoners in Zamek Lubelski before they retreated from the city. *The Tragic City of Lublin*, an edited version of original Russian footage of Lublin and part of the series *The Voice of Britain*, opens with a panoramic panning shot of the city, partly in ruins as a result of the Soviet offensive against the Nazis.[15] Several tanks can be seen advancing through the streets of the inner districts of the city; one of them fires against the castle. A rapid montage sequence shows a number of

106

mortars firing against the Nazis and the Red Army soldiers advancing in the streets of Lublin and opening fire toward the windows of the surviving buildings. Several scenes are likely to have been re-staged for the camera, yet the film is a valuable record of the final phases of the Soviet offensive. The viewer is then introduced to images of the castle, while the voiceover explains the use the Nazis had made of this building. A series of shots filmed inside the castle present a large number of corpses, victims of the final act of Nazi violence before their retreat. *The Tragic City of Lublin* records the aftermath of the massacre and shows the victims in the courtyard of the castle and the men and women of Lublin mourning their losses. The following scenes focus on the Roman Catholic memorial service held outside the castle to commemorate the victims, and show the priests and nuns attending the service. In the courtyard we can see a large cross, erected next to the walls of the castle. The final images of the film represent large crowds welcoming the Red Army and the members of the Polish resistance movement. *The Tragic City of Lublin* anticipates a recurring absence in post-war Polish cinema: the Holocaust. A demonstration of the ways in which texts can signify by what they leave out, by their structured absences, as much as by what they include, *The Tragic City of Lublin* erases all traces of pre-war Jewish life and later persecution in and near Zamek Lubelski. It does not reveal the fact that the area around the castle had been Jewish, and does not make reference to the fact that the ghetto had been established there or to the destruction and conspicuous absence of the *Marashal-shul*, the Great Lublin Synagogue which used to stand next the castle. The Soviet footage used in this newsreel thus uses Zamek Lubelski to establish two reoccurring narratives in the cinematic image of post-war Lublin and inscribes them in the cinematic space of the castle: the heroism of the Red Army and, perhaps paradoxically, the Roman Catholic identity of the country.

According to Lefebvre in his discussion of the spatialization of history, the impact of the events that take place at a particular location becomes inscribed in space. And yet, although the past leaves its traces in specific locations, space is always a present space, whole and complete, at once product and part of the production process of historical events. The location, continues Lefebvre, is never owned by the past and is continuously processed through the connection between past events and their actuality.[16] Accordingly, the historical events of 1944 are inscribed in Zamek Lubelski and processed in post-war films by means of their juxtaposition with the present. The funeral scene presented in *The Tragic City of Lublin* was recreated 33 years later in *Soldiers of Freedom*. This Soviet film covers the history of Poland from the capitulation in 1939 to the creation of the national government in Lublin and reflects the post-war Sovietization of Poland and its persisting actuality. Ozierov recreates the memorial service for the victims of the 1944 massacre on location in the courtyard of Zamek Lubelski. One of the final sequences presents an actor impersonating Bolesław Bierut, a former president of Poland, speaking over the coffins aligned in the courtyard, while a religious service is held and a large crowd of Lublin citizens is shown outside the castle. The film focuses on the Polish resistance and on the events of 1944 in Lublin as key to the birth of the People's Republic of Poland; and yet, despite the topographical coherence of its use of locations, it largely evades the crucial question of the fate of Lublin's Jewry. *Soldiers of Freedom* thus reiterates the narrative established in the Soviet footage used in *The Tragic City of Lublin*, and its structured absences reflect the ways in which history was reshaped by the communist regime in a nationalist re-appropriation of the fight against Nazism.

TRACING TOPOGRAPHIES

Zamek Lubelski can be understood in terms of representational space, a site defined by Lefebvre as a place that has its source in the history of people and individuals belonging to that site.[17] Conflicts can occur between representational spaces and their symbolic systems, in particular where two or more people claim an ownership of their past. Zamek Lubelski is a site of both Jewish and Christian martyrdom and, while Polish films exclusively inscribed the latter in this space, a more recent Western film returned the site to Jewish history. *The Aryan Couple* tells the story of a rich Jewish Hungarian industrialist (played by Martin Landau) who, in order to ensure his family's passage to Switzerland, is forced to hand over his business and estate to the Nazis. Despite the fact that Lublin is here "playing" the role of an unnamed Eastern European city, the use of the castle as a location is particularly meaningful because of the associations with Lublin's Jewry outlined above. Joseph Krauzenberg, Landau's character, meets a Nazi leader in the castle and can be seen walking through the courtyard previously filmed by Ozierov and Pathé. Krauzenberg is wearing the Star of David on his coat and his frail figure is surrounded by threatening elements, including swastikas, weapons, and German soldiers, and this sequence thus identifies the castle as a site, or representational space, of Jewish martyrdom. Nevertheless, administrative offices of the occupation forces were located in Litewski Square and thus Krauzenberg's visit only loosely reflects the role of this site on the map of Nazi-occupied Lublin.

The Aryan Couple uses other locations with a flexible or creative approach to the specificity of the city's historical topography. Located at 1 Rynek, the building known as Trybunał Koronny (the Crown Court) was used in *The Aryan Couple* as the location of Krauzenberg's residence. In a long sequence, Krauzenberg observes from the balcony a large group of Jewish men, women, and children escorted by the Gestapo in the direction of Grodzka Gate, the city gate that historically separated Stare Miasto from the Jewish quarter. This building was never a private residence and no Jews lived in this part of the city. Also, this would have been an unlikely route for the resettlement of the Jews from other regions to the main ghetto and again the film is not following a coherent topography of the city.

The narrow alleys near the Rynek are also used in Uri Barbash's *Spring 1941* (2007), the first Israeli film to use Lublin as a location. *Spring 1941* focuses on a Jewish family seeking shelter from Nazi persecution and includes scenes filmed in Archidiakońska, Jezuicka and Dominikańska streets in Stare Miasto, behind the Rynek. However, Lublin is not named in the film and the city plays the more generic role of an unnamed eastern border town during the war. The scene of mass deportation of the Jews through the streets of Lublin resembles the scene observed by Krauzenberg from the balcony of the Crown Court in *The Aryan Couple*. Several buildings are decorated with swastikas and three Jewish man executed by the SS can be seen hanging from the balconies of the old houses of Stare Miasto. This implies that the Jews are made to march through the streets of the ghetto, while the scene is filmed on streets that never belonged to the Jewish district or to the ghetto. Ultimately, both *Spring 1941* and *The Aryan Couple* use the city in a creative manner that is not consistent with its historical topography and with the development of the eradication of Lublin's Jewry.

Like in *Spring 1941* and *The Aryan Couple*, cinematic Lublin has often played the role of other cities, including Warsaw, Moscow, Paris, and Rivne.[18] A particularly interesting example of this creative use of locations is provided by Andrzej Wajda's *Kronika*

108

TRACING TOPOGRAPHIES

Wypadków Miłosnych (*A Chronicle of Amorous Accidents*, 1985), which is set in Vilnius and includes a sequence filmed at Grodzka Gate and Grodska Street.[19] However, Wajda's film presents the same paradox seen in *The Aryan Couple* as it inscribes Jewish heritage in the cinematic topography of Lublin despite being set elsewhere. *A Chronicle of Amorous Accidents* looks at the years that preceded the annihilation of the Jews and is a nostalgic view of a youthful summer in 1939, just before the German invasion of Poland. In a sequence portraying one of the first encounters between the two young Polish protagonists, we can see the couple walking through the Grodzka Gate and surrounded by Ashkenazi Jews engaged in their trades. The iconography of this scene is reminiscent of the photographs taken in the Jewish districts and ghettos before and during the war and – despite the fact that the film is not meant to be set in Lublin and thus presents a creative geography – the sequence filmed at Grodzka Gate presents the Jewish quarter of this cinematic version of Vilnius in accordance with the pre-war topography of Lublin. In this scene life in the small town looks idyllic; Wajda implies that anti-Semitism was largely absent in inter-war Poland and consequently he avoids the issue of the problematic coexistence of Poles and Jews in pre-war Lublin. Ultimately, *A Chronicle of Amorous Accidents*, *The Aryan Couple*, and *Spring 1941* belong to what Penz and Lu have discussed in terms of "narrative geographies where urban fragments are collaged into spatial episodes."[20] And yet their use of locations is based on what Hay describes as the intrinsic value of the cinematic city, its capacity to produce or reproduce the past as part of a series of relations "among changing cites where the production of memory for its inhabitant is also an issue of environment."[21]

Spatial issues resulting from the selective gaze of the filmmakers and the employment of a creative approach to location shooting in recent films also affect the cinematic portrayal of the camp at Majdanek. Despite the fact that 59,000 victims out of a total of 79,000 were Jewish, cinematic representations of the camp in Polish and Soviet films largely focused on the camp as a site of Polish suffering.[22] Like Auschwitz-Birkenau, Majdanek was both a labor camp and a site of political and racial extermination; when the camp was liberated on 24 July 1944, Soviet cameramen turned their attention to the discovery of this site of murder on an industrial scale at the outskirts of Lublin. In *Majdanek: Cmentarzysko Europy* (*Majdanek: Burial Ground in Europe*, Aleksander Ford, 1944) the role of the camp in the extermination of the Jews was not made explicit. Ford's film, as Jeremy Hicks suggests, illustrates the crimes committed by the Nazis against the Polish people and Soviet prisoners of war and does not address the real extent of the genocide perpetrated against the Jews.[23] Similarly, Irina Setkina's newsreel *Majdanek* (1944) presents what Hicks has called a *Sovietized* interpretation of the events resulting from a tendency in Polish and Soviet cinema of the liberation to suggest that the victims belonged to the same group as the spectator, the Polish and Russian people.[24] These films were consequently seen in the West as an example of Soviet propaganda and, largely neglected outside Poland, they downplayed the specificity of the Jewish catastrophe only to suggest that the Nazis chose their victims in an indiscriminate manner from all nations and largely because of political convictions.[25] Again in 1948, Ludwik Perski and Jerzy Bossak filmed *Lublin. Uroczystości na Majdanku* (*Lublin: Commemoration at Majdanek*) as part of one of the 10-minute-long newsreels known as *Polska Kronika Filmowa* ("Polish Film Chronicle") and neglected to address the role of the camp in the Final Solution. Shown in Polish theaters prior to feature films, *Lublin: Commemoration at Majdanek*

TRACING TOPOGRAPHIES

includes various shots of the population of Lublin visiting the camp and laying flowers on the site of the crematorium and it also includes scenes of the Supreme Court judge Wacław Barcikowski as he delivers a speech. A number of close up shots show the women of Lublin crying and mourning the victims of the Nazis at Majdanek. A large cross can be seen in the background and a Catholic service is shown taking place on the grounds of the former camp. In 1948 the association between Majdanek and the Final Solution was again merely implied and the camp presented as a site of martyrdom for POWs, Poles and Jews alike and thus, like Zamek Lubelski, as a contested representational site inscribed in the idea of Polish national martyrdom.[26] Early newsreels of Majdanek did what *The Tragic City of Lublin* had done for the castle and paved the way to a persistent tendency to underplay the role of the camp in the destruction of the Jews. Polish fiction films have primarily used the camp at Majdanek to portray the suffering and courage of the Poles and used the location creatively rather than coherently at a topographical level. For example, Leszek Wosiewicz's *Kornblumenblau* (*Cornflower Blue*, 1989) is based on Kazimierz Tyminski's memoir *Uspokic Sen* (*Calm My Dreams*, 1985) and focuses on the experience of a Polish Catholic who was arrested in 1941 under suspicion of hiding stolen guns and sent to Auschwitz and to the Montelupich Prison in Cracow.[27] The film is set in Auschwitz and filmed both in Field III at Majdanek and in Auschwitz itself. Tyminski was never taken to the Lublin district and here Majdanek merely "plays" the role of the most notorious death camp.

According to Pierre Nora, the absolute nature of memory is constantly challenged by the relative nature of history, and through this perspective the cinematic image of Majdanek can be seen as discontinuous and, to adopt Nora's words, one that "proceeds by strategic highlighting, selecting samples and multiplying examples."[28] Majdanek as a site of the destruction of the Jews was thus underplayed in Polish films and has only been made explicit in a more recent German-American production, Stephen Daldry's *The Reader* (2008). This is an adaptation of Bernhard Schlink's novel of the same name (1995) and it focuses on the post-war affair between young Michael Berg (David Kross) and Hannah Schmitz (Kate Winslet), a former German female SS guard at Auschwitz accused of letting over 300 Jewish women die in a burning church after the evacuation of the camp. Following the revelation about the woman's past, Michael visits the barracks, gas chamber, and crematorium of Majdanek. In the sequence introduced by the iconic sight of the barbed wire fence, he enters the camp through the former SS sector and goes to the barracks in Field III. Michael then enters one of the barracks and silently observes the wooden bunkbeds. He continues his visit with the shower room in Barrack 41; he is distressed as he looks at the showerheads, although these are indeed real showers and not part of the gas chamber. In the following shot, Michael makes his way to the gas chamber at the back of Barrack 41. The viewer is offered a glimpse of the Prussian blue residues on the wall of the gas chamber resulting from exposure to Zyklon B. Michael enters the room while Daldry's camera respectfully maintains the distance from the gas chamber. As recorded in the Soviet film *Majdanek* (1944), thousands of shoes and other items were found by the Red Army when they liberated the camp.[29] In *The Reader*, the protagonist visits the display in Barrack 45, possibly containing the same shoes filmed by Soviet cameramen 64 years earlier in *Majdanek*. Finally, Michael visits the crematorium and stands by the ovens. No dialogue or narration accompanies the camp sequence and there is a lack of topographical specificity. None of the sights

TRACING TOPOGRAPHIES

that could facilitate the identification of Majdanek as the location of this sequence – such as the mausoleum and Wiktor Tołkin's *Fight and Martyrdom* monument – are included in the film. In *The Reader* Majdanek is finally presented as a site of racial extermination; and yet Auschwitz-Birkenau was the camp where Hannah worked during the war, and it is implied that Michael is indeed visiting the camp in the south-west of Poland. It can thus be argued that Majdanek is again playing the role of the most notorious concentration and extermination camp. Nevertheless, *The Reader*'s narrative rings true to history. For German guards, who were often trained in the Reich territory's concentration camps, the experience of "going east" often increased their violent behavior.[30] Both Auschwitz and Majdanek are thus suitable locations for *The Reader*, a narrative that focuses on the darkest experience of the Nazis' system of concentration and extermination, one where apparently "normal" individuals like Hannah could be transformed into perpetrators. Ultimately, Daldry uses Majdanek in a symbolic way by means of a cinematic creative geography; the camp stands for Auschwitz or any site of Nazi persecution and it is not filmed in a way that makes use of the specificity of this location in a topographically coherent manner.

The re-elaboration of history, place, and images in the representational space of Majdanek is completed in Micha Wald's *Simon Konianski* (2009), where the former camp is finally acknowledged as a site of extermination of the Jews and also recognized for its regional specificity, with iconic images of its relics and the *Fight and Martyrdom* memorial. Landmarks can be used in the cinematic space to define and reveal the specific geographical coordinates of the location, and thus its history and significance in the diegesis of the film. The inclusion of the memorial, which had been avoided by Daldry in *The Reader*, thus provides the film with a specific location and, arguably for the first time, here Majdanek finally "plays itself." Filmed in several locations in Eastern Europe, *Simon Konianski* is a Franco-Belgian road movie where the title character aims at fulfilling his father's last request to be buried in the Ukrainian village where he was born. Members of the Konianski family were murdered by the Nazis and during the trip Simon and his six-year-old son Hadrien decide to visit Majdanek. As they approach the camp in their car, the *Fight and Martyrdom* monument appears in the background. They then park the car near the barracks of Field III and enter the camp from the gate near the replica of the original *Column of Three Eagles*, another iconic sight specific to Majdanek.[31] Hadrien runs through the field and disappears; Simon looks for him inside one of the barracks and he is visited by the ghost of his dead father. He will eventually find his son outside the barracks. In *Simon Konianski* we do not see the gas chambers or the crematorium, and yet Hadrien's brief disappearance is reminiscent of what happened in the death camps during the war, when families were separated at the moment of arrival at the camps and loved ones were last seen as they vanished in the extermination process. This is what happened in all death camps and yet *Simon Konianski* inscribes this pre-existing narrative in the specific representational space of Majdanek by revealing iconic landmarks of the camp. In particular, the presence of the *Fight and Martyrdom* monument and the Column of Three Eagles inscribes *Simon Konianski* in a specific geographical space and emancipates Majdanek from a location hitherto devoted to playing the role of Auschwitz to an identifiable site and context.

This article has focused on two spatial issues emerging from the urban cinematic of Lublin and Majdanek. On the one hand, the destruction of the Jews of Lublin as a specific

TRACING TOPOGRAPHIES

historical event in the context of the Holocaust has struggled to emerge from Polish films which used key locations to inscribe the events of 1939–1944 into a broader idea of Polish national martyrdom. On the other hand, Western films have re-established the association between the Holocaust and significant locations such as Zamek Lubelski and Majdanek. However, they have done so by means of a consistent use of creative cinematic geographies that both failed to reflect the historical topography of the city and often transformed cinematic Lublin and Majdanek into other cities and camps. Nevertheless, what emerges here is a cinematic space intrinsically related to the history of Lublin during the war and to various ways of reassessing its past. The topography of war-time Lublin and Majdanek is traceable in films mapping what Homi Bhabha has defined as "third space," a location where the events of the past are still inscribed in the environment of their happening.[32] Here, as Edward Soja suggests, the apparent oppositions between "the abstract and the concrete, the real and the imagined, the knowable and the unimaginable, the repetitive and the differential, structure and agency, mind and body, consciousness and the unconscious, the disciplined and the transdisciplinary, everyday life and unending history" come together by means of a critical spatial engagement with the past and its repercussions in the present.[33] Film can thus articulate a space that is both imagined and rooted in the history of place; in the case of cinematic Lublin and Majdanek this is a place where creative geographies and coherent topographies wrestle one another and reveal sites of memory that are not frozen in time but framed in the act of looking back at their past.

Notes

1. Speigelman, *Maus*, 230.
2. Hay, "Piecing Together," 219.
3. Penz and Lu, "Introduction," 9.
4. Ibid., 12.
5. Ibid., 14.
6. Cf. Haltof, *Polish Film and the Holocaust*.
7. Hay, "Piecing Together," 212.
8. Steinlauf, *Bondage to the Dead*.
9. Haltof, *Polish Film and the Holocaust*.
10. Miron, *The Yad Vashem Encyclopaedia*, 421.
11. One and a half million Jews were murdered at these death camps between 1942 and 1943 as part of Aktion Reinhard. Named after the deceased *SS-Obergruppenführer* Reinhard Heydrich, this was the most deadly phase of the Final Solution.
12. Black, "Rehearsal for 'Reinhard'?"
13. The square and the adjacent streets became recurring locations for political and military demonstrations and parades, and were often filmed in Polish official newsreels. For example, Helena Lemańska's *5 marca 1953: roku zmarł Józef Stalin* (*5 March 1953: Józef Stalin is Dead*) portrays the memorial services held in several Polish cities on the occasion of Stalin's death, and includes images of a large crowd gathered in Litewski Square to commemorate the Soviet dictator. On this occasion the square previously known as Adolf Hitler Platz was officially renamed after Józef Stalin. This film includes a panning long shot of the square which is followed by medium shots of an image of Stalin hanging from the balcony of Lubomirskich Palace and the commemorative banners prepared and held by the men, women, and children of Lublin. The funeral was staged as a tribute to Stalin and a further acknowledgment of his role as a commander in the Red Army's offensive against the Nazi occupation of Poland. Lemańska's film, however, confirms the repression of the memory of Lublin's Jewry. In 1953, anti-Semitism was on the rise both in Poland and the Soviet Union, with Jewish doctors

TRACING TOPOGRAPHIES

accused of poisoning Stalin, and on that day no banners or speeches acknowledged the specific role of the Red Army in the interruption of the Nazi extermination of Jews in the Lublin district (Steinlauf, *Bondage to the Dead*, 67).

14. Liquidated between 17 March and 11 April 1942, the ghetto of Lublin was hardly ever filmed during the occupation. The only existing original footage of the Lublin ghetto was filmed in 1940 by Fritz Hippler for his anti-Semitic propaganda documentary *Der ewige Jude* (*The Eternal Jew*). Based on a book published in 1937 by the Nazi Party, this film includes footage from several Polish ghettos; here the Jews are presented as uncivilized and parasitic people, often engaged in what are presented as barbaric religious rituals and ceremonies. Its message is well exemplified in the opening commentary: "The civilized Jews that we know in Germany give us only an incomplete picture of their racial character. This film shows genuine shots of the Polish ghettos. It shows the Jews as they really are, before they conceal themselves behind the mask of the civilized European" (cited in Taylor, *Film Propaganda*, 175). This commentary introduces the viewer to the overcrowded, narrow alleys of the ghettos, bustling with trade, and claims that Jews had always lived in ghettos and had chosen to appear poorly dressed and unhealthy despite their wealth. As Robert Reimer suggests, the film is effectively showing the result of Nazi rule in Poland, while claiming to display the natural depravity of the Jews (Reimer, *Cultural History*, 135). By the end of 1939, Jewish stores were marked with Stars of David and Jews were ordered to wear a white armband with a blue Star of David. The *Judenrat* of Lublin was established in January 1940, during a particularly harsh winter which contributed to the suffering of the Jews; one year later, on 24 March 1941, the ghetto was established in the designated area of the city. It was sealed with a barbed wire fence at the end of that year and, despite the high mortality rate, its population continued to grow as a result of continuous relocation and infiltration of Jews from other parts of Poland (Miron, *The Yad Vashem Encyclopaedia*, 422–5).

15. The castle appears in what is likely to be one of the earliest films of the city; *Lublin: Obrazek turystyczny* (*Touristic Lublin*) was filmed in 1914 during the Austro-Hungarian occupation and includes images of the cathedral and Zamek Lubelski. The castle was destined to become a reoccurring location in films of Lublin, for example both in Wanda Jakubowska's *150 na godzine* (*150 per Hour*, 1971), a film focusing on the youth of Lublin in the 1970s, and Gerard Zalewski's *Tetno* (*Heartbeat*, 1985), the story of Polish writer Halina Poświatowska, the castle can be seen in scenic long shots taken from Po Farze Square. The building's association with Polish patriotism continued after the communist era and the castle was chosen as a location by Jerzy Hoffman for his film *Ognim i Mieczem* (*By Fire and Sword*, 1999), set during the Cossack rebellion known as the Khmelnytsky Uprising (1648–1657). This film includes a scene shot in the Holy Trinity Chapel at Zamek Lubelski: here Catholic convert and patriot Jarema Wiśniowiecki takes an oath in front of the altar. During the communist era Wiśniowiecki was described as an "enemy of the people"; made in 1999, *By Fire and Sword* presents him as the hero of the battle of Berestechko.

16. Lefebvre, *The Production of Space*, 37.

17. Ibid., 41.

18. Grodzka Gate, in particular, can also be seen in Andrzej Konic's *Czarne Chmury* (*Black Clouds*, 1973), a costume drama made for Telewizja Polska, this time as the set for a street in seventeenth-century Warsaw. In Jerzy Antczak's biopic *Chopin. Pragnienie miłości* (*Chopin – Desire for Love*, 2002), Lublin plays both Warsaw and Paris, with several scenes filmed near Brama Grodzka. Lublin is Vilnius in Antoni Bohdziewicz's *Rzeczywistość* (*Reality*, 1960). In Adek Drabiński's *Kryptonim <PUCH>* (*Codename "Down,"* 2005) Lublin is Rivne, Ukraine. Lublin is Warsaw again in Adek Drabiński's *Tajna Sprawa* (*A Matter of Secrecy*, 2005), where it also plays Moscow.

19. Vilnius is located in Wilno Voivodeship, a region of Lithuania which was part of Poland between 1926 and 1939. The Jews of Vilnius shared the same fate as the Jews of Lublin and during the Nazi occupation its almost entire Jewish population was exterminated.

20. Penz and Lu, "Introduction," 14.

21. Hay, "Piecing Together," 229.

TRACING TOPOGRAPHIES

22. The death toll for the Majdanek camp is difficult to estimate and ranges from early over-estimations suggesting that over a million people died in the camp to a more realistic estimate of 79,000 victims (Kranz, *The Extermination of Jews*, 70–77).
23. Hicks, *First Films of the Holocaust*, 253.
24. Ibid., 158–66.
25. Ibid., 165.
26. Alain Resnais's pivotal documentary *Nuit et Brouillard* (*Night and Fog*, 1955) notoriously presents the same perspective. Partly filmed on the grounds and ruins of Majdanek, the entire film uses the word "Jew" only on one occasion and Nazi crimes are portrayed as perpetrated equally against a range of victims from different national, political, and religious backgrounds.
27. The same perspective appears in other Polish films. In 1979, the camp at Majdanek was used as a location for Roman Wionczek's *Sekret Enigmy* (*The Secret Enigma*), the story of Henryk Zygalski, Jerzy Różycki, and Marian Rejewski, the three Polish mathematicians who cracked the Enigma code used by the Germans during the war. The same story appears in the television series *Tajemnice Enigmy* (*Secrets of the Enigma*, 1979) also directed by Roman Wionczek and filmed in Majdanek.
28. Nora, "Between Memory and History," 19.
29. During the war Majdanek was also used as a storage facility for the belongings of the victims of Aktion Reinhard.
30. Cf. Koslov, "'Going East'."
31. The Column of Three Eagles was based on Albin Maria Boniecki's design and made by Polish prisoners in 1943 on the occasion of a visit by the International Red Cross. Prisoners were demanded to decorate the camp in order to create an impression of order and attractiveness (Wiśnioch, *Majdanek*, 42).
32. Bhabha, *The Location of Culture*, 55.
33. Soja, Thirdspace, 57.

Disclosure statement

No potential conflict of interest was reported by the author.

Bibliography

Bhabha, Homi K. *The Location of Culture*. London and New York: Routledge, 2004.

Black, Peter R. "Rehearsal for 'Reinhard'? Odilo Globocnik and the Lublin *Selbstschutz*." *Central European History* 25, no. 2 (1992): 194–226.

Haltof, Marek. *Polish Film and the Holocaust: Politics and Memory*. New York and Oxford: Berghahn Books, 2012.

Hay, James. "Piecing Together What Remains of the Cinematic City." In *The Cinematic City*, edited by David Clarke, 209–229. London: Routledge, 1997.

Hicks, Jeremy. *First Films of the Holocaust: Soviet Cinema and the Genocide of Jews 1938–1946*. Pittsburgh: University of Pittsburgh Press, 2012.

Koslov, Elissa M. "'Going East': Colonial Experiences and Practices of Violence among Female and Male Majdanek Camp Guards (1941–44)." *Journal of Genocide Research* 10, no. 4 (2008): 563–582.

Kranz, Tomasz. *The Extermination of Jews at Majdanek Concentration Camp.* Lublin: Państwowe Muzeum na Majdanku, 2010.

Lefebvre, Henri. *The Production of Space.* Trans. Donald Nicholson-Smith. Oxford: Blackwell, 1991. First published 1974 by Anthropos as *La production de l'espace.*

Miron, Guy, ed. *The Yad Vashem Encyclopaedia of the Ghettos during the Holocaust.* 2 vols. Jerusalem: Yad Vashem, 2010.

Nora, Pierre. "Between Memory and History: Les Lieux de Mémoire." In "Special Issue: Memory and Counter-Memory," *Representations*, no. 26 (Spring 1989): 7–24.

Penz, François, and Andong Lu. "Introduction: What is Urban Cinematics?" In *Urban Cinematics: Understanding Urban Phenomena through the Moving Image*, edited by François Penz and Andong Lu, 7–19. Bristol: Intellect Books, 2011.

Reimer, Robert C. *Cultural History through a National Socialist Lens: Essays on the Cinema of the Third Reich.* Rochester, NY: Camden House, 2000.

Soja, Edward W. *Thirdspace.* Malden, MA: Blackwell, 1996.

Spiegelman, Art. *Maus.* New York: Pantheon Books, 1991.

Steinlauf, Michael C. *Bondage to the Dead: Poland and the Memory of the Holocaust.* New York and Syracuse: Syracuse University Press, 1997.

Taylor, Richard. *Film Propaganda: Soviet Russia and Nazi Germany.* London and New York: I.B. Tauris, 1998.

Wiśnioch, Maria. *Majdanek: A Guide to the Historical Buildings.* Lublin: Państwowe Muzeum na Majdanku, 2012.

Transcultural engagement with Polish memory of the Holocaust while watching Leszek Wosiewicz's *Kornblumenblau*

Victoria Grace Walden

Queen Mary, University of London, UK

ABSTRACT

Kornblumenblau (Leszek Wosiewicz 1989) is a film that explores the experience of a Polish political prisoner interned at Auschwitz I. It particularly foregrounds issues related to Polish-Jewish relations during the Holocaust in its diegesis. Holocaust films are often discussed in relation to representation and the cultural specificity of their production context. However, this paper suggests thinking about film and topographies, the theme of this issue, not in relation to where a work is produced but in regards to the spectatorial space. It adopts a phenomenological approach to consider how, despite *Kornblumenblau*'s particularly Polish themes, it might address the transcultural spectator and draw attention to the broader difficulties one faces when attempting to remember the Holocaust. Influenced particularly by the writing of Jennifer M. Barker and Laura U. Marks, this paper suggests that film possesses a body ¬¬ a display of intentionality, beyond those presented within the diegesis, which engages in dialogue with the spectator. During the experience of viewing *Kornblumenblau*, this filmic corporeality draws attention to the difficulties of confronting the Holocaust in particularly haptic ways, as the film points to the unreliability of visual historical sources, relates abject sensations to concentrationary spaces and breaks down as it confronts the scene of the gas chamber.

Introduction

Thinking about this issue's theme, "tracing topographies" in relation to Holocaust film might suggest a review of screen representations of specific historical sites, such as Auschwitz or Majdanek, or a survey of a particular nation's engagement with Holocaust history as has been fashionable in a range of disciplines.[1] However, the spectatorial space is one that has been much neglected in discourse about Holocaust film, despite its vital significance to the film experience. Films play a significant role in constructing Holocaust memory, evidenced, for example, by the impact of *Schindler's List* (USA, 1993).[2] However, little attention has been given to the ways in which films engage spectators with this past during the screening and the significance of the viewing space to the meaning attributed to the experience of watching a Holocaust film. From Edward W. Soja's writing about thirdspace to Henri Lefebvre's Marxist-phenomenological and

TRACING TOPOGRAPHIES

Doreen Massey's geographical work, many scholars consider space to be fluid and defined by the elements that meet within it.[3] This article extends this idea phenomenologically, particularly thinking through the work of Jennifer M. Barker and Laura U. Marks to argue that the viewing space is defined by a fleshy encounter between spectator and film bodies.[4] It is these bodies in dialogue that, I argue, help define the meaning (both corporeal and intellectual) of the cinematic space and enable a transcultural engagement with Holocaust memory.

Using the Polish film *Kornblumenblau* (1989) as an example, I examine how such a historical-realist film seemingly rooted in particular national concerns enables a transcultural engagement with the complexities of Holocaust memory through the spectator's mimetic relationship with the film body.[5] While the film exposes a particularly Polish memory of this past, I suggest that turning to a phenomenological reading enables one to understand the film's potential transcultural significance and begins to explain how the spectator engages with Holocaust memory as they watch the film.

While much has been written about the types of Holocaust films produced by particular countries, there has been a turn in recent years, influenced by the work of Daniel Levy and Natan Sznaider, toward thinking about Holocaust memory on transnational terms.[6] Levy and Sznaider suggest that in the age of globalization, "alongside nationally bounded memories a new form of memory emerges [...] 'cosmopolitan memory'."[7] This new type of memory, they argue, acknowledges the significance of global concerns to local communities, transcending the specifics of national or ethnic boundaries.[8] Valentina Glajar acknowledges the negotiation of transnational and national concerns regarding Holocaust memory in the Romanian context, an issue relevant beyond this particular country.[9] I prefer the term "transcultural" to acknowledge that it is not only national boundaries that the cinematic encounter of watching *Kornblumenblau* transcends, but other identity values too.

Levy and Sznaider's argument suggests that thinking about *Kornblumenblau* only in terms of its distinct Polishness negates its potential resonance beyond its country of origin. Focusing on the viewing space rather than place of production of the film enables one to consider this potential wider significance. A close study of the film body and the spectator's engagement with it in the viewing space, rather than solely focusing on its national and representational value, reveals that this filmic body is in tension with the images it presents, highlighting the many difficulties that characterize any attempt to remember the Holocaust, particularly for those who did not experience it first-hand (as most spectators and films did not). The spectator is invited to mimetically engage with this complexity during the film experience.

Film phenomenology – the study of the viewing experience and materiality – is particularly interested in the film body. This "body" is not understood as one particular physical site; to describe either camera or projector as such is quite inadequate. Rather, it is implied through the film's revelation of its intentionality – its temporal and spatial movement expressed diegetically, subjectively (the term Vivian Sobchack uses to refer to camera motion), optically and cinematically (through the edit). All of these types of movement express the direction of the film's consciousness (its phenomenological intentionality).[10] While it may seem peculiar to suggest film possesses "consciousness," this is understood in terms of its ability to experience spatiality and temporality, rather than a spiritual or psychic sense of being. Alongside film phenomenology, thing theory and object-orientated ontology have, in recent years, drawn attention to the significance of non-human ways of being and highlighted the relevance of non-anthropocentric ways of thinking about the lived-world.[11] None of these approaches assume things can experience the world like humans, but consider the different engagements with the world they might offer through their material specificity. Thinking about a film "body" then means thinking about how film perceives and expresses the world, or in the case of *Kornblumenblau*, how it attempts to remember the Holocaust.

Kornblumenblau and Polish Holocaust memory

Before continuing with my argument, it is useful to explain how *Kornblumenblau* might be perceived as specifically Polish in relation to the Holocaust memory with which it engages. The film explores Tadeusz Wyczyński's experience at Auschwitz I. The Polish musician almost dies after being injected with typhus in the infirmary. Desperate to survive, he is saved by a Kapo who appreciates his musical talent. This enables Tadeusz to work through the camp's ranks, from potato peeler to waiter, then musician in the camp orchestra. At the film's climax, Tadeusz pretends to play the tuba at an SS festival; elsewhere victims are herded into a gas chamber. The performance is interrupted by an air strike that liberates prisoners. Though loosely based on the testimony of Kazimierz Tyminski, *Kornblumenblau* clearly exhibits fantastical elements.[12] It condenses Tyminski's experiences of Auschwitz and Buchenwald into the one synecdochical site and fabricates a Soviet salvation (when in reality the majority of inmates had been evacuated on "death marches" by the time troops arrived). *Kornblumenblau* is a productive example to use for this investigation because it particularly foregrounds issues relevant to Polish memory of the Holocaust, but, as I will argue, also has the potential to engage the spectator with more general, transculturally relatable difficulties one encounters when confronting this past.

To some extent, *Kornblumenblau* attempts to portray a photo-realist, historical image of Auschwitz. It was filmed at the former sites of Auschwitz and Majdanek, and the props, costumes, and decor simulate an "authentic" representation of a functioning concentration camp. It was shot on film, in color and black-and-white, the latter giving certain sequences a particularly archival aesthetic. The film has had a limited release beyond Poland. Today, the non-Polish spectator is most likely to discover it on YouTube where digital compression offers a further distancing effect, not only between the spectator and a past that looks archival, but also between the present of the viewing experience and the time of production, as analog film is distorted by the digital signal.

Marek Haltof considers *Kornblumenblau* within the context of Polish Holocaust cinema, noting that it is illustrative of the renewed interest in Polish-Jewish relations after the release of *Shoah* (France and UK, 1985) and Jan Błoński's controversial publication "The Poor Poles Look at the Ghetto" in 1987.[13] Haltof positions *Kornblumenblau* within the first major wave of second-generation films – those produced by film-makers who did not experience the Holocaust.[14] The film expresses a particularly Polish memory of the Holocaust in many ways. It is based at Auschwitz and adapts a Polish survivor's testimony, whose name is interestingly changed from Kazimierz – a particularly poignant name in the history of Poland[15] – to Tadeusz, reminiscent both of Polish survivor Tadeusz Borowski's particularly macabre writing, thus hinting at the film's dark tone (as suggested by Haltof), and national poet Adam Mickiewicz's 1843 epic poem "Pan Tadeusz," which offers one of the earliest positive representations of the Jew in Polish culture.[16] The different name offers a subtle but significant change, implying that Jewishness is fundamental to Polish culture, rather than separate from it.

Furthermore, the film's protagonist is a witness-victim, as were many Polish people; he is persecuted by the Nazis and witness to the Jewish Holocaust. While there has been much debate in Poland regarding the so-called "hierarchy of suffering" between Poles and Jews, *Kornblumenblau* expresses the two traumatic narratives simultaneously, albeit from a Polish point of view, thus the Jewish experience is marginalized.[17] Furthermore, the film engages with archive material, a trope of Polish Holocaust film.[18] However, unlike other films that use this technique to represent the missing Jewish culture, *Kornblumenblau* manipulates the archival image in ways that suggest unease about film's ability to portray an objective, official history of the Holocaust, as will be discussed in more detail later. Like the other films, however, this too points to the country's missing Jewish population.

While an understanding of the film's cultural context is useful, it is important not to forget the international dimension of film production. Many of the films Haltof discusses in his survey of Polish Holocaust film are co-productions involving foreign companies (though *Kornblumenblau* is distinctively Polish). Furthermore, one must consider the transcultural composition of film audiences. While specifically Polish themes are foregrounded in *Kornblumenblau*, it can enable the spectator, Polish or otherwise, to reflect on their knowledge and engagement with the Holocaust and negotiate with the film, even if it may challenge their preconceptions. Nationally focused studies underplay the significance of this dialogue between film and spectator, and thus do not fully consider the implications of this relationship and the potential for the experience to inform an act of "bearing witness" to the Holocaust, understood here not in relation to seeing this event first-hand, but in terms of later "witnesses" engaging with the past through mediated means.[19]

Watching *Kornblumenblau* as transcultural experience

My proposal in this article is that adopting a phenomenological reading of *Kornblumenblau* highlights its transcultural relevance to Holocaust memory. The Holocaust has long been considered of transnational import. In their work about transnational memory, Chiara De Cesari and Ann Rigney consider the Holocaust "a moral benchmark in a new world order," echoing Levy and Sznaider's idea of a "global memory imperative" in relation to the Holocaust.[20] Holocaust memory is informed by international committees such as the International Holocaust Research Alliance (IHRA); its victims were born in, transported to, and survivors emigrated to a range of different countries; Auschwitz, a Nazi German camp in what is once again Polish land, had an international mix of inmates and is now a site of transcultural learning and memorialization, with visitors from a wide range of countries remembering victims who were imprisoned based on a range of national, sexual, cultural, or religious identifiers. However, the Holocaust has also been integrated into national myths by countries both directly and not directly affected by it. The transcultural dimensions of the film experience are particularly apt for engaging with the multifaceted issues of Holocaust memory.

TRACING TOPOGRAPHIES

The transnational in relation to film studies has generally been used to refer to particular texts that engage with journeys across borders, such as stories about Diaspora, or international co-productions, rather than spectatorial experience.[21] In film studies, "the spectator" has generally been considered an abstract term. In this sense, it does not refer to a specific individual, but rather considers the presence of a body with which the film communicates or engages. Spectator studies tend to think about how a film suggests a particular reading. Feminist approaches, among others, have stipulated a certain kind of body, but, as bell hooks's work on black female spectators suggests, this denies the many identities that formulate a body, including, but not limited to, class, gender, age, disability, nationality, and ethnicity.[22] Thus, the spectatorial body might always be considered transcultural in its negotiation of different identities.

Phenomenologists, with their focus on experience, seem to acknowledge the transcultural potential of bodies. Beyond film studies, Emmanuel Levinas points to the significance of the Other – a body that is not ours, and is potentially dissimilar from our own – in shaping our ethical responsibility.[23] In Marks's understanding of mimesis in the cinematic experience, she argues that what she calls "intercultural spectatorship … is the meeting of two different sensoria, which may or may not intersect. Spectatorship is thus an act of sensory translation of cultural knowledge."[24] Marks argues that the cinematic experience is deeply sensuous and engages taste, touch, and smell, as well as sight and hearing, and that sensual experience is culturally learned. For Marks, then, the spectator can mimetically engage with film on a haptic level and in doing so they are able to exchange cultural knowledge: to get closer to memories they have not experienced in the lived-world. Marks's work, which negotiates Deleuzian philosophy and phenomenology, suggests that mimesis is related to the spectator's experience with the film rather than any potential realism claim of the image. She differentiates haptic looking from optical thus:

> Optical visuality depends on a separation between the viewing subject and the object. Haptic looking tends to move over the surface of its object rather than plunge into illusionary depth, not to distinguish form so much as to discern texture. It is more inclined to move than to focus, more inclined to graze than to gaze.[25]

Marks suggests that spectators can mimetically engage with a film by grazing over such images. While the majority of her work emphasizes diegetic images that provoke sensations of touch, for example close-ups of fabric or pouring water, her theory can also be applied to the movement and materiality of the film body itself (as she suggests in her later work).[26] Following Marks, I argue that by mimetically engaging with the textural surfaces and intentionality of the film, the spectator watching *Kornblumenblau* can relate to the way in which the film grapples with an attempt to remember the Holocaust.

Despite its dominant historical-realist style, *Kornblumenblau* draws attention to the film body on many occasions, most strikingly with its pseudo-archival imagery, use of color and sound, and a gas chamber sequence in which the film seems to literally break down. Expanding on the phenomenological work of Marks and Sobchack, Barker draws attention to the specificity of film materiality, suggesting that the medium has a "skin," "viscera," and "musculature" – terms she applies phenomenologically, rather than biologically, to refer to the film's experience of materiality, temporality, and spatiality.[27] Three particularly striking revelations of the film body in *Kornblumenblau* are the opening pseudo-archive sequence, in which it foregrounds a particular material skin and a relationship with temporality and spatiality reminiscent of early cinema; affectively charged use of sound and color which at times seems to break the film's historical-realist verisimilitude; and the gas chamber sequence in which the combination of diegetic, subjective, and cinematic movement culminates in an expression of corporeal breaking down. These particular sequences encourage the spectator to engage with the complexities of Holocaust memory revealing a material pastness, repulsion of concentration camp violence, and the corporeal difficulty of confronting the gas chamber – issues with transcultural resonance beyond the specificity of Polish Holocaust memory. Following Marks's suggestion that the engagement between spectator and film bodies is a mimetic encounter, we can see that the spectator of *Kornblumenblau* confronts the complexities of Holocaust memory through an engagement with a foreign non-human body, that of the film.

The experience of engaging with *Kornblumenblau* is transcultural on several levels then: firstly, it is a Polish film available beyond the nation's borders; secondly, the spectator is always negotiating with their own plurality of identities alongside those shared by the film; thirdly, it offers an encounter between Polish (on screen) and potentially non-Polish bodies (viewing the film); and finally, it presents an encounter between a foreign, non-human body (the film) and the spectator. The following analysis focuses on the relationship between film and spectatorial bodies in order to explore how transcultural concerns about Holocaust memory can be translated during the viewing experience.

I work through the corporeal layers of the filmic body to excavate how this fleshly encounter points to potentially transcultural Holocaust memory issues, but without ignoring the film's national significance (for this does not disappear as soon as we begin to think on transcultural levels; rather nationality is one of its many features).

Archival skin

Kornblumenblau opens with a black-and-white semi-archival sequence of pre-war Poland. Several Polish fiction films about the Holocaust use archive images to represent the Jewish experience as if attempting to fill in the gap left by an absent culture. However, the opening sequence of *Kornblumenblau* challenges such portrayals by interrogating the archive and drawing attention to its gaps. In doing so, the sequence reveals a tension between the absent and present, fiction and history, while evoking sensations of loss and critiquing official history.

The sequence embeds Tadeusz's developmental years, from birth to marriage, within the history of Poland: from the Prussian Empire, represented by processions at Brandenburg Tor, Berlin; through the factory lines of industrialization; war (expressed through fiction footage, interestingly including Sergei M. Eisenstein's *Strike* [Soviet Union, 1925] and *October* [Soviet Union, 1928]); the decadence of independent Poland to Nazi occupation. While some footage seems archival, some is ambiguous, and some clearly staged as Adam Kamień, who plays Tadeusz, performs as the protagonist and his father. The staged scenes mimic the speed, color, and materiality of the archival film. Thus it is difficult for the spectator to differentiate between "real" archive and fiction images. This is further complicated by the old fictional footage.

A tension between the present and absent emerges as the sequence expresses a non-Jewish Poland. A specific "Polishness" is emphasized through snippets of the national anthem in the title cards, and the image of Father Christmas (hinting to a Christian culture); there are no prominent signs of Jewishness, despite the country's prevalent, particularly Orthodox, Jewish population in the 1930s. The speed and texture of the archival-like footage invites the spectator to feel a sensation of the past and to mimetically engage with the film's way of remembering it. However, they cannot feel a sensation of closeness with the country's pre-war Jewish culture because it is absent. While this sequence does not explicitly draw attention to Jews, the contemporary spectator, in particular, will notice this aberration, which is reinforced by Tadeusz's witnessing of Jewish culture later in the film – a violinist whom he hears from a distance and a ballerina he sees dancing in slow motion in an image defined by a de-saturated palette, itself somewhat reminiscent of the archive here. The similarity of the ballerina scene to the pseudo-archival sequence draws the spectator's attention back to these opening images of Poland, from which Jews are missing. Thus, Jews are only traces; they have disappeared from the official narrative (particularly true during Soviet times). The detached, later image of the female Jew evokes sensations of loss.

These sensations provoked by archival materiality can encourage the spectator to identify with those absent from the image and sidelined in official history and memory, as well as those present. Thus, attention is drawn to the gaps in the archive, rather than the archive "filling in" for a missing culture, as it seems to in other Polish films. The fakedness of the opening sequence draws attention to the instability of the archive as an authority on the past and thus subtly draws attention to the history it does not tell, that of Poland's Jewish community. Jews are not only missing from official archives by the time of the film's production, but due to the Holocaust and postwar anti-Semitism, they were physically missing from the majority of Poland. The sequence questions the reliability of the archival texture as a stable material through which to fully access the past. The fakedness and lacunae that characterize the opening montage suggest the archive offers only a construction of memory. This instability of memory is transculturally relatable.

In recent years the concept of the "missing Jew" has become a symbol of remembrance in Poland, for example Israeli artist Ronen Eidelman's photographic installation "Coming Out in Lublin," in which he places images of the city's missing Jews on building exteriors; the project "Tęsknię za tobą Żydzie" ("I Miss You Jew") by Polish artist Rafał Betlejewski, in which the title statement is spray-painted in Polish streets; and Gordzka Gate's "Mysteries of Memory" installation – a single street lamp that continuously shines in the old Jewish district of Lublin. The opening of *Kornblumenblau* encourages the modern spectator, aware of the larger discourse about remembering Jewishness in Poland, to adopt a critical position and to reflect on the film's corporeal vulnerability as it attempts to remember this past through a pseudo-archival narrativization.

The absent Jew becomes prominent retrospectively as the film progresses. Read in dialogue with the archival-like image of the Jewish ballerina, the opening reveals distrust on the part of the film, of its own ability to recall and remember the past accurately and appropriately through the memory images of its archive. Furthermore, the archive is explicitly related to memory later in the film when Tadeusz reminisces about pre-war Poland and dreams in archival images. By mimetically engaging with these sequences, the spectator is encouraged to reflect upon the difficulties of confronting Holocaust memory. Thus they are encouraged to consider whether any official history or memory of the Holocaust is necessarily the only one and whether archive images really offer the closeness to the past their obvious aged tactility suggests. Therefore issues that might seem specifically

Polish – the disputes about the hierarchy of suffering between Polish and Jewish victims – have transcultural affect here as the film encourages the spectator to reconsider their relationship with any history of the Holocaust with which they are familiar. Jewish people and culture, after all, became "missing" from many locations beyond Poland.

While Marks refers particularly to experimental cinemas when she states that "unrepresentable memories [for her, this includes stories of Diasporic trauma and the Holocaust] find their expression in [its] … characteristic gaps," this can also be related to the opening sequence of *Kornblumenblau*.[28] Missing memories are exposed through the archival skin of this Polish imagining of the past and its juxtaposition of fiction and archival imagery (both historical and fictional) that destabilizes the authority and truth value of the archive and thus encourages the spectator to attend to the lacunae of the images, reminding them that memory is characterized by incompleteness, a feature particularly prominent in Holocaust memory when so many victims died, unable to share their stories.[29] Coming into contact with images of the past, the film's opening archival skin then draws attention not only to the Jew missing in Polish memory of the Holocaust, but encourages the spectator to reflect on what is absent from their own landscape, communities, cultures, and their knowledge of this complex past: the images that are materially out of reach.

The pronounced archival materiality of the opening encourages a haptic relationship with the image: its graininess, fadedness, black-and-white color and slow speed draw attention to its pastness as it expresses a decaying image (for such film did not seem grainy and faded to its original viewers). While the footage appears to offer an interaction with the historical as the past seems to become present before us, it also reveals its distance from the spectator's time because of its material "damage" (however fake this might be in this particular example). In *Kornblumenblau,* the spectatorial relationship with the past is complicated by the foregrounding of tensions between the absent and the present, and the "real" and fiction, emphasizing the instability of memory. Archival moving images are a particularly filmic form of memory, or history, thus these tensions reveal the film's distrust in its own particular way of engaging with the past. It encourages the mimetic spectator to critique histories of the Holocaust they know and offers a tool for exploring its supposed unrepresentability, to find another, haptic way of connecting with this past.

Marks considers vision to dominate historical discourse, while alternative memories are often evoked through other senses as a reaction against official narratives.[30] For her, memory of the unrepresentable (or unrepresented because it is missing from official archives) emerges from haptic images because they attempt to critique official ways of expressing the past. Thus, one might consider films that underplay the privileging of vision and the symbolic to highlight the complexity of memories (by revealing other stories) of the past, not only in terms of their content and point of view, but also in their approach to remembering. It is particularly interesting that Marks considers such memories to be those that are "unrepresentable," a term often used to describe the Holocaust.

Following this thinking suggests that *Kornblumenblau*'s opening sequence, which draws attention to an archival materiality and temporality, and in doing so encourages the spectator to graze the image rather than solely gaze at it, emphasizes not only its lacunae, and therefore the complexities of memory (there is not one dominant narrative of the past, but rather a wide range of stories), but also the ability we have to confront the

TRACING TOPOGRAPHIES

past in multisensory ways, through our skin, viscera, and musculature, challenging the dominance of vision and the symbolic. This haptic relationship with images invites the spectator to acknowledge the diverse, transcultural dimensions of Holocaust memory and encourages them to challenge official ways of engaging with the past within their own cultural context and beyond.

Beneath the skin

Barker suggests that "touch is not just skin-deep but is experienced at the body's surface, in its depths and everywhere in between ... touch is a 'style of being'" and *Kornblumenblau* offers haptic encounters that resonate deep within the viscera.[31] There are moments in the film when color overlays cover the screen and sound seems unsynchronized with the image. Such qualities announce the material presence of the film's body. Such moments reveal the tension between the film's images of Auschwitz and the body of the film grappling with this complex past; they interrupt the historical-realist verisimilitude foregrounding the film's corporeality, evidencing an uneasy relationship between the remembered past and the affect of memory. Barker notes that generally the film body is rarely visible, but in some instants it is "explicitly announced" through certain movements or material qualities.[32] These moments in *Kornblumenblau* create startling affect and encourage reflection on the ability to remember the Holocaust.

Kornblumenblau is mostly in color; however, its dominant gray and brown tones create a de-saturated feel. Even the blue stripes on the victims' uniforms look faded. Thus, the film expresses a somewhat historical aesthetic. Sepia, black-and-white, and de-saturated tones are often used in film to express the fadedness of the past, which now only appears to the spectator as a trace of its former self. Color and black-and-white are often understood as representing a "now" and a "then" respectively, a technique often used in Holocaust films.[33] *Kornblumenblau* too uses black-and-white and color, though interestingly, as previously noted, the former expresses unstable memories of pre-war life, rather than somehow authenticating the film's relationship with a real past. The film's color sequences are denoted by a de-saturated palette, reflecting a horizon dimmer than the spectator's lived-world. Such an aesthetic might be considered particularly appropriate for expressing traumatic pasts distinguished as specifically different types of experiences from modern quotidian life.

However, the film's historically suggestive palette is invaded by moments of vivid red which are deeply affective. Like Steven Spielberg's infamous girl in the red coat, the use of color in such instances in *Kornblumenblau* could be read in terms of its narrative function: evoking a foreboding sense of death. However, its powerful resonance, as in Spielberg's film, suggests it has strong affective, as well as representational, significance. While color is often considered to heighten realism, before color celluloid became standard early films often used color tinting for quite different purposes.[34] It would be difficult to assume that the lurid, vivid colors used in films such as *Annabelle Serpentine Dance* (USA, 1895) or *Joan the Woman* (USA, 1916), for example, pertain to realism.

Though some early film-makers attempted to create more "realist" images using color, during the first few decades of cinema it was more often used to provoke affective response in the spectator. *Kornblumenblau* introduces redness in a similar manner to these early films. The film's overlay of color does not belong to the verisimilitude, in fact it disturbs and interrupts historical realism. Yet it establishes a certain mood and provokes particular sensations. It is significant that the film occasionally returns to a coloring technique particularly prevalent in early cinema: as with the slowed speed of the opening pseudo-archive sequence, once again the film body recalls a specifically cinematic sense of pastness, negotiating between a screen representation of the Holocaust and the affect remembering it cinematically has on the film body.

In *Kornblumenblau*, red tinting is prevalent during sequences in the barracks and prison cells where it is often accompanied by a monotonous chorus of moaning. These scenes create a sensory overload; there is an excess of information attacking the spectator's sensory organs: too much color, too much sound, which accompany an image of human bodies claustrophobically crammed into spaces. The color and sound foreground the filmic body's attempt to remember these sites that were inhumane; places of death as much as sleep. The filmic body's expression in *Kornblumenblau*, which seems to spew color and sound (and I purposefully use the analogy with vomiting here), provides moments of sensorial excess. They draw attention to the difficulty of comprehending the affect of inhumane conditions upon the material body. They have the potential to make one feel physically sick. As the film's material excess is exposed, the spectator can mimetically engage with it, experiencing sensations of the abject deep within their viscera. Mimetically engaging with the tension between different filmic elements here provokes sensations of bodily excess for the spectator, who can feel this in the tension of their own muscles, in the depths of their gut, and on the surface of their skin.

For Julia Kristeva, the abject is that which is of the body, yet opposed to it. It reveals the fragile limitations of the body and expresses itself in substances such as vomit, phlegm, and blood that the body wishes to expel. Though she writes from a psychoanalytical perspective, Kristeva's work has phenomenological potential because it considers abjection to be an excess of the body. She regularly refers to the body in her descriptions of abject experiences. For example, she states:

> When the eyes see or the lips touch that skin on the surface of milk – harmless, thin as a sheet of cigarette paper, pitiful as a nail paring – I experience a gagging sensation and, still farther down, spasms in the stomach, the belly; and all the organs shrivel up the body, provoke tears and bile, increase heartbeat, cause forehead and hands to perspire.[35]

For Kristeva, abjection is felt not only on the surface of the body – the forehead and hands – but deep within its musculature and visceral recesses, as spasms, gagging, and shriveling organs. Thus the body is central to thinking about the abject.

As the filmic body in *Kornblumenblau* expels color and sounds, it reveals its difficulty in confronting Auschwitz – it expresses the abject affect of dealing with this particular traumatic memory as it pushes certain elements to the foreground, disturbing the illusion of a seamless diegetic world. Significantly, none of these moments refer specifically to the Jewish Holocaust. The red therefore emphasizes that the filmic body is beyond a particular cultural identity. Auschwitz after all would have impinged abjection on individuals from many different cultures, and is a site today that people, despite their origins, often feel pushes their minds and bodies beyond any experiential limits previously experienced. These color overlays in *Kornblumenblau* draw attention to an embodied memory of this site: a mediated layer placed over the image of the film's verisimilitude.

The appearance of these red overlays and sounds of nauseating moans not only enable the spectator to mimetically engage with the act of remembering; they lay bare the vulnerability of the film body as it tries to remember these past scenes of violation. It is common practice in narrative film-making to attempt to render the film body invisible, thus sound and image tend to complement each other to create a believable verisimilitude. The majority of *Kornblumenblau* complies with these expectations. However, the moments when red floods the screen and moans invade the soundscape reveal that another conscious, sensing body is present: a body trying to engage with the realist image on an affective level. It is a body that attempts to empathize with the historical narrative it constructs and in doing so expels excess, violently releasing it toward the spectator in a projectile attack on the senses. Mimetic engagement allows the spectator to feel these sensations of abjection. We can all engage with these feelings of excess, whether we experienced Auschwitz or not. Such foregrounding of the film body is emphasized further in the film's gas chamber sequence.

Confronting the gas chamber

In the film's penultimate sequence, while Tadeusz is busily engaged in a grand ceremony for the SS, pretending to play the tuba, it is the cinematic spectator – without the protagonist – who witnesses mass murder in the gas chamber in a scene that is cross-cut with the macabre and bizarre celebrations. Tadeusz is absent from the gas chamber scene, therefore it is not the protagonist that the spectator identifies with as much as the film's body. Watching this sequence is a particularly visceral experience because it invites the spectator to engage with a filmic body that appears unable to cope with this historical scene. While clichés commonly found in representations of the gas chamber on screen, such as the spy hole, are included, they are disrupted by reminders of the presence of the film's body, thus the spectator is abruptly shifted from identification with diegesis and characters to a conscious identification with the film body.

Debates about the representability of the gas chamber on screen have been at the forefront of Holocaust discourse. Saxton particularly highlights the dispute between Jean-Luc Godard and Lanzmann. She notes that both film-makers "see conventional forms of representation as unable to bear witness to the horror of the camps," yet offer radically different responses to this dilemma.[36] The former, considering cinema as having failed to film the Holocaust, searches for a redemptive quality in the medium and believes that if a mythic image of the gas chambers (the so-called *pellicule maudite* – the "confounded reel") exists, then it should be shown. The latter, voraciously against using the Holocaust archive, claims he would destroy such an image if it was found.[37] Such disparate thoughts about this scene highlight its ethical complexity and thus the challenges it offers to Holocaust memory – challenges that have transcultural significance.

In *Kornblumenblau*, when the victims are herded into the gas chamber the shot is framed from the other side of a fence. The camera moves from left to right, as the people move right to left. The effect of these contrasting movements appears to slow down the image as fragments of it are caught in the gaps of the fence, like single frames of the film or images of a zoetrope. This effect gives the sensation that the spectator is staring at the physical, material film rather than a seamless diegesis. However, there is a quick cut to a realist composition of women in long-shot walking into the gas chamber, which pulls the spectator back into the film world. A tension emerges between the presence of the film body and the diegesis it is trying to express. Mimetically the spectator can empathize with the film's corporeal destruction as they also struggle to relate to the experience of the characters, for death in the gas chamber is an experience one can never fully understand corporeally (or arguably intellectually).

The film begins to reveal its fragility, divulging its illusionary status as a moving image; it starts to break down as it confronts this scene, yet abruptly switches back to a more realist style recognizing a responsibility to bear witness to it (which can also be interpreted as "to remember" in the context of Holocaust memory). As the gaps in the fence are successively replaced by the dark space of its panels, we are reminded of what Barker calls:

> [t]he phenomenological ambivalence between stillness and motion ... [that] defines the very nature of cinema, where the tension is experienced and expressed viscerally through what Andrei Tarkovsky described as the "time that pulsates through the blood vessels of the film."[38]

Barker is quick to remind us that this pull between stillness and motion, and wholeness and fragments, is not unique to film but is also phenomenologically inherent to the human body. She explains that the "fits and starts" that define cinema's 24 frames per second are similar to the intermittences in the human interior that allow it to function – the flow of the blood in the heart, the breath in and then out.[39] Thus Barker recognizes that the film's corporeal wholeness is illusionary: it usually hides from us the mechanical fragments that allow it to move through time and space, just as humans don't reveal every tiny movement that happens inside their bodies to others. When the film body reveals the fragility of its viscera in a sequence such as *Kornblumenblau*'s gas chamber scene, it encourages the spectator to recognize their own corporeal vulnerability as they mimetically engage with the film.

When the gas chamber appears, seemingly from the SS officer's point of view, the spectator is once again reminded of the film's presence as borders on the screen appear to divide the image into four framed areas. Frames are commonly used to express voyeurism in the film: Tadeusz watches two men speaking about escape plans through a door frame; sees the Jewish ballerina through the open doors of the cattle cart on which she arrived; and watches an execution through a window in the kitchen store room. However, in the film's climax, the distinct frame lines do not serve to help the spectator see anything clearly; rather they disrupt the aesthetic of the image, making it difficult to distinguish action.

Thus, the sequence throws any potential reliability of the film's previous frames into question, which implicitly emphasizes the unreliability of a vision-centric and hegemonic comprehension of the past. In fact, the dominance of the darkness left by the framing disrupts the image, making it more abstract. The inclusion of four separate frames in the image reminds the spectator that celluloid is composed of several micro-elements, foregrounding the materiality of the film. When people enter the gas chamber, beyond the fence, we identify with the temporality and spatiality of frames as the film appears to emphasize its frame-by-frame movement; during the victim's suffering, with the physical borders of frames, and in the sequence's finale we see the most simplistic element of film: the single, still, aestheticized filmic frame.

When the door is opened and the bodies revealed, their organization is clearly constructed – it could be construed to symbolize a human skull. This shot is heavily aestheticized, drawing the spectator's attention to its existence as image. The camera is still and two Sonderkommando open the door slowly as if releasing theatre curtains before they stand in the darkness at the edge of the frame they have created. The fleshy death mask constructed from several corpses is perfectly centered in the frame for the audience to appreciate as image. Stillness haunts the frame, momentarily allowing the audience to survey the devastation. Despite the harrowing features of the image, the camera lingers on it and the stillness of the frame encourages the spectator to fully digest everything they see on screen. Both the content of the image – the strange skull-like construction composed of human bodies – and the film body's unusual display of intentionality – characterized by stillness which draws attention to the existence of the single frames of which the film is constructed – draw attention to a corporeal foreignness about this scene. It feels strange in both human and filmic bodily terms. From a perceived slowing down of the film's moving image to the revelation of the frame borders and finally to the individual framed image, the film presents a fragile breaking down as it confronts the gas chamber. As the sequence progresses, the film negates any illusion of continuous filmic movement, and reveals its vulnerability and its inability to confront this past without reflecting on its own material fragility.

It is also significant that the diegetic human forms move in more abstract ways as the scene progresses. Firstly they run into the gas chamber and we see their physical human form, then they perform choreographed awkward movements across the screen as the camera glimpses only segments of their bodies in the chaotic space of the gas chamber. Finally they appear as a collective skull-like image – no longer recognizable as individual human bodies, but as one aesthetic mass. Normative bodily expression, by both the film and diegetic human bodies, is challenged in this sequence. The gas chamber as a historic scene is not only difficult to comprehend linguistically but is impossible to know sensually. Thus *Kornblumenblau* materially shuts down as it attempts to confront this image from the past that it can never fully recall. The spectator is invited to engage with this mimetically and to appreciate their own corporeal vulnerability and their inability to fully know this traumatic scene. This is one moment in *Kornblumenblau* in which the Polish narrative is sidelined (Tadeusz pretending to play in the orchestra is intercut with this sequence, but for relatively brief moments). In the film's climax, the foregrounding of corporeal breaking down draws attention to shared transcultural experiences with Holocaust memory: a problem all encounter when confronted with this past – what did it mean to experience death in the gas chamber? Thus, how should it be remembered?

Conclusion

Many elements of *Kornblumenblau* foreground a specifically Polish memory of the Holocaust, so it would be tempting to focus solely on the film's national context. However, turning toward the relationship between spectator and film reveals its transcultural significance. *Kornblumenblau* encourages the spectator to challenge the singularity of official histories and to consider the Holocaust a complex event characterized by a multiplicity of memories, many of which are often suppressed. Furthermore, the film provokes an embodied rather than solely intellectual engagement with the past, and thus opens up the potential for not only different memories to be appreciated, but also different ways

TRACING TOPOGRAPHIES

of thinking and feeling about the past. These issues are particularly foregrounded by the haptic resonance of the opening pseudo-archival sequence.

Furthermore, color and aural overlays that disrupt the verisimilitude throughout the film draw attention to the corporeal difficulties one has in confronting the space of the concentration (and death) camps – a repulsion toward such violation of the body. In the climax, the spectator is encouraged to mimetically engage with the film body's difficult confrontation with the gas chamber: an image neither film nor spectator has or could ever witness first-hand and survive to remember. The sequence challenges mythic depictions of this scene, encouraging the spectator to relate to the experiential distance between their lived-world and this particularly challenging moment of the past. All of these sensations are knowable across cultures and different bodies.

Kornblumenblau is thus not only a film of national significance, but of transcultural import too. While this focused study of one particular Holocaust film cannot speak for every screen interpretation of this past, I hope to have evidenced the potential the medium has to engage the spectator not only with the Holocaust as a real event that happened or its memory as defined on national terms, but with the complex transcultural dimensions of memory of this traumatic past. Turning attention to the topography of the spectatorial space, reading it phenomenologically, and identifying it as characterized by the meeting of film and spectatorial bodies, reveals the significance of the relationship between film and spectator, and enables analysis of the affect Holocaust films may provoke for the spectator: a grossly understudied yet incredibly important issue. To fully appreciate the potential significance of film to Holocaust memory, more detailed studies of the relationship between film and spectator are necessary, rather than continuing to solely focus on such films' national or representational value. The Holocaust continues to have transcultural resonance and film is one particularly affective medium through which we can engage with this. *Kornblumenblau* may be a Polish film in terms of its production context and several of its dominant themes, but it has the ability to speak to audiences beyond the nation's borders and to engage them with issues related to remembering the Holocaust. Such a transcultural transmission is meaningful and powerful. It is a shame then that the film has had such a limited release beyond Poland.

Notes

1. For examples of works that focus on film's role in constructing national memories of the Holocaust, see Doneson, *The Holocaust in American Film*; Haltof, *Polish Film and the Holocaust*; Litchner, *Film and the Shoah*; and Hicks, *First Films of the Holocaust*.
2. One can take Schindler's List tours of Kraków, and several years after the film's release, Oscar Schindler's former factory was transformed into the exhibition "Kraków under Nazi Occupation 1939–1945." Furthermore, beyond Poland, Spielberg's film has had a phenomenal effect on international Holocaust memory as the profits were used to establish the USC Shoah Foundation, which has recorded more than 50,000 survivor testimonies.
3. Soja, *Thirdspace*; Lefebvre, *Production of Space*; Massey, *Space, Place and Gender*.
4. Marks, *Skin of the Film*; Barker, *The Tactile Eye*.
5. I use the word "transcultural" here to expand beyond the transnational as only relating to crossing borders between states (an issue I will discuss further later in this article).
6. Levy and Sznaider, "Memory Unbound."
7. Ibid., 87–8.
8. Ibid.

TRACING TOPOGRAPHIES

9. Glajar, "Introduction."
10. Sobchack, "The Active Eye," 22.
11. For further discussions about non-anthropomorphic approaches to thinking about being, see Bennett, *Vibrant Matter*; and Bogost, *Alien Phenomenology*.
12. Tyminski, *To Calm My Dreams*.
13. Błonski, "The Poor Poles.".
14. Haltof, *Polish Film and the Holocaust*, 138–86.
15. King Kazimierz "the Great" was considered friendly to the Jews, and created Kraków's Jewish quarter, which was named after him. However from the mid-1400s, Jews moved to Kazimierz en masse after being expelled from cities, and it was later destroyed by the Nazis.
16. Borowski, *This Way to the Gas Chambers*; Haltof, *Polish Film and the Holocaust*, 162.
17. The many dimensions of this complex debate are outside the remit of this article, but are explored further in Błonski, "The Poor Poles"; Santorski and Wydawnicza, *Difficult Questions*; Engelking, "Murdering and Denouncing Jews"; Frommer, "Postscript"; Gross, "Holocaust in Occupied Poland"; Piotrowski, *Poland's Holocaust*; Żbikowski, "'Night Guard'"; and Zimmerman, *Contested Memories*.
18. Fictional films such as *Korczak* (Poland, Germany and UK, 1990), *The End of Our World* (*koniec naszego swiata*, Poland, 1964), and *According to the Decrees of Providence* (*Wedle wyroków twoich*, Poland and West Germany, 1984) use archive imagery to authenticate their relationship to history, while several documentaries interrogate the relationship between photography and memory, including *Photographer* (*Fotoamator*, Poland, France and Germany, 1998) and *I Am Looking at Your Photograph* (*patrzę na twoja fotografię*, Poland, 1979).
19. Marianne Hirsch particularly explicates this idea that later witnesses (or in her words "post-memory" generations) can only access the Holocaust through mediated forms, in *Generation of Postmemory*, 33.
20. De Cesari and Rigney, "Introduction," 3.
21. For an example of such an approach, see Ezra and Rowden, "General Introduction."
22. hooks, *The Oppositional Gaze*.
23. Levinas, *Totality and Infinity*.
24. Marks, *Skin of the Film*, 153.
25. Ibid., 162.
26. Marks, *Sensuous Theory*.
27. Barker, *The Tactile Eye*, 151. One can see, in Barker's terms, the limitations human scholars have in attempting to think in non-anthropomorphic ways about the world when the language we have available to discuss corporeality is so reliant on features of the human body.
28. Marks, *Skin of the Film*, 194.
29. While it might seem a far stretch to suppose one should turn to what is not shown in footage, Hicks, *First Films of the Holocaust*, reveals the insightfulness of such an approach in his reading of the Jewish Holocaust in Soviet films, many of which avoid or suppress Jewishness.
30. Marks, *Skin of the Film*, 40–41.
31. Barker, *The Tactile Eye*, 2.
32. Ibid., 7.
33. This distinction between "now" and "then" through color and black-and-white can be seen in *Night and Fog* (*Nuit et brouillard*, France, 1955), *Schindler's List* (USA, 1993) and the recent *Auschwitz-Birkenau: The Place Where You Are Standing* photography album published by the Auschwitz-Birkenau State Memorial Museum.
34. For examples of writing that relates color to film realism, see Kalmus, "Colour Consciousness," 24; Barsam and Monahan, *Looking at Movies*, 211.
35. Kristeva, *Powers of Horror*, 2–3.
36. Saxton, *Haunted Images*, 48.
37. Ibid., 48–52.
38. Barker, *The Tactile Eye*, 122.
39. Ibid., 128.

Disclosure statement

No potential conflict of interest was reported by the author.

Bibliography

According to the Decrees of Providence (Wedle wyroków twoich), directed by Jerzy Hoffman. Poland and West Germany: Central Cinema Company Film (CCC)/Film Polski/PRF "Zespol Fimowy"/ Sender Freies Berlin (SFB), 1984.

Annabelle Serpentine Dance, directed by William K. L. Dickson. USA: Edison Manufacturing Company, 1895.

Auschwitz-Birkenau State Museum. *Auschwitz-Birkenau: The Place Where You Are Standing.* Edited by Jadwiga Pinderska-Lech. Oświęcim: Auschwitz-Birkenau State Museum, 2013.

Barker, Jennifer M. *The Tactile Eye: Touch and the Cinematic Experience.* Berkeley, CA: University of California Press, 2009.

Barker, Jennifer M. *"Touch and the Cinematic Experience." In Art and the Senses, edited by Francesa Bacci and David Melcher, 149–159.* Oxford: Oxford University Press, 2006.

Barsam, Richard, and Dave Monahan. *Looking at Movies: Introduction to Film.* New York: W. W. Norton & Company, 2010.

Bennett, Jane. *Vibrant Matter: A Political Ecology of Things.* Durham, NC: Duke University Press, 2010.

Błonski, Jan. 1987. "The Poor Poles Look at the Ghetto." *Tygodnik Powszechny*, January 11. http://www.ucis.pitt.edu/eehistory/H200Readings/Topic4-R1.html.

Bogost, Ian. *Alien Phenomenology or What It's Like to Be a Thing.* Minneapolis: University of Minnesota Press, 2012.

Borowski, Tadeusz. *This Way to the Gas Chambers, Ladies and Gentlemen.* Middlesex: Penguin, 1980.

Chamarette, Jenny. *Phenomenology and the Future of Film: Rethinking Subjectivity beyond French Cinema.* Basingstoke: Palgrave Macmillan, 2012.

Coates, Paul. *"Colour and Suffering." Chap.* 8 in Cinema and Colour: The Saturated Image. London: Palgrave Macmillan, 2010.

De Cesari, Chiara, and Ann Rigney. *"Introduction." In Transnational Memory: Circulation, Articulation, Scales,* edited by Chiara De Cesari and Ann Rigney, 1–28. Berlin: De Gruyter, 2014.

Doneson, Judith E. *The Holocaust in American Film.* 2nd ed. New York: Syracuse University Press, 2002.

The End of Our World (koniec naszego swiata), directed by Wanda Jakubowska. Poland: Zespól Filmowy "Start," 1964.

Engelking, Barbara. "Murdering and Denouncing Jews in the Polish Countryside, 1942–1945." *East European Politics & Societies* 25 (2011): 433–456.

TRACING TOPOGRAPHIES

Ezra, Elizabeth, and Terry Rowden. "General Introduction: What is Transnational Cinema?" In *Transnational Cinema: The Film Reader*, edited by Elizabeth Ezra and Terry Rowden, 1–13. New York: Routledge, 2006.

Frommer, Benjamin. "Postscript: The Holocaust in Occupied Poland, Then and Now." *East European Politics & Societies* 25 (2011): 575–580.

Glajar, Valentina. "Introduction." In *Local History, Transnational Memory in the Romanian Holocaust*, edited by Valentina Glajar and Jeanine Teodorescu, 1–18. Basingstoke: Palgrave Macmillan, 2011.

Gross, Jan T. "Holocaust in Occupied Poland: New Findings and New Interpretations: Special Issue Introduction." *East European Politics & Societies* 25 (2011): 391–392.

Haltof, Marek. *Polish Film and the Holocaust: Politics and Memory*. New York: Berghahn Books, 2012.

Hicks, Jeremy. *First Films of the Holocaust: Soviet Cinema and the Genocide of the Jews, 1938–1946*. Pittsburgh: University of Pittsburgh Press, 2012.

Hirsch, Joshua. *After Image: Film, Trauma and the Holocaust*. Philadelphia: Temple University Press, 2004.

Hirsch, Marianne. *The Generation of Postmemory: Writing and Visual Culture after the Holocaust*. New York: Columbia University Press, 2012.

hooks, bell. "The Oppositional Gaze: Black Female Spectators." In *Film and Theory: An Anthology*, edited by Robert Stam and Toby Miller, 510–523. Malden, MA: Blackwell Publishers.

I Am Looking at Your Photograph (*Patrzę na twoja fotografię*), directed by Jerzy Ziarnik. Poland: Wytwórnia Filmów Dokumentalnych (WFD), 1979.

Joan the Woman, directed by Cecil B. DeMille. USA: Cardinal Film/Paramount Pictures, 1916.

Kalmus, Natalie. "Colour Consciousness." In *Colour: The Film Reader*, edited by Angela D. Vacche and Brian Price, 24–29. New York: Routledge, 2006.

Korczak, directed by Andrzej Wajda. Poland, Germany and UK: British Broadcasting Corporation (BBC)/Erato Films/Erbograph Co./Regina Ziegler Filmproduktion/Telmar Films Intl./Zespol Filmowy "Perspektywa"/Zweites Deutsches Fernsehen (ZDF), 1990.

Kornblumenblau, directed by Leszek Wosiewicz. Poland: Studio Filmowe im Karola Irzkowskiego, 1989.

Kristeva, Julia. *Powers of Horror: An Essay on Abjection*. New York: Columbia University Press, 1982.

Laub, Dori. *"An Event without a Witness: Truth, Testimony and Survival." In Testimony: Crises of Witnessing in Literature, Psychoanalysis, and History, by Shoshana Felman and Dori Laub*, 75–92. New York: Taylor & Francis Group, 1992.

Lefebvre, Henri. *The Production of Space*. Translated by Donald Nicholson-Smith. Malden, MA: Blackwell Publishing, 1991.

Levinas, Emmanuel. *Totality and Infinity*. Pittsburgh: Duquesne University Press, 1961.

Levy, Daniel, and Natan Sznaider. "Memory Unbound: The Holocaust and the Formation of Cosmopolitan Memory." *European Journal of Social Theory* 1 (2002): 87–106.

Lichtner, Giacomo. *Film and the Shoah in France and Italy*. London: Vallentine Mitchell, 2008.

Marks, Laura U. *Sensuous Theory: Touch and Multisensory Media*. Minneapolis: University of Minnesota Press, 2002.

Marks, Laura U. *The Skin of the Film: Intercultural Cinema, Embodiment and the Senses*. Durham, NC: Duke University Press, 2000.

Massey, Doreen. *Space, Place and Gender*. Cambridge: Polity Press, 1994.

Metz, Christian. *The Imaginary Signifier: Psychoanalysis and the Cinema*. Bloomington: Indiana University Press, 1982.

Mulvey, Laura. "Visual Pleasure and Narrative Cinema." *Screen* 3 (1975): 6–18.

Night and Fog (*Nuit et Brouillard*), directed by Alain Resnais. France: Argos Films, 1955.

October (Ten Days that Shook the World) (Oktyabr), directed by Sergei M. Eisenstein. Soviet Union: Sovkino, 1928.

Photographer (*Fotoamator*), directed by Dariusz Jabłoński. Poland, France and Germany: Apple Film Productions/Broadcast AV/TVP1/Arte/Canal+ Polska/Mitteldeutscher Rundfunk (MDR), 1998.

TRACING TOPOGRAPHIES

Piotrowski, Tadeusz. *Poland's Holocaust: Ethnic Strife, Collaboration with Occupying Forces and Genocide in the Second Republic, 1918–1947*. Jefferson, NC: McFarland & Company, 1998.

Santorski, Jacek, and Agencja Wydawnicza. *Difficult Questions in Polish-Jewish Dialogue: How Poles and Jews See Each Other: A Dialogue on Key Issues in Polish-Jewish Relations*. Warsaw: Jacek Santorski & Co Agencja Wydawnicza, 2006.

Saxton, Libby. *Haunted Images: Film, Ethics, Testimony and the Holocaust*. London: Wallflower Press, 2008.

Schindler's List, directed by Steven Spielberg. USA: Universal Pictures/Amblin Entertainment, 1993.

Shoah, directed by Claude Lanzmann. France and UK: Historia/Les Films Aleph/Ministère de la Culture de la Republique Française, 1985.

Sobchack, Vivian. "The Active Eye: A Phenomenology of Cinematic Vision." *Quarterly Review of Film and Video* 3 (1990): 21–36.

Sobchack, Vivian. *The Address of the Eye: A Phenomenology of Film Experience*. Princeton, NJ: Princeton University Press, 1992.

Soja, Edward W. *Thirdspace: Journeys to Los Angeles and Other Real-and-Imagined Places*. Cambridge, MA: Blackwell Publishers, 1996.

Strike (Stachka), directed by Sergei M. Eisenstein. Soviet Union: Goskino/Proletkult, 1925.

Tomkins, Silvan S. Exploring Affect: The Selected Writings of Silvan S. Tomkins. Edited by E. Virginia Demos. Cambridge: Press Syndicate of the University of Cambridge, 1995.

Tyminski, Kazimierz. *To Calm My Dreams*. Sydney: New Holland Publishers, 2011.

Witt, Michael. *Jean-Luc Godard: Cinema Historian*. Bloomington: Indiana University Press, 2013.

Żbikowski, Andrzej. "'Night Guard': Holocaust Mechanisms in the Polish Rural Areas, 1942–1945." *East European Politics & Societies* 25 (2011): 512–529.

Zimmerman, Joshua D. *Contested Memories: Poles and Jews during the Holocaust and Its Aftermath*. New Brunswick, NJ: Rutgers University Press, 2003.

Post-witnessing the concentration camps: Paul Auster's and Angela Morgan Cutler's investigative and imaginative encounters with sites of mass murder

Diana I. Popescu

Birkbeck, University of London, UK

ABSTRACT
This article offers a critical analysis of British writer Angela Morgan Cutler's and Jewish American author Paul Auster's accounts of their encounters with the Nazi sites of mass murder Auschwitz-Birkenau and Bergen-Belsen. Having no personal connection to the history of the Holocaust, Cutler and Auster post-witness the past through experiencing contradictory sensorial and cognitive reactions to the memorial sites, which resemble cognitive dissonance.

In a letter buried in a soil of ashes, Auschwitz *sonderkommando* Salmen Gradowski makes the following plea: "Dear finder," he summons, "search everywhere, in every inch of soil. Tens of documents are buried under it, mine and those of other persons, which will throw light on everything that was happening here."[1]

The search for hidden traces that may reveal the truth of history continues to be of relevance for those who visit sites of murder. What is the purpose of a visit to Auschwitz or Bergen-Belsen? How can our senses help us better see and perform the investigative activity to seek and find commended by Gradowski? Is an investigative mode good enough in our approach of the past? It may endow us with knowledge, but can it narrow the gap between knowledge and understanding resulting from the Holocaust? How could a contemporary visitor establish a meaningful connection with the past from this distance in time and position of unavoidable ignorance?

This article maps the experiences of visiting sites of mass murder of two contemporary writers, Paul Auster and Angela Morgan Cutler. In particular, I will explore these authors' activities of *post-witnessing*, a concept I employ to denote the condition of belatedness that characterizes individuals, irrespective of their familial connection, who engage in investigative, reflective, and creative thinking about what the Holocaust means to them and to the times they live in. I argue that the condition of post-witnessing[2] the concentration camps – as explored through the works of the above-mentioned authors – implies both an investigative and imaginative effort, and can be associated with the psychological response known as cognitive dissonance. While Marianne Hirsch's articulate definition of "postmemory" serves as a source of inspiration and informs to a great degree the relationship with the traumatic past developed by the writers here discussed, I adopt the term "post-witnessing" for reasons I explain in what follows. Postmemory describes the relationship members of generations born after the Holocaust develop in relation to a past mediated through testimonies, stories of survival, of trauma and of loss, contact with material artifacts, and by witnessing the difficulties of living after having survived. These experiences, explains Hirsch, "were transmitted to them so deeply and affectively as to seem to constitute memories in their own right."[3] Postmemory generations, explains Hirsch, connect with the past not by means of remembering or recall, as is the case with survivor generations, but through acts of "imaginative investment, projection and creation." Hirsch further explains these structures of transmission of memories to subsequent generations as follows:

> To grow up with such overwhelming inherited memories, to be dominated by narratives that preceded one's birth or one's consciousness, is to risk having one's own stories and experiences displaced, even evacuated, by those of a previous generation. It is to be shaped, however indirectly, by traumatic events that still defy narrative reconstruction and exceed comprehension. These events happened in the past, but their effects continue into the present. This is, I believe, the experience of postmemory and the process of its generation.[4]

The after-effects of the events experienced by earlier generations continue to reverberate and shape an emotional connection with the past experienced vicariously by later generations. Even though initially developed to refer to direct descendants of Jewish survivors and refugees of World War II, the term postmemory was further extended to designate subsequent generations of individuals with no direct connection to this history.

Since postmemory is primarily related to the ability to construct imaginative and emotional investments in the past, for the purposes of my argument, the term does not fully encompass another dimension I will be exploring in this article, namely the postmemory generations' intention to establish a direct connection with the past through an investigative effort to search for traces of the past by visiting sites of mass murder. Post-witnessing refers here to the urge to investigate the past by undertaking a real and not only an imaginary journey of discovery, and by conducting forensic work on these sites grounded in the here and now. In other words, post-witnessing denotes a position of immediate and unmediated personal relationship developed with a place of trauma in the present moment. It is an act of acknowledging in an active way the temporal and spatial remoteness from the past. Post-witnessing implies the investigative effort of visiting the real sites of mass murder and the imaginative effort of understanding how and what they might have been like. The work of the two novelists presented here is a result of their real encounters with the sites of murder, encounters driven by a search for answers in the hereness and nowness of these spaces. The act of "post-witnessing" resembles also the condition described as "cognitive dissonance," which involves an impossibility to reconcile two or more contradictory realities and states of awareness. These will be discussed at length in my analysis of Cutler's and Auster's narrated experiences of encountering the sites of the concentration camps. While this discussion of experiences of "post-witnessing" the concentration camps focuses strictly on two contemporary writers' biographical accounts, post-witnessing can be extended to investigations of any individual experiences of visiting murder sites. Certainly, scholarly work about visitor experiences of concentration camps, and in particular from Israel and Poland, as well as work on the development of dark tourism, sheds important light upon the ideological, political, and social narratives these spaces are used to effect.[5] However, there has been little work done to examine visitors' cognitive, perceptual, and affective involvement with these sites, and to observe whether these mental processes work together or apart to construct a personal and memorable experience of these sites. Naturally, one expects a variety of interactions that make up a complex fabric of unique individual responses and encounters with sites of murder. Given the assumed hybridity of the psychological responses to the physical spaces of mass murder, one may cautiously suggest that these encounters inevitably create spaces of dynamic interpretation, as suggested by the editors of this volume, or to employ Homi Bhabha's terminology, they conjure "third spaces" by giving rise to "something different, something new and unrecognisable, a new area of negotiation of meaning and representation."[6] In creating these spaces of meaning and representation, the power of direct contact with the physicality of the site should not be underestimated, since the materiality of the site acts as an anchoring device for sedimentation of memory, rather than an impediment to it.

In what follows, I will make the case that the post-witness is an individual who engages with this past both through the body and the mind, through perception and imagination. Hence, the plea to investigate is inevitably also a plea to imagine.

In answer to Gradowski, George Didi-Huberman proposes imagination as "a response [perhaps the only response] that we must offer, as a debt to the words and images that certain prisoners snatched for us, from the harrowing Real of their experience."[7] Didi-Huberman reminds us that any historical evidence of the Holocaust, whether in the form of an archival image or the site of mass murders, "is merely an object ... indecipherable and insignificant ... so long as I [the subject] have not established a relation – [here I stress] *an imaginative and speculative relation* – between what I see here and what I know from elsewhere."[8] To extrapolate, post-witnessing the concentration camp implies, as I hope to show in this article, a practice of establishing an imaginative and speculative (or investigative) relation between what I see *here and now*, and what I know from *elsewhere*. In order to fill the gap between knowledge and understanding, then, the investigative and the imaginative mode work together to establish a practice of post-witnessing. Post-witnessing here entails the closeness with the physical space where crimes were committed. It is the activity undertaken by few to visit the sites and develop on the site memories and personal connections of their own.

Building imaginative and investigative relations with the sites of murder

At first glance, Paul Auster's memoir *Winter Journal* (2012) and Angela Morgan Cutler's autobiographical novel *Auschwitz* (2008) may appear unlikely partners of conversation. Yet, as I will show, the juxtaposition here is not only for the sake of merely comparing and contrasting two narrations, but to make sense of how these authors' encounters with the sites of murder are remembered from a viewpoint which involves both imaginative and investigative efforts to internalize real experiences of visiting Bergen-Belsen and Auschwitz within the reflective narrative form of the memoir and autobiographical novel.

I aim to offer an understanding, albeit limited to these examples, of what happens to the body and the mind when encountering sites of murder. In particular, I am interested to investigate the psychological tensions emerging from the clash between the reality of the camp as one experiences it through the body and the senses (seeing, hearing, and touching) and the reality of the camp as one processes it through imagination, cognition, and previously acquired knowledge of this past. In order to make sense of the psychological processes involved in the encounters with the sites, I will invoke Leon Festinger's theory of cognitive dissonance as well as Jacques Lacan's understanding of the Real.[9] The clash between what one perceives in the present and what one imagines about the past creates a space of liminality whereby the past and the present superimpose and merge; or rather, this clash creates a gap between the past and the present, one blocking the presence of the other. It is this liminal condition, described as cognitive dissonance, that can become the locus of the post-witnessing experience of the concentration camps.

For both Paul Auster and Angela Morgan Cutler, the experience of visiting concentration camps contains three well-defined stages to be explored in further detail in what follows. These are: (1) the anticipation or expectation stage; (2) the arrival or physical encounter with the site; and (3) the moments after, or the post-encounter which takes place at the stage of writing. Within this sequence the whole of the experience of the encounter with the sites is processed, analyzed, and organized in narrative form.[10]

Angela Morgan Cutler's encounter with Auschwitz

Angela Morgan Cutler's autobiographical fiction *Auschwitz* (2008) documents the struggle between locating Auschwitz within the contemporary Polish landscape and containing the symbolic place of Auschwitz within her personal life and understanding. Written in an autobiographical diary form, in the first person, Cutler introduces the reader to the process of writing about Auschwitz, and her experience of visiting the site with her husband En and sons Max and Seth. It is important to note that even though Cutler may not have any direct personal connections to these events, her husband is the son of a Holocaust survivor, Elise. Elise lost her parents at Auschwitz, a place she had visited previously with her son. Cutler's visit, on 22 July, a hot summer's day, is recounted in great detail and forms the backbone of the novel. Divided into chapters each carrying a title to describe the stages and foci of the visit – "hair and tears," "photographs," "the gas chamber," "the shoe," "the pond" – the novel is interspersed with lengthy reproductions of what appear to be the author's real email exchanges with Franco-American author Raymond Federman, referred to in the text as Moinous, a child survivor and writer, as well as detailed accounts of the author's dreams seemingly related to the Holocaust. The novel paints a complex portrayal of an individual's process of writing[11] about Auschwitz consciously, at the intellectual and emotional level, as well as unconsciously, at the level of unrecognized emotions and thoughts that surface in dreams.

The structure of the novel renders the author's experience dissonant. The text is disjointed and non-linear, made up of an intermittent travelogue recounting Cutler's experiences of visiting Auschwitz, Minsk, and Berlin; the exchange of emails between Cutler and Moinous, and her experience of conceiving and writing the novel. Cutler's anticipation of the encounter is laden with conflicting questions which create unease and discomfort, such as whether one should go or not go, and how one should behave on the site. Is it okay to eat while visiting Auschwitz? To cry? To not cry? The writing reflects deep uncertainties in regard to how to approach the site from a psychological point of view. What is one supposed to feel and think when being on the site? What mental state of mind is desirable, or recommended? How can one reach it? Arriving at the site unavoidably means confronting the distance, elusiveness, and absence of Auschwitz, and the inability to grasp its meaning.

Anticipation is recognized as the unavoidable entry pass for anyone contemplating the visit: "Auschwitz. And who hasn't done this. Anticipated everything on the way there. Composed a whole book on the way."[12] Then there is the prevailing feeling of shame in being a tourist who can arrive at Auschwitz freely and leave undamaged; and discomfort at having to repeat the name Auschwitz to buy a ticket. Cutler feels the need to distinguish herself from other tourists, as a creative and informed individual whose visit is somehow different from the other visitors who take the guided tour instead. Being guided at Auschwitz means not possessing the knowledge of what Auschwitz the site is, as well as uncritically becoming a part of the tourist industry, which Cutler seems to allude to. The notion of being "different" stands out:

> we are making our way on the local bus. We are not on the guided tour. This is something I feel I must mention, as if I am making a distinction. Of course I am – repeat the line quietly – as if by making our own way there we become – or rather, like to think of ourselves – as a different kind of tourist, a different kind of voyeur.[13]

This difference is also made apparent in Cutler's narrated thought process and decision in regard to what outfit is most appropriate to wear at Auschwitz. Can one visit Auschwitz on sunny summer afternoons, wearing bright colors? Can one touch the dank walls of the gas chamber and eat lunch in the Auschwitz café? Every small decision becomes a source of self-doubt and uncertainty. Every gesture becomes awkward and inappropriate. The visit makes Cutler self-conscious and vulnerable. She recounts:

> Yes, I think I must have chosen the wrong colour; that such a colour must be in bad taste that I, who always insist on wearing black, today impulsively decide on a turquoise skirt as if some colour were needed – as if it matters. Yes, I prepared this morning, thinking of what to wear. What to wear for such an occasion. What would seem appropriate? Saying to myself: Look at me, dressing for Auschwitz.[14]

Cutler's visit has got a purpose, that of writing about Auschwitz. Yet, through self-questioning one continues to find deeper layers of motivation for the visit:

> and of course I question and ask myself on the way, on the way to Auschwitz, what are the reasons for being here, for wanting to go there, for thinking I could write anything here, there; should I even be seen on this bus? No. The way I tried to ease myself onto the bus without being seen. And of course I did not expect, had not expected to see the destination spelled out so acutely.[15]

The confusion of arrival and the questioning continues as one enters the site. The term Auschwitz appears written in capital letters on an entire page (see page 7 in the novel). This compulsive rewriting of the name can be also regarded as a form of preparation for the encounter, of turning the encounter into something less strange, less daunting, something that one may be able to grasp. Yet the arrival is marked by hesitation, the inability to participate in the moment, to fully acknowledge it, as well as an impossibility to escape it. This hesitation is made apparent in the moving and turning of the bus, in the circular movements and the repetition of the word Auschwitz. Cutler's account of arrival

TRACING TOPOGRAPHIES

marked by the to-and-fro may mean that arrival is not static, but dynamic; it is an activity in its own right. The following passage captures the dynamic nature of arrival:

> unsure – tentative, for sure – we hesitate on arrival. I can not deny, as the driver turns, turns again, shouts again, the word again: Auschwitz … The word turning in his mouth, turning over in ours, turning our heads to his, straightening, standing up and down to his telling: it's here. Here … here, he says. Come. Come. In our repeating, in our arriving we do not move. Move. We only repeat.[16]

The dissonant experience continues as Cutler describes an arrival tinged with anxiety and fear:

> the temporary relief of arrival tinged with the solitude of what-now, of abandon: to be or not to be on the bus, run after the bus, change our minds, on or off the bus, startled now by the sudden heat, the bus disappearing from view.[17]

Cutler's experience of arrival is not unlike that of other tourists. Studies of tourist experiences at concentration camps show that there is a mismatch between what is expected and what is experienced on the site. Expectation is inherent to any act of traveling and affects the experience of it. Research on tourist perceptions of the camps conducted by Israeli anthropologist Jackie Feldman shows that if visitors have expectations as to how the destination will look or how they will react to it that are not met by the experience, they will feel let down, even be left with a feeling of emptiness. Feldman notes a student's reaction which points to how expectations may have the effect of completely blocking real experience of the site, leading to a feeling of frustration because of the inability to connect:

> We were in Treblinka and they were telling me that people died here, and I see myself staring at the grass and trying to understand what happened here. And I find myself, trying, by force to imagine, but I don't want to do it by force. If it does not speak to me it doesn't, maybe it will come in time. But I am unable and it is very frustrating.[18]

Derek Dalton's account of encountering Auschwitz documents similar psychological processes, where expectations have accumulated via exposure to multiple forms of Holocaust representation in popular culture, and through education, which inevitably interfere with the actual experience of the site. Dalton's visit to Auschwitz carries both imaginative and investigative undertones. He argues that imagination plays a vital role in "animating the artefacts and geography of a place and investing them with meaning." His actions are investigative, as he confesses: "I have come to Auschwitz-Birkenau to dig in the fertile soil of my imagination – my memories of the Holocaust," and he acknowledges that "the mental images that shaped my personal historical consciousness of the Holocaust were powerfully invoked and evoked by new sights and images that I encountered in the camps."[19]

Cutler's account resembles the psychological processes documented by Feldman and Dalton. In Cutler's case, however, the dissonance between expectations of what the visit will be like and the reality of the moment of being on the site create a blockage, a form of blindness or blankness. The sight of material relics overwhelms the viewer, leaving him or her to wrestle with making sense of them. One remains clueless when faced with the question of how to respond to the sight of the material relics displayed in the museum at Auschwitz. Cutler recounts the state of emotional unknowing caused by the encounter with the relics:

TRACING TOPOGRAPHIES

the familiar buckled suitcases painted with oversized names that have become so symbolic of this museum, I wonder how am I to respond to these, to the chewed-over toothbrushes, the baby chupetas, the mountains of cooking pots, and to the empty gas cans now before me, I say to En [her husband] … I don't know what I am supposed to be feeling.[20]

Furthermore, Cutler doubts what she sees and asks whether the objects arranged in glass displays resemble art objects. She asks how real can they be? What kind of contact with the reality of the past can they provide for the visitors? These thoughts are unsettling since the search for the real of Auschwitz evades Cutler. Being on the site may not necessarily mean being met with the real of Auschwitz, since, "even though I know this is the real thing, what does real thing mean anymore, when the look of them only keeps returning me to art objects."[21]

These stages of mental blockage find a psychological explanation in Leon Festinger's theory of cognitive dissonance. Festinger suggests that we have an inner drive to hold all our attitudes and beliefs in harmony and therefore avoid dissonance. This theory starts from the idea that we seek cognitive consistency in our beliefs and attitudes in any situation where two cognitions are inconsistent.[22] In the case of a visit to a concentration camp, the two cognitions that are in dissonance are: (1) the perception of the camps as they *are now*; and (2) the expectation of connecting with the site, seeing through the mind's eye how they *were then*. The experience of post-witnessing defined as I argue by the effort to investigate what there is and to imagine what was, falls within the traps of cognitive dissonance. Hence, while the senses experience the site of Auschwitz-Birkenau as *it is* – a ruin overtaken by nature's force – the imaginative faculty conjures images of what the site might have been, namely a place of extreme human suffering which horrifies the senses. This clash of cognitions creates a state of discomfort and anxiety. In order to reach a position of cognitive consonance, one must, therefore, find strategies to diminish the dissonance.

Angela Cutler's encounter with Auschwitz falls within the traps of cognitive dissonance. Though Cutler is able to see and touch, this does nothing to alleviate her confused reactions. Cutler manages only to tangibly interact with Auschwitz. The senses alone cannot bridge the gap between the here and now of the site and what the site might have been in the past. The encounter with the now of the site is, as one may tell from the following passage, startling and incongruent with what Cutler has pictured it to be. The arrival at the site seems from the passage below to be perceived as the goal of the journey. But what happens when Cutler arrives inside the site? The incongruence between the anticipation of the visit and the reality of it is rendered as a state of numbness since for Cutler and other visitors, nothing happens on the site. Furthermore, the perception of the real site does not follow Cutler's imagination of the site; "the scale here is all wrong," she argues.

> Yes, when I leave the bus that brought us here, when I walk the small distance into, when I enter what I have seen so many times before, beneath the words – Work Shall Set You Free – *Arbeit Macht Frei* – there it is, here it is, to pass beneath, what happens, nothing happens, not now, look up, look into; you're inside already, already finding yourself inside Auschwitz finding yourself agreeing, agreeing with a stranger that the scale here is all wrong.[23]

What one can sense is that the place Auschwitz is not and cannot be connected with the name Auschwitz. Hence, expectation does not match the reality of the visit. In order to diminish dissonance, the imaginative faculty refuses to collaborate. The subject remains grounded in the realm of the here and now. The narrator is preoccupied with searching and finding, and collecting small things, feathers, stones, some clues of what happened there. This search for clues presupposes an investigative eye, but the force of the site leaves no room for creative thought. What prevails is the mere condition of the post-witness, the actualization of a sense of afterward-ness and of distance: "Look here I am at Auschwitz. Here now but after the event. This can only ever be after the event. Look, here I am already. Already collecting."[24] The act of collecting emerges as a prevailing theme in Cutler's account of Auschwitz – the visit, and of her struggle with Auschwitz – the book she has committed herself to write. The collecting of small pieces of broken items found on the grounds of Auschwitz is a common practice among many visitors. In this case, Cutler may be no different from other tourists who feel they would like to bring something back home with them, mementoes, reminders of having been there. While there are risks of sacralizing these material relics[25] I would like to argue that collecting items found on the site is an appealing practice especially because they offer a tangible connection with the past. These are broken pieces of what used to be objects belonging to victims or survivors; objects that may have saved their lives by preventing them from starving, such as spoons and bowls, or getting injured, such as shoes and clothes. These items offer to the investigative eye of the post-witness a chance to decipher the stories of their owners. The simple act of collecting objects allows tourists such as Cutler to interact with the site and to anchor oneself in the reality of the site. They gather the pieces of what has yet to be discovered. Hence, collecting small things becomes a practice of appropriating pieces of the past to create personal links to a site that remains alien and silent. Searching the grounds of Auschwitz and collecting relics defines the condition of the post-witness whose investigation and search for meaning becomes tangible via this sensory contact with broken objects. To reconstruct the story of Auschwitz one needs a tangible connection that opens up the possibility to imagine what the past may have looked like. Cutler continues:

> Already collecting. My head on the ground ... digging in the path for some small stones, some clue, yes, here I am already collecting small mementoes for Moinous as I said I would, asking myself if as a child I was short-changed on tragedy.[26]

Collecting objects may appear to be the only activity that Cutler can engage in, and which can offer an answer to the persistent question: what to do after arriving at the site? The small things found in the ground create a unique relation to the site.

A short digression into the meaning of collecting objects as a form of investigation and observation seems useful at this point. Material objects can become active agents of memory. Cutler's collecting of objects is a form of memory work, since it is expected that through attentive observation, the owners of the objects can be revealed and can step out of anonymity. Objects allow an interpersonal relationship with their lost owners, brought forth through the act of close observation. For Cutler, collecting objects is an act of acknowledging the palpable reality of the crimes. The contact with material remnants creates the experience of post-witnessing. This particular individual–object interaction is especially reflected in a recent work by artist Esther Shalev-Gerz called "Menschen Dinge: The Human Aspect of Objects" (2006).[27] This artwork testifies to post-witnessing as an investigative and imaginative activity through which members of

TRACING TOPOGRAPHIES

later generations create their own personal memories and fabricated connections with the past. Invited to create a project for the Buchenwald Concentration Camp Memorial, Esther Shalev-Gerz asked museum professionals – the director, a historian, an archaeologist, a female restorer, and a female photographer – to talk about the objects found in the grounds of the camp. Each tells about his or her encounters – professional, personal, and imaginary – with objects such as a comb, a bowl, a brooch, modified, engraved, repurposed, and personalized by the detainees during their imprisonment. The objects are presented in video films and photographs slightly out of focus. The five videos show representatives of the memorial interact with objects, by turning them around and investigating them while talking. Esther Shalev-Gerz's choice of title, "The Human Aspect of Objects," resonates how in the absence of people, the objects that remained – a comb, a bowl, tin mugs – embody the past but also create material links that connect us to those lost. The human aspect of objects points to the communicative capacity, agency, and power of things as they trigger in us – those who contemplate them – a process of translation and interpretation of history. Through observation of the objects, the participants in Shalev-Gerz's exhibition are asked to create their own relations to the past by interpreting, translating, and endowing the objects with meaning, and thus recognizing the "human value" of objects. Translating this connection between the objects and the site proves difficult to capture in writing. Indeed, Cutler's struggle to make sense of her visit and to find a form to narrate it is a good example. Not only does Cutler repetitively attempt to write about her connection to this history and to the site, but her exploration becomes an exploration of the limits of language. Hence, what becomes apparent is the circularity of her prose as a strategy to capture the meaning this place has for her. After her visit, Cutler attempts to send an email to Moinous, using a Polish keyboard. Unsurprisingly, her attempt to put the experience into words fails:

> we tjhen went to berkenau and sat beside a pond full of ashesz – waht a factory of death […] sorry abouyt this – this oinpoossible keybporadf […] max telling me that someone in the cornere is watchong porn on their screem – 0 i wondeered why he wsa so quiet.[28]

Cutler renders the nonsense of writing about Auschwitz, exposing the limits of herself, her body and mind, and the limits of language. The creative process and the experience of writing about the visit can be read as an attempt to break into the "Real" theorized by Lacan as that which is pre-mirror and pre-imaginary, and which resists representation in language, or loses its reality once it is rendered through language.[29] This awareness gains force during a visit to some woods near the site. Cutler and her family stumble upon a pond – the pond which she knows by now held the ashes of tens of thousands of gassed victims. "It was the 22nd of July when we found ourselves on a coach to Auschwitz, the 22nd of July when we found ourselves circling the pond, this Birkenau pond, a pond I knew nothing of until the day before our visit, from a small guide book given to me by a Jew from Krakow."[30] The pond reflects nothing back but her own figure. "There is nothing to gaze at nor into – the water that is clear no more – that reflects only the need to keep staring and searching for … whom … for what."[31] Cutler thinks of how "Auschwitz cannot be written directly – one must make circles around it."[32] To write, therefore, is to circle around its truth, to approach the opaqueness that "reflects only the need to *keep staring and searching*."[33] In circling the ash-pond, Cutler attempts to find a balance between encountering Auschwitz through the investigative effort and

TRACING TOPOGRAPHIES

understanding it through the creative process. Hence, writing about the visit to Auschwitz is a form of "not arriving" at the truth of it. The Real of Auschwitz is what interpreters of Lacan describe as "the aspect where words fail,"[34] "the in-eliminable residue of all articulation, the foreclosed element, which may be approached, but never grasped."[35]

A sense of profound dislocation is experienced when writing about Auschwitz. Dislocation comes from the expectations Cutler may have of the site, which has gained mythical and sacred dimensions, and the duty to engage in remembering through behavior that seems appropriate in the place. The anticipation of a life-changing experience has its burdens. Can one appreciate the quietude and peacefulness of the place as a positive experience of the site, and without feeling guilty? Can one embrace the beauty of its transformation, and the naturalness of time passing? Can one integrate this space within the present, and accept that a return to what was is impossible? Cutler's writing is a record of her struggles to integrate conflicting perceptions of Auschwitz and what it stands for and Auschwitz the current site.

Paul Auster encounters Bergen-Belsen

A different kind of cognitive dissonance experience is narrated by the Jewish American writer Paul Auster. Unlike Angela Cutler's visit to Auschwitz, Auster's visit to Bergen-Belsen occupies little space in his memoir, *Winter Journal* (2012), a moving meditation on self-growth, aging and death, memory and the body narrated chronologically in the second person. Paul's choice of second person "you" to address in an open dialogue his past selves creates a surprising sense of intimacy with the narrator's both present and former selves. The perspective of the second person does not have a distancing effect; on the contrary, it conveys a freshness and closeness to the character Paul Auster as we, the readers, encounter him anew at different ages and under different circumstances. As if talking about someone else, Auster establishes a powerful connection with the reader, which lends an immersive quality to his account of Bergen-Belsen. While this episode does not occupy a lengthy space, approximately three pages in a narrative more than 150 pages long, its brief presence is worth exploring. The passage of interest appears at the end of Auster's memoir, unexpectedly, as a final stage in the exploration of an identity defined through the body and its memory.

"You heard the dead calling out to you – but only once, once in all the years you have been alive."[36] Thus starts the account of the visit. Indeed, it is an anti-climactic beginning, since the reader is already given a hint of what follows, an account of the dead calling. Auster goes on to reassure the reader that his is a stable relationship with reality which has been put to the test during his visit to Bergen-Belsen. Since one defines oneself more easily by what one is not, the narrator establishes the framework of his reality: "you are not someone who sees things that are not there." This statement seems well grounded in a concrete and stable notion that one can trust one's senses. Seeing in this case means what the eyes allows one to observe in one's surroundings. The author admits to his confusion over what his senses tell him: "and while you have often been confused by what you are seeing, you are not prone to hallucinations or fantastical alterations of reality." The event that happens next severely alters the author's perception of reality. The event is located in a distant past and in a remote geographical setting: "some 25 years ago and under circumstances far removed from the flow of your daily life." The authorial

TRACING TOPOGRAPHIES

self is dislodged from what is familiar, what is ordinary, and experiences something outside of the parameters of reality: the experience of an auditory hallucination, which continues to "bewilder with its vividness and power."[37] There is no sense of mistrust in what actually happened, or denial of it. Indeed, the experience is represented as no doubt pertaining to the domain of the Real. The location is Germany, and the episode happened during a visit to Bergen-Belsen, or rather, the author makes it clear, "the site where Bergen Belsen had once stood." Hence, the experience could not have happened somewhere else, and more so, it was triggered by being in a place. We also learn about the thoughts that preceded this experience and the presence of an inner conflict. The moments before the visit are described in similar terms to Cutler's; the narrator is gripped by indecision at the thought of visiting the place: "you wanted to go, even if a part of you was reluctant to go." Auster makes up his mind to visit the site when his German publisher agrees to accompany him. In preparation for his encounter with Bergen-Belsen, Auster's mind conjures images and previous knowledge about the history of the site, as depicted in the following passage:

> There you were sitting in the car and thinking about Anne Frank and her sister, Margot, who had both died in Bergen-Belsen, along with tens of thousands of others, the many thousands of others who perished there from typhus and starvation, random beatings, murder. The dozens of films and newsreels you had seen of the death camps were spooling through your head as you sat in the passenger seat of the car.[38]

The state of anxiety grows. The senses are again bewildered, as what was seen through the mind's eye did not find a match on the site itself. Instead the dissonance intensified. One's internal landscape did not and could not match what the eyes saw on the site. The nothingness of the site prevails. As a blank canvas, time and events of history erased the signs of past events. "Nothing was left of the camp itself." How can one read the site? In the place of what was then "the building, the barracks, the barbed-wire fences," what stood there now was "a small museum, a one-story structure filled with poster-sized black-and-white photographs along with explanatory texts." How could one connect with what it was? The place, grim and awful, blocks the possibility to imagine the reality of the place as it had been during the war. The return in time, through the efforts of imagination, is impossible. The anticipation of the site and the preparation to experience the event does not help either. Connection with the people who perished on this site – the expectation or the objective of the visit to such a place – does not happen. While the mind summons knowledge of what the place looked like *then*, the eyes can only register the site as "denuded and antiseptic." "You couldn't feel the presence of the dead, the horror of so many thousands crammed into that nightmare village surrounded by barbed wire."[39]

Then something else happens. The beauty of the site clashes with the reality of what this site had seen, opening up a space for the sensations to take a grip over the reality of the authorial self. The hallucinatory experience took its toll. Once expectation fails to match the reality of the visit, the anticipation of a life-changing experience also disappears. This pause or stillness of the mind allows the creation of a liminal space and the conditions of an embodied experience of post-witnessing. Imagination takes hold and shapes the experience of the senses as the narrator undergoes a form of post-witnessing which dissolves the distance between the self and the past. The senses and the imagination merge and become indistinguishable. The gap between the two forms of cognition involved in the encounter

TRACING TOPOGRAPHIES

with the site – how the external senses record the site and how the mind imagines the past to be – disappears for a moment, overtaken by the hallucinatory experience:

> Then you went outside, onto the grounds where the death camp had stood, but it was a grassy field now, a domain of lovely, well-tended grass stretching for several hundred yards in all directions. Then you came to a patch of grass that was slightly elevated, three or four inches higher than the rest of the field a perfect rectangle that measured about twenty feet by thirty feet, the size of a large room, and in one corner there was a marker in the ground that read: Here lie the bodies of 50,000 Russian soldiers. You were standing on top of the grave of fifty thousand men. It didn't seem possible that so many dead bodies could fit into such a small space, and when you tried to imagine those bodies beneath you, the tangled corpses of fifty thousand young men packed into what must have been the deepest of deep holes, you began to grow dizzy at the thought of so much death, so much death concentrated in such a small patch of ground, and a moment later you heard the screams, a tremendous surge of voices rose up from the ground beneath you, and you heard the bones of the dead howl in anguish, howl in pain, howl in a roaring cascade of full-throated, ear-splitting torment. The earth was screaming. For five or ten seconds you heard them, and then they went silent.[40]

In Auster's case, the convergence of the senses and of imagination cancels momentarily the distance between two dissonant forms of experiencing the site, through the senses and through imagination, that thus far tend to remain disjointed.

What constitutes the personal experience of post-witnessing the murder sites? Can one engage in a commemorative act by simply being in the space? What do these spaces summon? How do our body and mind create the conditions for a commemorative experience? What remains after the visit? Imagination seems a necessary or rather indispensable faculty when writing about such a visit. Simply accepting the ruin and the loss, and acknowledging that the sites do not speak, is not easy to come to terms with. One is compelled to draw on imagination to animate the artifacts and the geography of the place and invest them with meaning. Searching for meaning means creating a meaningful experience.

As a way of concluding, one can argue then that both Cutler's and Auster's acts of post-witnessing the concentration camps draw on the potential, though limited, of the body and the mind to recreate an embodied connection with the past whereby the past becomes tangible through senses and imagination as well as memory. Perhaps central to the experience of encounter with Auschwitz the site and the search for its meaning is the willingness to move *toward* death, to quote Helen Cixous, toward "the known unknown, where knowing and unknowing touch, where we hope we will know what is unknown."[41]

Notes

1. Gradowski, "Letter," 75.
2. Post-witnessing as an activity that summons imaginative faculty, and the intertwined relationship between memory and imagination in artistic engagements with the Holocaust, is further developed in the introduction to Popescu and Schult, *Representing the Holocaust*.
3. Hirsch, "The Generation of Postmemory," 107.
4. Ibid.
5. See scholarly works on dark tourism by Lennon and Foley, Derek Dalton, and Emma Willis; Jackie Feldman's work on Israeli students' experiences at camps; and Tim Cole's work cited in this article.

TRACING TOPOGRAPHIES

6. Rutherford, "The Third Space," 211.
7. Didi-Huberman, *Images in Spite of All*, 3.
8. Ibid., 112.
9. See works by Festinger, *A Theory of Cognitive Dissonance*; and Lacan, "Symbol and Language" in *The Language of the Self*.
10. Many visual artists have worked through these stages of their experiences of visiting murder sites. See Tanja Schult's "To Go or Not to Go?"
11. For a detailed interpretation of writing processes and writing styles in Cutler's novel, see Rine, "Making the Silence Speak."
12. Cutler, *Auschwitz*, 11.
13. Ibid., 9–10.
14. Ibid., 10.
15. Ibid., 9.
16. Ibid., 12.
17. Ibid., 13.
18. Feldman, "In Search," 230.
19. Dalton, "Encountering Auschwitz," 189.
20. Cutler, *Auschwitz*, 31.
21. Ibid.
22. See Festinger, *A Theory of Cognitive Dissonance*.
23. Cutler, *Auschwitz*, 17.
24. Ibid., 18.
25. See works by Tim Cole, Oren Baruch Stier, and James Young.
26. Cutler, *Auschwitz*, 18.
27. Shalev-Gerz's artistic engagement with material relics and the Holocaust is discussed at length by Jacob Lund and James E. Young, in *Revisiting Holocaust Representation in the Post-Witness Era*.
28. Cutler, *Auschwitz*, 90.
29. See Lacan, "Symbol and Language."
30. Cutler, *Auschwitz*, 141.
31. Ibid., 231.
32. Ibid., 242.
33. Ibid., 231 (emphasis added).
34. Vogler quoted by Amanda Loos, 'Symbolic, real, imaginary', University of Chicago online glossary, retrieved from http://csmt.uchicago.edu/glossary2004/symbolicrealimaginary.htm, accessed on 20 February 2016.
35. Miller, 1981, 280.
36. Auster, *Winter Journal*, 147.
37. Ibid., 147–8.
38. Ibid., 148.
39. Ibid.
40. Ibid., 148–9.
41. Cixous, *Three Steps on the Ladder*, 38.

Disclosure statement

No potential conflict of interest was reported by the author.

Bibliography

Auster, Paul. *Winter Journal*. Toronto: McClelland and Stewart, 2012.

Cixous, Hélène. *Three Steps on the Ladder of Writing*. Translated by Sarah Cornell and Susan Sellers. New York: Columbia University Press, 1993.

Cole, Tim. "Holocaust Tourism: The Strange yet Familiar/the Familiar yet Strange." In *Representing the Holocaust in the Post-Witness Era*, edited by Diana I. Popescu and Tanja Schult, 93–107. Basingstoke: Palgrave Macmillan, 2015.

Cole, Tim. *Selling the Holocaust: From Auschwitz to Schindler, How History is Bought, Packaged, and Sold*. New York: Routledge, 2000.

Cutler Morgan, Angela. *Auschwitz*. Ullapool: Two Ravens Press, 2008.

Dalton, Derek. *Dark Tourism and Crime*. London: Routledge, 2014.

Dalton, Derek. "Encountering Auschwitz: A Personal Rumination on the Possibilities and Limitations of Witnessing/ Remembering Trauma in Memorial Space." *Law Text Culture* 13 (2009): 187–225.

Didi-Huberman, Georges. *Images in Spite of All: Four Photographs from Auschwitz*. Translated by Shane B. Lillis. Chicago: University of Chicago Press, 2008.

Feldman, Jackie. *Above the Death Pits, beneath the Flag: Youth Voyages to Poland and the Performance of Israeli National Identity*. Oxford: Berghahn Books, 2008.

Feldman, Jackie. "In Search of the Beautiful Land of Israel: Israeli Youth Voyages to Poland." In *Israeli Backpackers and their Society*, edited by C. Noy and E. Cohen, 217–50. New York: New York State University Press, 2005.

Festinger, Leon. *A Theory of Cognitive Dissonance*. Stanford, CA: Stanford University Press, 2009.

Gradowski, Salmen. "Letter." In *Amidst a Nightmare of Crime: Manuscripts of Members of Sonderkommando*, edited by Jadwiga Bezwinska and Danuta Czech. Oswiecim: State Museum, 1973.

Hirsch, Marianne. "The Generation of Postmemory." Accessed October 10, 2015. http://www.columbia.edu/~mh2349/papers/generation.pdf.

Lacan, Jacques. "Symbol and Language." In *The Language of the Self*, edited by J. Lennon and M. Foley. Baltimore, MD: The Johns Hopkins University Press, 1956.

Lennon, J., and M. Foley. *Dark Tourism: The Attraction of Death and Disaster*. London: Continuum, 2000.

Lund, Jacob. "Acts of Remembering in the Work of Esther Shalev-Gerz – From Embodied to Mediated Memory." In *Revisiting Holocaust Representation in the Post-Witness Era*, 28–44. Hampshire: Palgrave Macmillan, 2015.

Miller, Jacques-Alain. "Translator's Note." In *The Four Fundamental Concepts of Psychoanalysis*. New York: W.W. Norton & Company, 1981.

Popescu, Diana I., and Tanja Schult, eds. *Revisiting Holocaust Representation in the Post-Witness Era*. Basingstoke: Palgrave Macmillan, 2015.

Rine, Abigail. "Making the Silence Speak: Angela Morgan Cutler's *Auschwitz*." *Oxford Journals Forum for Modern Languages Studies* 44, no. 3 (2008): 340–351.

Rutherford, Jonathan. "The Third Space: Interview with Homi Bhabha." In *Identity: Community, Culture, Difference*, 201–221. London: Lawrence and Wishart, 1990.

Schult, Tanja. "To Go or Not to Go? Reflections on the Iconic Status of Auschwitz, its Increasing Distance and Prevailing Urgency." In *Revisiting Holocaust Representation in the Post-Witness Era*, edited by Jonathan Rutherford, 107–132. Hampshire: Palgrave Macmillan, 2015.

Stier, Oren Baruch. *Committed to Memory: Cultural Mediations of the Holocaust.* Amherst: University of Massachusetts Press, 2003.

Willis, Emma. *Theatricality, Dark Tourism and Ethical Spectatorship: Absent Others.* Basingstoke: Palgrave, 2014.

Vogler, Candace. *Notes on Lacan.* MAPH 301 Core Course. Autumn 2001.

Young, James E. "Countermonuments as Spaces for Deep Memory." In *Revisiting Holocaust Representation in the Post-Witness Era*, 44–53. Basingstoke: Palgrave Macmillan, 2015.

Young, James. *Texture of Memory. Holocaust Memorials and Meaning.* New Haven, CT: Yale University Press, 1993.

Extra-territorial places in W. G. Sebald's *Austerlitz*

Melanie Dilly

Department of Modern Languages, School of European Culture and Languages, University of Kent, UK

ABSTRACT
W.G. Sebald's *Austerlitz* (2001) demonstrates how narrative technique can still open up new ways of personal engagement with the past of the Second World War: hybrid constructions of the documentary and the fictional as well as a shift of focus from an objective to a subjective truth put the active reader into the foreground. This article will focus on examples from Sebald's book where the temporal gap between a place's history and its visitor is most striking. The protagonist's coping strategy is to pick up on the traces distributed in the text so that as the result of constant negotiations new meanings in the sense of a Third Space are revealed.

Seventy years after Auschwitz, we are facing a turn in Holocaust literature. The opportunity to collect further first-hand accounts of victims and survivors, often held to be the only reliable and authentic voices, is rapidly disappearing. But does this mean that memory will now become fully institutionalized through museums and history books? While these certainly fulfill an important function, contemporary literature suggests that personal memory may not yet be at its end. By looking at W. G. Sebald's *Austerlitz* (2001), this article will argue that through hybrid constructions of the documentary and the fictional, literature attempts to open up new ways of personal engagement with the past and its places, such that we seem to be witnessing a shift of focus from an objective to a subjective truth, from victims' narratives to the reader's perception of these narratives.

Scholarship on Sebald's writing widely agrees on the metaphor of archeology to describe his approach to the topic of memory: just like the text is characterized by narrative layering, memory and history, too, can be recovered by working one's way through layers of the present and the more recent past.[1] Along these lines, Laura García-Moreno demonstrates how "locations […] are marked by layers of history."[2] Silke Arnold-de Simine further argues how the historical layers stand for various atrocities, which are sometimes only partially uncovered by the protagonist, and we find similar positions to García-Moreno's and Arnold-de Simine's trains of thought, for example, in works by Ben Hutchinson or Mary G. Wilson.[3] Stephan Seitz adds how this temporal layering in one location opposes a linear concept of time.[4] He thus introduces the potential conflict of these place-time constellations. While the archeological memory project is certainly adequate to describe Sebald's and his narrator's approach to the past, James L. Cowan rightly criticizes that the question of historical authenticity is often avoided:[5] the archeological object might turn out to be a fictional one, which can nevertheless represent a metaphorical truth.[6] Expanding on Cowan's metaphorical reality, the following examples and arguments will show that it is the act of excavating itself, to stick to the archeology metaphor, which brings about a reality that is different to the object to be excavated.

This article will focus on a selection of places visited by the book's protagonist which are characterized by a gap between the past of the place and the present-day location that is visited as well as by a lack of personal transmission of memory so that a dialogue between the place and its visitor is not possible. Starting with Iver Grove, demonstrating the clash of two temporalities, and the French national library, where the temporal clash is complemented by a deviation from historical fact, a development can be traced which leads up to the example of the ghetto of Terezín, which the protagonist calls "that extra-territorial place":[7] Terezín is a place beyond the reality we live in and beyond our ability to conceptualize and as such challenges its visitor and *Austerlitz*'s reader to reconsider their relationship to the place and its past. What remains possible for the protagonist and the active reader is to pick up on the traces distributed in the text: through the examples of the Bibliothèque nationale in Paris and the ghetto of Terezín, it will be shown how in Sebald's text even the historically inaccurate can offer access points for further engagement with the topic of National Socialism. This engagement, however, can only revolve around – and not fully grasp – the traumatic core. Sebald stresses that the topic of the Holocaust can only be approached obliquely, citing Primo Levi's image of the gorgon, and uses these hybrid constructions to talk about the Holocaust not directly but in a mediated way, stretching truths through fictionalization. Meaning is thus the result of constant negotiations between different elements of the text, elements that eventually reach out to the reader. This approach goes hand in hand with an understanding of topographies as "markers of allusions and connotations that must be properly eked out," as set out by the editors of this volume in the introduction; Terezín as the extra-territorial place can be read as a trace, triggering the process of negotiation which eventually leads to the production of new meanings. This process of negotiation in the literary mode of fictionalization and deviation from fact functions to ensure the active engagement of the reader in order to replace the static past with dynamic memory.

"A curious confusion": the experience of temporal gaps

The protagonist Austerlitz visits the abandoned house of Iver Grove as a boy with his history teacher Hilary. Iver Grove is presented as a place where time seems to stand still. It thus provides an extreme instance of the past clashing with the present, and helps us to understand better the complex system of a distanced past as opposed to dynamic memory before the next examples add another level with the distortion of historical fact.

Inside the house of Iver Grove, Austerlitz comments that everything is exactly as it must have been 150 years earlier, with even the furniture in good condition.[8] This is in stark contrast to other, decayed parts of the house. A large reception hall has been filled with corn and a second hall, decorated with stucco, now provides space for hundreds of potato sacks. What once must have been a proud bourgeois estate is now a barn.

TRACING TOPOGRAPHIES

Another particularity of Iver Grove as stuck in the past concerns the billiards room. Its blinds have always been shut so that no daylight ever entered the room. In a place where light and darkness do not alternate, where time does not pass, days cannot be measured. As a result, the historian Hilary senses "a curious confusion of emotions" while Ashman, the current owner of Iver Grove, experiences this "chasm of time" as overwhelming.[9] Ashman tells the two visitors that 10 years after having sealed off the billiards room as well as the nursery during the war, he entered for the first time and almost went mad due to the unnatural nature of the experience. His reaction is that of rage and aggression, which makes him shoot at the clock tower in the backyard, at the object signifying the problem at hand: power and control. The clock tower renders visual the discrepancy of the temporal experience; while for Ashman time continued, it did not in the nursery. Ashman realizes this disconnectedness of the two time zones. Rebelling against the workings of time, Ashman in fact repeats the actions of his ancestors. By making the clock at the clock tower stop, he tries to stop the continuation of time. This is not commented upon by Hilary, Austerlitz, or the narrator, and the scene returns to the frame narrative.

Perspective, as always in Sebald's works, is crucial. One must not confuse Austerlitz's, or even the narrator's, perception with that of Ashman. The building represents Ashman's family history and its rupture. As they cannot connect to this history, Austerlitz and the narrator have withdrawn to the background of the narrative and the text is focalized through Ashman. Mediating someone else's story, they refrain from any judgment. However, Ashman cannot relate to Iver Grove's history either. His ancestors had attempted to maintain the past, but this very fixation on the past forecloses any possibility for their descendants to connect to it; this was a doomed undertaking.

A similar experience of disconnectedness is described in Terezín, which Austerlitz visits as an adult and where he believes his mother Agáta to have been interned. Here he stares at a shop window, closely examining everything that is displayed.[10] In both cases – Iver Grove and the shop window – the places are abandoned. They represent a dissociated and dead past. There is no opportunity for Ashman or Austerlitz to connect to these places, as there is no one or nothing left that could establish a link between Austerlitz's reality and the past he sees. There is nothing that he can *remember*. Amir Eshel's description of the Terezín shop window passage, which would be equally valid for Iver Grove, as the place of a "timeless kingdom of the dead" where "the time of the dead had never passed,"[11] is not entirely accurate. It is not "timeless" because the categories associated with time are still functional. And it is not that the time had never passed; it is precisely *because* it passed that we can identify it as past and not the present. Eli Friedländer also states that according to Walter Benjamin, an event only becomes historical in the aftermath: "Similarly for Benjamin, history is not merely colored by the perspective of the present; rather history achieves full reality and the historical object is actualized by the way of the involvement of the present."[12] And still this description does not entirely grasp what we can observe at Iver Grove; what is missing is the actualization. Even though time is certainly ambiguous in the sense of being subject and object at the same time,[13] we cannot speak with Walter Benjamin of dialectics at a standstill, as the time zones at Iver Grove are separate. "Standstill" is a utopian concept for Benjamin and does not allow for this separateness. In the standstill, past and present coincide:

TRACING TOPOGRAPHIES

It is not that what is past casts its light on what is present, or what is present its light on what is past; rather the image is that wherein what has been comes together in a flash with the now to form a constellation. In other words: image is dialectics at a standstill.[14]

Dialectic as a dynamic concept is not appropriate, then, to describe the encounter with a static and dead past. Benjamin's concept might perhaps be more appropriate in the context of memory, where the past is kept alive in the present. The present determines the past and this retrospection has the consequence that temporality is not necessarily causal or chronological;[15] the past can only exist through the present. As a place of the past rather than a place of memory, Iver Grove is an early example in the novel where past and present are not coexisting different temporal layers but violently clashing ones.

A parallel example to Iver Grove is Austerlitz's visit to Věra, his family's neighbor in Prague and his former nanny. Here, too, past and present collide. Through the possibility of personal memory, however, the temporal violence as experienced at Iver Grove is indeed replaced by coexistence. When Austerlitz enters her apartment building again for the first time, he too, like his teacher Hilary before him at Iver Grove, experiences an "anxious confusion."[16] Before entering, he gives detailed descriptions of the building, so that the reader can easily follow his gaze. Noticing the stones under his feet and the cool air in the entrance area, the subjective experience of something that should be familiar to him is at the core of this *déjà vu* even though he does not yet know for sure that this is indeed a memory. Austerlitz feels the "uneven paving," thinking he "had already been this way before."[17] This mirrors Marcel Proust's narrator in *Finding Time Again*: he "could not help tripping up against the unevenly laid paving-stones."[18] Trying to find balance again, "I set my foot down on a stone which was slightly lower than the one next to it" and suddenly he has a *déjà vu* in the form of a happiness that he had earlier experienced at seeing the steeples of Martinville, or during the famous madeleine episode.[19] Austerlitz's confusion, however, is not equally blissful. It is described as "blissful yet anxious," leading to physical exhaustion and building up tension in Austerlitz and the reader before the meeting with Věra.[20] Proust's narrator feels immediately how "all uneasiness about the future and all intellectual doubt were gone"[21] – a sorrowlessness that Austerlitz hopes to achieve from the following meeting with Věra, but does not actually attain. Recalling that Austerlitz suffers from several mental breakdowns, this can be traced back to the fact that he does not have an idea or ambitions for his future. Petra Strasser argues that without a notion of one's own future, the past is equally a void.[22] Time plays a crucial role here – as another element of rising tension, time is stretched for Austerlitz: "It may have been as much as an hour before I finally rang the bell of the right-hand flat on the top floor, and then half an eternity seemed to pass before I heard movement inside […]."[23] Story time here is longer than discourse time; Austerlitz's subjective experience of the same time span, however, is considerably longer. The words "may" and "seem" reveal not only a degree of uncertainty but also an awareness of its subjectivity.[24] This culminates in the actual encounter between Věra herself, who "despite her fragility […] seemed quite unchanged," and Austerlitz.[25] Similarly, neither her flat nor her furniture – which she took over from her great-aunt in 1933 – has changed, because "once she had lost me and my mother, who was almost a sister to her, she could not bear to alter anything."[26] This time the descendant, Austerlitz in this case, does not have to despair, because Věra herself is the link to connect him to the past and represents communicative memory.[27] Ashman had no one to connect to, but Věra was so close to the family that she can be considered a family member. Claire Feehily illustrates how "[t]he role of the family as the institution for memorializing is repeatedly shown to have broken down,"[28] but through the character of Věra, Sebald refuses to let personal and familial memory end with the death of biological relatives.

The Bibliothèque nationale in Paris as an example of the monumental in memory

With the building of the new Bibliothèque nationale in Paris, which Austerlitz visits regularly, the reader is presented with monumental architecture that introduces an impersonal element to the topic of memory, but that once again goes hand in hand with destruction. Seitz speaks of the annihilation of the past, which destroys all traces of the past through demolition and reconstruction,[29] an interpretation that is reflected in Austerlitz's account of his conversations with the library assistant Henri Lemoine, who says history "is buried in the most literal sense beneath the foundations of our pharaonic President's Grande Bibliothèque."[30] While on the one hand Marianne Hirsch with her concept of postmemory fears that memories of the parent generation are "so powerful, so monumental, as to constitute memories in their own rights,"[31] this view is countered by Sebald: the old memory is not monumental, the new one is rather visualized as a new building, destroying and replacing the past, which can now only be recovered if the reader engages in active research beyond the words of the book. Behind this project stands again a powerful ruler, who can be either the president of the national library or the president of France at the time.

In the case of the Bibliothèque nationale, the buried past is that of a former warehouse, where goods that previously belonged to deported Jews were collected and redistributed during the war. It has, however, recently been noticed that the location of the warehouse was not at the exact site of the library, as is claimed in Sebald's book, and that research has avoided the question of historical authenticity. In fact, the warehouse was 500 meters south of today's library; it was bombed by the Germans in 1944, rebuilt as a warehouse after the war, and eventually demolished in 1997 to enable the construction of the Université de Paris 7.[32] While the question of historical authenticity is always important to raise, the deviation from factual truth supports an underlying metaphorical truth: "the modern warehousing of information threatens to destroy the traces of the site of human suffering."[33] The railway system and the nearby Gare d'Austerlitz "mimic[ ] the network of iron supports that connect the glass panes in nineteenth-century railway stations as well as in the Paris arcades"[34] and at the same time establish a link between the Paris national library, and monumental buildings more generally, and the deportations during the Holocaust. *Pace* Hirsch, then, not only does this mean that one does not come to terms with the past, it also means that a confrontation with the past is actively avoided.

Due to "the utter unsuitability, from a librarian's perspective, of the glass towers for the storage of books,"[35] the library not only fails to fulfill its aim of social, cultural, and scientific education, but it also restricts the possibility for progress itself; "the hypermodern is really a regression." The Babylonian building takes the reader back to earlier ages "where semi-divine rulers exercised absolute domination and power."[36] Furthermore, the library's

TRACING TOPOGRAPHIES

holdings are merely a selection of what is judged valuable for a society by some; its visitors can only acquire knowledge within the limits of this canon. Sebald's critique has its foundation in the inherent absurdity of the subject matter. A comparison with the national library at its former site, rue de Richelieu, reveals that this is a fundamental problem of all libraries and archives rather than just of the Bibliothèque François Mitterrand. Austerlitz experienced the library at the Richelieu site as a place of solidarity[37] where the green desk lights have a positive and soothing effect. He has a sense of connectedness to those who are in the same reading hall and those who were there before him.[38] Sebald includes a picture here of the "Salle Labrouste," which is described by Benjamin as follows:

> These notes devoted to the Paris arcades were begun under an open sky of cloudless blue that arched above the foliage; and yet – owing to the millions of leaves that were visited by the fresh breeze of diligence, the torturous breath of the researcher, the storm of youthful zeal, and the idle wind or curiosity – they've been covered with the dust of centuries. For the painted sky of summer that looks down from the arcades in the reading room of the Bibliothèque Nationale in Paris has spread out over them its dreamy, unlit ceiling.[39]

While Austerlitz obviously enjoys working there, he also feels "a kind of continual regression expressed in the form of my own marginal remarks and glosses, which increasingly diverged into the most varied and impenetrable ramifications."[40] Trying to read and to write in order to complement his own work, he is hindered by the very same action. The protagonist's frustration peaks when he watches a film with the title "*Toute la mémoire du monde*."[41] The title discloses the overambitious project of the national library. It wants to be more than a collection of historical accounts; it wants to preserve the living and dynamic side of time as well: memory. All memories of the whole world shall be stored in this archive. As an archive it will never be able to live up to these expectations and Austerlitz's "regression" shows precisely the limitations of canonization. Eventually the fellow readers at the library and those before them seem to "have vanished from the face of the earth,"[42] mirroring the library's failure.

Austerlitz gets his information from Henri Lemoine. As an employee of the library, Lemoine's position is expected to be one of authority when it comes to its past. Initial doubts, however, become manifest in his conversation with Austerlitz about the "dissolution […] of our capacity to remember."[43] While historical facts might be subject to forgetfulness, Lemoine nevertheless has a sense of temporality. When he is on the 18th floor of the library he feels "the current of time streaming round his temples and brow."[44] Like Ashman at Iver Grove, Lemoine is at a literary and metaphorical abyss. The quest for (historical) truthfulness and an objective reality is misleading. The reality that can be found in Sebald's book lies in the mechanisms of memory. *Who* and *what* are secondary questions. Their deviation from the truth serves the purpose of the *how*. The issue of reliability is also secondary, as Austerlitz either refers to the possibility of uncertainty himself or truly believes what he has learned or knows. Echoing Theodor Adorno, according to whom the "aim of the artwork is the determination of the indeterminate,"[45] the aim here is to raise doubts about the dominance of truth as a singular perspective by showing the possible flaw inherent in all narratives. With the example of the French national library, it could be shown how the reader needs to adopt an active role in order to uncover flawed, hidden, or distorted truths. This is taken a step further in the following section on Terezín where the process of uncovering creates yet another version of truth. If

TRACING TOPOGRAPHIES

previously the reader already had to look beyond the text, she now has to look beyond her conception of reality as represented in the extra-territorial place.

Terezín: one recording, two films

Terezín is one of the central places in *Austerlitz* as this is the last known location of the protagonist's mother. This time, he does not visit the place again but consults different sources with the hope of finding reliable accounts in order to get a complete understanding of the situation and living conditions in Terezín. Temporal distortions of both the reading of H. G. Adler's book about the ghetto as well as a film document lead to a differentiated understanding that is neither the past's actual reality nor the present document's version of it but a truth found through the continued renegotiation of meaning. Austerlitz reads Adler's book during his breaks from gardening, an activity that he takes up for two years after a mental breakdown. The mental breakdown was a consequence of the discovery of his true identity; interestingly he did not suffer because of the loss of his true, biological parents but because he feels estranged to the childhood he had in Wales even though he had not liked it. In the time leading up to the breakdown, Austerlitz describes himself as "that child suddenly cast out of his familiar surroundings."[46] The traumatic component is not the Holocaust and *Kindertransport* but the fact that his true identity has been revealed to him: "reason was powerless against the sense of rejection and annihilation which I had always suppressed, and which was now breaking through the walls of its confinement."[47] A period of physical and mental suffering ends for Austerlitz in a psychiatric hospital. When he can leave the hospital again, he takes up gardening as a kind of rehab program and makes it part of his daily routine for two years. His preoccupation with family history continues incessantly. With Adler's book, Austerlitz does not try to restore family bonds but rather to establish new ones to his biological parents and more specifically his mother.

Austerlitz explains here that the lack of knowledge was responsible for his not having been able to picture more precise details:

> Reading this book, which line by line gave me an insight into matters I could never have imagined when I myself visited the fortified town, almost entirely ignorant as I was at that time, was a painstaking business because of my poor knowledge of German [...].[48]

When he visited the fortified town, he described the houses as mute and the windows as blind, almost repeating Hilary's words about Iver Grove. Knowledge and imagination are linked dialogically. *Vorstellen* refers on the one hand to real facts but on the other hand also to a non-realistic mode of imagination, to something that bypasses the actual impossibility of knowing. Furthermore, Adler's book is written in German and Austerlitz claims that his language skills were not good enough to read the book fluently. He compares the process of reading this book in German with "deciphering an Egyptian or Babylonian text in hieroglyphic or cuneiform script."[49] With the comparison to the old Egyptian language, Austerlitz picks a sign system in which signifier and signified were not arbitrary. This was initially also the case for the Babylonian cuneiform script. Thus, Sebald's comment fulfills two functions: it is another example of the inadequacy of (modern) language and the expression of the wish for visualization. Yet Austerlitz's reliability has to be called into question again with regard to his claim about his language skills, as only a couple of

155

TRACING TOPOGRAPHIES

lines later the narrator remarks: "to my surprise, Austerlitz articulated these heterogeneous German compounds unhesitatingly and without the slightest trace of an accent."[50] His reappropriation of the German language seems as wondrous as the sudden remembering of his Czech mother tongue. Eventually, Austerlitz has to acknowledge that his language and reading problems are just part of a larger problem of understanding. He has difficulties putting the individual words and phrases into a larger, meaningful context: "in its almost futuristic deformation of social life the ghetto system had something incomprehensible and unreal about it, even though Adler describes it down to the last detail in its objective actuality."[51] The "last detail" and "objective actuality" reveal again Austerlitz's wish for complete understanding and, thus, what he *hoped* to find in Adler's book rather than what Adler's book actually offers. But it also shows how the documentary approach in the form of a historical account based on facts reaches its limits. Even if it were able to describe every detail of the entire ghetto reality, it would still not suffice to stimulate and enable the *imagination* to picture it. A second reason for this unsuccessful venture into the past of Terezín through Adler's book is precisely the lengthy reading process. Austerlitz could not find meaning in the book "because it quite often took me until midnight to master a single page, and a good deal was lost in this lengthy process," which Sebald stylistically mimics in a sentence that stretches over 10 pages.[52] Reading time exceeds both story and discourse time of Adler's work. This stretching out of time ("Zerdehntheit"[53]) is accountable for lost meanings. The text lacks coherence due to the stretched reading process. Austerlitz's reading of Adler's book can therefore serve as a first example of where time is distorted for the purpose of better understanding a past reality, even though the project remains unsuccessful; Terezín seems to Austerlitz *more* distanced after reading Adler's book, and not less.

The ghetto of Terezín has become, in other words, "that extra-territorial place."[54] Through Adler, Austerlitz can neither understand nor imagine what the ghetto must have been like. It stays surreal – beyond reality ("incomprehensible and unreal"), beyond time ("futuristic deformation") and beyond space. Extra-territoriality in the first instance refers to a space free from local jurisdiction, which might be an apt description of the situation during the National Socialist period, but in this context it can literally be seen as being beyond space. This second understanding can be gained from an etymological analysis of "extra-territorial" when it is broken up into its originally Latin components "extra" and "terra." "Terra" can refer to land in the sense of those parts of the earth that are dry but also to the earth as a whole. "Extra" can be translated as outside, except or beyond. Thus, "extra-territorial" refers to something beyond the world or reality we live in. It is not identified what or where this extra-territorial place is; Sebald indeed uses it in some of his other works as well, for example for an abandoned military base in the UK. As Sebald offers a term that only describes what it is not – not part of this place or reality – it must be understood as a term that wants to express that it is also beyond our ability to conceptualize it. The link to our reality is nevertheless existent; extra-territorial does not mean alien. In the case of *Austerlitz* and the ghetto of Terezín the link of the extra-territorial place to *terra* is the fact that the ghetto has been built up and sustained by men and that it was occupied by people who appear in Austerlitz's narration in a list of professions and places of origin.[55] Though not an alien place, it has become extra-territorial for those who came after: the personal link is missing and Austerlitz's

TRACING TOPOGRAPHIES

lengthy reading process with the aim of understanding the past has the effect of estranging the reader from it even more.

Austerlitz then puts all his hopes into a Terezín propaganda film, which Adler himself could not get hold of. Austerlitz identifies a gap in Adler's account and seems to believe that if he could fill the gap in Adler's book on Terezín, he must be able to get the whole picture: "I kept thinking that if only the film could be found I might perhaps be able to see or gain some inkling of what it was really like," longing to know a reality that he here defines as "to cast my mind back to the ghetto," which, so he says, is impossible through Adler's book.[56] This goes beyond the mere understanding and knowing of (historical) fact as he wants to see the ghetto through the detainees' eyes. Even before he has a copy of the film, Austerlitz indulges in fantasies and images of the film he invents in his mind; expressions such as to "picture" or "imagine" clearly illustrate the subjective nature of his fantasies.[57] Austerlitz imagines his mother to be an actor in the role of Olympia in *Hoffmanns Erzählungen* – a story about the distortion of truth. Olympia, an automaton, seemingly comes to life because the protagonist is given a special pair of glasses or rather because he creates this reality in his mind. This reflects what happens to and through Austerlitz when he analyzes the Terezín film and eventually even thinks he is able to physically feel how his mother steps out of the film to become one with him.[58] Such fantasies, however, are doomed to be disappointed: "At first I could get none of these images into my head; they merely flickered before my eyes as the source of continual irritation or vexation [...]."[59] Is this the film's flaw, "the sluggish reaction of the human eye" or rather a symptom of an eye disease as experienced by the narrator?[60] All of these might in fact represent the inability to perceive this past with the senses and methods we conventionally use. The list of things Austerlitz sees in the film shows how he again cannot meaningfully integrate the information he is given.[61]

Austerlitz's first strategy is to watch the 14-minute-long film repeatedly, but again without success, because he could "not see Agáta anywhere, however often I ran the tape."[62] Then he has the idea of watching the film in slow motion in order to properly analyze "those pictures, which seemed to dissolve even as they appeared."[63] At first, the copy of the film in slow motion seems to bring about the hoped for change: "and indeed once the scant document was extended to four times its original length, it did reveal previously hidden objects and people, creating, by default as it were, a different sort of film altogether, which I have since watched over and over again."[64] The changes, however, all contribute to a perception of dehumanization. Movements are shown so slowly that it seems to Austerlitz as if the workers depicted were asleep: "so heavily did their eyelids sink, so slowly did their lips move as they looked wearily up at the camera. They seemed to be hovering rather than walking, as if their feet no longer quite touched the ground."[65] Not only is Austerlitz's viewing of the film slowed down but so is the workers' gaze. These slow and heavy movements remind the reader of the sick and old and culminate in the levitating moribund, who have found another grave in the sky, echoing Paul Celan's "Death Fugue." The shapes of the bodies blur until they literally disappear: "The contours of their bodies were blurred and [...] had dissolved at the edges."[66] Physical decay also affects the material of the film and is only noticed by Austerlitz in the slow version of the film with the consequence that images are annihilated and replaced by white patches with many black dots, again reminding the reader of the narrator's eye problems earlier in the book.[67] This also highlights the nature of the source

157

TRACING TOPOGRAPHIES

material as a historical document. The document "simultaneously evoke[s] the material survivals of the past, and the ephemerality of those survivals": it is subject to decay itself and does not remain a timeless eyewitness.[68]

The material's status as an objective and reliable source must be questioned, which we are beginning to see through the analysis of the different film Austerlitz gets to see, when he slows down the film's speed. The joyful dance music is turned into "a funeral march dragging along at a grotesquely sluggish pace."[69] These pieces of music, according to Austerlitz, "moved in a kind of subterranean world, through the most nightmarish depth [...] to which no human voice has ever descended."[70] While earlier Terezín was beyond reality, it is now below the world that we know, establishing a link to the underworld and realms of the dead, which are also beyond the human voice's reach and beyond our reality. Terezín thus becomes the extra-territorial cemetery or underworld. Language has become unidentifiable and is now a "menacing growl."[71] While the signifier has been rid of its actual purpose, language as a whole still fulfills its function of conveying meaning. In this extra-territorial cemetery, however, the only meaning that needed to be conveyed was that of fear and threat, that of the looming extinction of life. The menacing growl reminds Austerlitz of a visit to the *Jardin des Plantes* in Paris where he heard the roaring of lions and tigers – another case of imprisonment and distorted time as they kept roaring "hour after hour without ceasing."[72] The comparison with the lions and tigers, however, does not necessarily make their suffering more human, but rather further dehumanizes Terezín. No longer is sound in the slow version of the film intelligible as human. While the film was ostensibly shot in order to show how sorrow-free and humane life in the ghetto was, a second narrative can be found in the film itself. Slowing it down enables Austerlitz – and *a fortiori* the attentive reader of Austerlitz's account – to identify a second truth. This truth is not "more true" or in a hierarchical relationship to the other one; it is simply a different one. Therefore, it does not hold the ultimate and complete truth either, but is flawed itself. What Adorno claims about truth content is consequently equally applicable to memory: it "presents itself in art as multiplicity, not as the concept that abstractly subordinates artwork."[73]

The biggest flaw that the distorted viewing creates is the case of the woman whom Austerlitz mistakenly identifies as his mother Agáta, although he does not actually know what his mother looks like. His picture of her is based on "faint memories" and "few other clues";[74] he does not know but only fantasizes and thinks he knows. He repeatedly watches a section of four seconds. The display indicating the time of the film partly hides her face and it is in this moment that Austerlitz has the impression that time moves too fast even in this slowed down version of the film: "the hundredths of a second flash by so fast that you cannot read and capture them";[75] slowing the film down has the consequence of it being too fast. Now it is not only the film and its individual images that Austerlitz cannot grasp, it is time itself. Věra later confirms that the woman in the film is not Agáta,[76] something that Austerlitz could not have found out through the film and its technical manipulation. It is in fact through the distortion of time of this historical document that Austerlitz was able to imagine and thus create a different, and in this case wrong, truth. Tracing the topographies of Terezín through Adler's book – to get back to the overarching theme of this volume – leads Austerlitz to the film and eventually its flawed interpretation, which in turn are traces for the active reader and offer access

TRACING TOPOGRAPHIES

points for further engagement with the ghetto of Terezín in particular and National Socialism more broadly.

George Lakoff and Mark Johnson emphasize that "truth is relative to our conceptual system, which is grounded in, and constantly tested by, our experiences and those of members of our culture in our daily interactions with other people and with our physical and cultural environments," illustrating how the reader contributes to the meaning of a text not only through cognitive action, but also through her social and cultural background.[77] Ansgar Nünning even goes so far as to define the group of "postmodernist historical fictions" as "retrospective projections" where singular truth is replaced by "a series of versions which are dependent on and constructed by the observer rather than retrieved from the past."[78] *Austerlitz*, as a representative of contemporary memory texts, in other words, shows how a message equally depends on sender and recipient. In this process of sending and perceiving, the message can alter: Sebald's protagonist goes on a quest to find out about his mother's fate, and yet the reader sees a slightly different text if she notices and follows the references and traces that Sebald scatters throughout his book. Truth is therefore not defined hierarchically or classified as objective, but rather as traces in an oblique variety that need to be discovered. As in the case of the national library in Paris, then, this second narrative can only be found by the attentive reader who perceives and challenges the references in the text. Multiplicity and the reader's role in co-creating it might broaden the scope of the concept of memory, which is no longer to be defined by the simple dichotomy between personal memory and historical fact.

Notes

1. Feehily, "Counter-Monument," 181.
2. García-Moreno, "Strange Edifices, Counter-Monuments," 364.
3. Arnold-de Simine, "Remembering the Future," 161; Hutchinson, "Narrative Status," 175; Wilson, "Sheets of the Past," 66.
4. Seitz, *Geschichte als bricolage*, 127.
5. Cowan, "W.G. Sebald's *Austerlitz*," 67.
6. Ibid., 76.
7. Sebald, *Austerlitz*, translated by Anthea Bell, 331.
8. Ibid., 149.
9. Ibid., 152–3.
10. Ibid., 274.
11. Eshel, "Power of Time," 78.
12. Friedlander, *Walter Benjamin*, 64.
13. "Ambiguity is the manifest imaging of dialectic, the law of dialectics at a standstill. […] Such an image is presented by the arcades, which are house no less than street. Such an image is the prostitute – seller and sold in one." Benjamin, *The Arcades Project*, 10.
14. Benjamin, *The Arcades Project*, 463. "Nicht so ist es, daß das Vergangene sein Licht auf das Gegenwärtige oder das Gegenwärtige sein Licht auf das Vergangene wirft, sondern Bild ist dasjenige, worin das Gewesene mit dem Jetzt blitzhaft zu einer Konstellation zusammentritt. Mit anderen Worten: Bild ist die Dialektik im Stillstand." Benjamin, *Das Passagen-Werk*, 578.
15. Friedlander, *Walter Benjamin*, 65.
16. Sebald, *Austerlitz*, translated by Anthea Bell, 215. It needs to be remarked that the phrasing in the German original is "Verwirrung der Gefühle" in both contexts of Iver Grove and the visit to Věra, but has been translated slightly differently by Anthea Bell.

TRACING TOPOGRAPHIES

17. Ibid., 212.
18. Proust, *Finding Time Again*, 174.
19. Ibid., 174–5.
20. Sebald, *Austerlitz*, translated by Anthea Bell, 215.
21. Proust, *Finding Time Again*, 175.
22. Strasser, "Blick zurück," 137.
23. Sebald, *Austerlitz*, translated by Anthea Bell, 215.
24. In the German original, "mochte" and "wie es mir vorkam" highlight even more Austerlitz's subjective perception. Sebald, *Austerlitz*, 219.
25. Sebald, *Austerlitz*, translated by Anthea Bell, 215.
26. Ibid., 216.
27. Pethes, "Metalepse der Erinnerung," 29.
28. Feehily, "Counter-Monument," 185.
29. Seitz, *Geschichte als bricolage*, 130.
30. Sebald, *Austerlitz*, translated by Anthea Bell, 403. The German "überhaupt die ganze Geschichte" can either refer to the story of the former warehouse at the site or to history more generally. Sebald, *Austerlitz*, 405. The latter seems to me more likely through the words "überhaupt" and "die ganze," which clearly take "Geschichte" beyond a specific (hi) story. This ambiguity is not reflected in Bell's translation, which reads "the whole affair."
31. Hirsch, "Surviving Images," 9.
32. Cowan, "W.G. Sebald's *Austerlitz*," 67–78.
33. Ibid., 76.
34. Ryan, "Fulgurations," 238.
35. Cowan, "W.G. Sebald's *Austerlitz*," 63.
36. Ibid., 61–2.
37. Sebald, *Austerlitz*, translated by Anthea Bell, 363.
38. Ibid., 385–6.
39. Benjamin, *The Arcades Project*, 457–8.
40. Sebald, *Austerlitz*, translated by Anthea Bell, 363.
41. Ibid., 364.
42. Ibid., 386.
43. Ibid., 398.
44. Ibid., 400.
45. Adorno, *Aesthetic Theory*, 165.
46. Sebald, *Austerlitz*, translated by Anthea Bell, 322.
47. Ibid.
48. Ibid., 327–30.
49. Ibid., 330.
50. Ibid.
51. Ibid., 331.
52. Ibid., 330–31, 331–42.
53. Sebald, *Austerlitz*, 335.
54. Sebald, *Austerlitz*, translated by Anthea Bell, 331.
55. Ibid., 331–3.
56. Ibid., 342.
57. Ibid. In the German original: "malte ich mir aus" and "bildete ich mir ein." Sebald, *Austerlitz*, 346.
58. Sebald, *Austerlitz*, translated by Anthea Bell, 343.
59. Ibid., 344–5.
60. Ibid., 131, 52–3.
61. Ibid., 344.
62. Ibid., 345.
63. Ibid.

64. Ibid. A substantial section of this quotation seems to have been inserted by Bell: "[…] creating, by default as it were, a different sort of film altogether, […]" does not have an equivalent in the relevant passage in the German text. Bell thus to a certain degree takes over the role of analyzing Sebald's text.
65. Ibid., 348.
66. Ibid.
67. Ibid., 348, 47.
68. Walder, *Postcolonial Nostalgias*, 100.
69. Sebald, *Austerlitz*, translated by Anthea Bell, 348.
70. Ibid., 349.
71. Ibid.
72. Ibid., 350.
73. Adorno, *Aesthetic Theory*, 173.
74. Sebald, *Austerlitz*, translated by Anthea Bell, 351.
75. Ibid.
76. Ibid., 353.
77. Lakoff and Johnson, *Metaphors We Live By*, 193.
78. Nünning, "Historiographic Metafiction and Narratology," 369.

Disclosure statement

No potential conflict of interest was reported by the author.

References

Adorno, Theodor W. *Aesthetic Theory*. Edited by Gretel Adorno and Rolf Tiedemann. Translated by Robert Hullot-Kentor. London: Continuum, 2004.

Arnold-de Simine, Silke. "Remembering the Future: Utopian and Dystopian Aspects of Glass and Iron Architecture in Walter Benjamin, Paul Scheerbarth, and W. G. Sebald." In *Imagining the City*, edited by Christian Emden, Catherine Keen, and David R. Midgley, 149–169. Cultural History and Literary Imagination, v. 7–8. Oxford: Peter Lang, 2006.

Benjamin, Walter. *The Arcades Project*. Translated by Howard Eiland and Kevin McLaughlin. Cambridge, MA: Belknap, 1999.

Benjamin, Walter. *Das Passagen-Werk*. Vol. 5 of *Gesammelte Schriften*, edited by Rolf Tiedemann and Hermann Schweppenhäuser. Frankfurt am Main: Suhrkamp, 1982.

Cowan, James L. "W. G. Sebald's *Austerlitz* and the Great Library: History, Fiction, Memory. Part I." *Monatshefte* 102, no. 1 (2010): 51–81.

Deiters, Franz-Josef, Axel Fliethmann, Birgit Lang, and Christiane Weller, eds. *Erinnerungskrisen*. Limbus: Australisches Jahrbuch für germanistische Literatur- und Kulturwissenschaft 1. Freiburg i. Br.: Rombach, 2008.

TRACING TOPOGRAPHIES

Denham, Scott, and Mark McCulloh, eds. *W. G. Sebald: History – Memory – Trauma.* Interdisciplinary German Cultural Studies 1. Berlin: de Gruyter, 2006.

Emden, Christian, Catherine Keen, and David R. Midgley, eds. *Imagining the City.* Cultural History and Literary Imagination, v. 7–8. Oxford: Peter Lang, 2006.

Eshel, Amir. "Against the Power of Time: The Poetics of Suspension in W. G. Sebald's *Austerlitz*." *New German Critique*, no. 88 (2003): 71–96.

Feehily, Claire. "'The Surest Engagement with Memory Lies in its Perpetual Irresolution': The Work of W. G. Sebald as Counter-Monument." In *W. G. Sebald: Schreiben ex patria / Expatriate Writing*, edited by Gerhard Fischer, 177–192. Amsterdamer Beiträge zur neueren Germanistik 72. Amsterdam: Rodopi, 2009.

Fischer, Gerhard, ed. *W. G. Sebald: Schreiben ex patria / Expatriate Writing.* Amsterdamer Beiträge zur neueren Germanistik 72. Amsterdam: Rodopi, 2009.

Friedlander, Eli. *Walter Benjamin: A Philosophical Portrait.* Cambridge, MA: Harvard University Press, 2012.

García-Moreno, Laura. "Strange Edifices, Counter-Monuments: Rethinking Time and Space in W. G. Sebald's *Austerlitz*." *Critique* 54 (2013): 360–379.

Hirsch, Marianne. "Surviving Images: Holocaust Photographs and the Work of Postmemory." *The Yale Journal of Criticism* 14, no. 1 (2001): 5–37.

Hutchinson, Ben. "Narrative Status and its Implications." In *W. G. Sebald: History – Memory – Trauma*, edited by Scott Denham and Mark McCulloh, 171–182. Interdisciplinary German Cultural Studies 1. Berlin: de Gruyter, 2006.

Lakoff, George, and Mark Johnson. *Metaphors We Live By.* Chicago: University of Chicago Press, 1980.

Mauser, Wolfram, and Joachim Pfeiffer, eds. *Erinnern.* Freiburger Literaturpsychologische Gespräche 23. Würzburg: Königshausen u. Neumann, 2004.

Nünning, Ansgar. "Where Historiographic Metafiction and Narratology Meet: Towards an Applied Cultural Narratology." *Style* 38, no. 3 (2004): 352–375.

Pethes, Nicolas. "Metalepse der Erinnerung: Zur Funktion von Fiktion bei der Restitution kollektiver Gedächtniskrisen – am Beispiel von W. G. Sebalds *Austerlitz*." In *Erinnerungskrisen*, edited by Franz-Josef Deiters et al., 13–33. Limbus: Australisches Jahrbuch für germanistische Literatur- und Kulturwissenschaft 1. Freiburg i. Br.: Rombach, 2008.

Proust, Marcel. *Finding Time Again.* Translated by Ian Patterson. Vol. 6 of *In Search of Lost Time*, edited by Christopher Prendergast. London: Penguin, 2003.

Ryan, Judith R. "Fulgurations: Sebald and Surrealism." *The Germanic Review* 82, no. 3 (2007): 227–249.

Sebald, W.G. *Austerlitz.* Translated by Anthea Bell. London: Penguin, 2002.

Sebald, W.G. *Austerlitz.* Bibliothek – Süddeutsche Zeitung 93. Munich: Süddeutsche Zeitung, 2008.

Seitz, Stephan. *Geschichte als bricolage: W. G. Sebald und die Poetik des Bastelns.* Göttingen: V&R unipress, 2011.

Strasser, Petra. "Blick zurück in die Zukunft: Erinnerung unter dem Aspekt der 'Nachträglichkeit'." In *Erinnern*, edited by Wolfram Mauser and Joachim Pfeiffer, 137–149. Freiburger Literaturpsychologische Gespräche 23. Würzburg: Königshausen u. Neumann, 2004.

Walder, Dennis. *Postcolonial Nostalgias: Writing, Representation and Memory.* Routledge Research in Postcolonial Literatures 31. New York: Routledge, 2011.

Wilson, Mary G. "Sheets of the Past: Reading the Image in W. G. Sebald's *Austerlitz*." *Contemporary Literature* 54, no. 1 (2013): 49–76.

British representations of the camps

Sue Vice

University of Sheffield, UK

ABSTRACT
This article analyses how the topography of various kinds of wartime camp are represented in British narratives. It does so in order to explore whether a specifically British experience or viewpoint is evident in these texts.

The camps under discussion include the internment camps, established from 1940 onwards on British soil for the incarceration of 'enemy aliens', and their representation in wartime memoirs and novels as well as in more recent fiction. The second category of camp to be analysed is that of the necessarily fictional deportation camp, imagined in recent novels to have been established in a Britain which has either been invaded or surrendered in 1940. Lastly, the terrain of the forced-labour and extermination camp at Auschwitz has appeared in recent British fiction in a way that draws on documentary sources by means of an anglophone perspective.

The article concludes by observing that, in each case, what might have seemed to be a comparison, drawing likenesses between the real or imagined British camp and those of occupied Europe, turns out rather to be a stark literary and moral contrast.

In this article, I will discuss the variety of ways in which the topography of wartime camps has been represented in some examples of post-war British writing. The nature of Britain's wartime history has meant that such material takes particular forms. These include testimonial and fictional efforts to represent the experience of internment; counterfactual versions of detention and transit camps, situated in a Britain imagined to have surrendered or to have undergone Nazi occupation; and fictive representations of the historical extermination camps of occupied Europe. In all these cases, the topography of the camp is constructed for a range of symbolic ends, and in ways that both assert and deny the actual or possible similarities of these British camps to their Nazi counterparts. Although the representation of these spaces is based on historical sources, which give them a realist appearance, the textual role of the British camps is more akin to that of Homi Bhabha's "third space" as analyzed in the present volume's introduction, as one that "enables other positions to emerge."[1] In the texts analyzed here, the elements of two apparently incompatible experiences – the British war effort and Nazi genocide – are hybridized in fictional form to what is often an uncomfortable effect.

TRACING TOPOGRAPHIES

Internment

In the 2014 centenary commemorations of the First World War, very little mention was made of the mass internment of around 30,000 "enemy aliens" that took place then in Britain. Although the government of the time was keen to avoid such an episode in the Second World War, and initially only small numbers were interned, after the fall of France in mid-1940 the process was indeed repeated: 25,000 men and 4000 women, including Germans, Austrians, and Italians, were interned. The very word "alien" reveals a disturbingly longer history to the kind of attitude to refugees and indeed immigrants than the war context might suggest, and some historians have argued for "at least bureaucratic continuity" in relation to internment from the First World War up to the contemporary so-called wars on terror.[2] In this article, I will consider the literary topography of the experience of internment in some examples of memoirs and fiction. Some of these are by refugees themselves, published close in time to the events, others much more recently, and I will explore internment's significance in relation to Britain's wartime self-image, as well as to individuals' conceptions of national identity.

In all of these kinds of text, the spaces of internment are implicitly compared to those used for more sinister purposes in Europe, while at the same time their specifically British identity is acknowledged. The British locations of internment included such sporting and exhibition venues as Olympia, Ascot, and Brighton racecourse, as well as disused factories in Lancashire, half-built housing estates, and seaside resorts such as those on the Isle of Man. Along with the experience of deportation, in these cases to commonwealth countries such as Canada and Australia, many of these locations are represented in the texts I will discuss here. Thus the topography of these spaces encapsulates British social and imperial history, but is invoked in varied metaphorical and symbolic ways: as a means of exploring differences and similarities between Nazi Germany and Britain; as counterfactual spaces, enabling or prompting questions in the form of Bhabha's "time-lag" about what would have happened in Britain if it had been invaded or had surrendered; or as internal and subjective locations.[3] Yet such spaces can also be unexpectedly liberating, at least in retrospect, as suggested by the title of Frederick Cohn's *A Lucid Interval*, a novel focusing on the internment of the young German refugee Martin Rosen, followed by his deportation to Canada.[4] As the novel's subtitle *A Young Poet behind Barbed Wire* implies, Martin associates internment with having the opportunity and impetus to write, despite the family separation and uncertainty he underwent. The internment camp in Britain has been revisited in more recent contemporary fiction, by writers such as David Baddiel, Natasha Solomons, and Alison MacLeod. In these examples, its dual role as a historical and a symbolic space is even more apparent: in Jonathan Burt's terms, the internment camps appear both diegetically, in the plot, and semiotically, in each text's metaphorical structure.[5]

The history of the British internment camp experience has been lost to sight in accounts of the war, partly because it is seen as a minor, internal event eclipsed by the rest of the war effort, and partly because it is in fact quite the opposite: an event that is extremely significant in its own right, and since it casts doubt on the British national myth of wartime triumph, in a military but also in a moral sense. As Tony Kushner argues, Britain is the only nation concerned to have retained a positive self-image after the war, as the country that withstood Nazi Germany for so long and all alone.[6] However, the terminology of internment itself reveals its compromising nature for the British self-image, because of its uncomfortable associations with Nazi institutions: this is evident in the use of the word "camp" at all, and is made much more uncomfortable when expressed in German. For instance, a watercolor by the Expressionist artist Margarete Klopfleisch is disturbingly but accurately entitled "Internierungslager Isle of Man"; with more overt irony, the Austrian writer Robert Neumann, who fled to Britain in 1934, entitled his diary of internment in the Isle of Man "*KZ auf Englisch*," or "The English Concentration Camp."[7]

In twenty-first-century fiction about the internment experience, the camp seems to figure in just this way, as a means of mediating between the "rival memory-work" of, on the one hand, British wartime triumph, and, on the other, Britain's failure to prevent genocide in Europe.[8] This is an embattled version of Bhabha's hybridity. As Kushner argues, it is not a coincidence that historical studies of both internment policy and the Allied response to the "crisis of European Jewry in the Nazi era" started to appear at the same time, in the 1980s.[9] In both Alison MacLeod's novel *Unexploded*, from 2013, and David Baddiel's *The Secret Purposes* of 2004, the internment camp has a clear role: it distinguishes British from German behavior, yet also makes us reconsider the myth of British moral superiority, through the plot device of a romance. In each case this is an unconsummated, perhaps transitional, love affair between a male German internee and a British woman, in a symbolic pattern: the identifiably Jewish man is somehow acceptable to a woman who is equally definitively non-Jewish, as if conveying that British acceptance will take place on its own terms. June Murray, the woman who falls in love with the rabbi's son Isaac Fabian in *The Secret Purposes*, is, even more symbolically, a translator at the Ministry of Information, a role which embodies access to fluent Britishness.

Both *Unexploded* and *The Secret Purposes* thus bring out those features of wartime internment which had previously been lost to sight: its existence at all, and its significance for the internees as well as for Britain's self-conception, arising from the novels' belated and fictional status. As David Cesarani argues, the wartime context of internment tended to produce accounts by eyewitnesses that downplayed suffering in the place of emphasizing fortitude and humor.[10] Mark Lynton's *Accidental Journey* (1998), his refugee memoir of life in Huyton camp near Liverpool, followed by deportation to Canada, describes what he calls "the best moments" of internment, placing the experience of being released among them with deliberately humorous irony.[11] The artist and novelist Fred Uhlman, best known for his 1971 novel *Reunion*, wrote in his diary of the time that internment might appear to be a "non-event" in contrast to the brutal murder of millions, but he still wants to relate his story because, "however small, it is part of the English history of the war, [and] for me and my friends it was not a trivial affair but a *traumatic* experience," as well as an "injustice and waste of energies."[12] Uhlman drew on this diary in writing his 1960 memoir, *The Making of an Englishman*, but, as is also the case with Robert Neumann's writing about internment, irony is emphasized in the memoir over horror and the "terrible, ghastly, sickening depression" recorded in Uhlman's diary.[13] Yet even irony can be revelatory. When he is due to be taken away for internment, Uhlman recalls that a British neighbor congratulated him: "You can play tennis all day and you won't need to worry about the war."[14] In his memoir, Uhlman substitutes humor for political argument: he describes sharing a room on the Isle of Man with a communist internee, but rather than detail any ideological conflict, he describes being irritated only by the way the other man brushed his teeth. Uhlman's noting the accomplishments of those interned, including sea-captains working for Britain who had never been naturalized, an architect who had helped design the penguin house at London Zoo, the author of a chess column for the *New Statesman*, and an athlete who had represented Britain at the Olympics, not only supports his positive contention that the Isle of Man became "one of Europe's best universities," but that all his fellow internees were already in effect "Englishmen."

Sacrificing anger for irony or humor in Uhlman's and Neumann's memoirs is likely to have been due to their authors' wish not to seem "ungrateful" to a country that had offered them asylum, as well as uncertainty about their eventual fate. This is coupled with the brief nature of the internment for most individuals, giving it a different cast with hindsight.[15] Verdicts such as that of the political émigré Erna Nelki, who called internment "not only cruel but wrong," and that of Walter Igersheimer, who was sent to Canada via Huyton, that he and his fellow internees felt "betrayed by the very country we wanted to belong to and fight for," are relatively rare.[16] Neither Nelki's nor Igersheimer's account shows evidence of hindsight's softening effects since both were written before the war's end. Indeed, the representation of the internment camp focuses largely on the danger of being an outsider, both nationally and spatially. This fear is evident in such varied phenomena as Mr Rosenblum's comic efforts to assimilate in Natasha Solomons' novel *Mr Rosenblum's List*, subtitled *Friendly Guidance for the Aspiring Englishman*; the anxiety about performativity expressed in the title of such refugee memoirs as Charles Hannam's *Almost an Englishman*, as well as that in Uhlman's *The Making of an Englishman*; and the leaflet entitled "Helpful Information and Guidance for Every Refugee," issued by the "German Jewish Aid Committee, London 1939," which advocated Anglicization so insistently that it has taken on the status of a literary device in its own right.[17]

Natasha Solomons' *Mr Rosenblum's List* also emphasizes the comic interlude over suffering or tragedy, despite its appearing as recently as 2010. Such humor and positivity apply not only to internment in this novel, but also to British antisemitism and refugees' wish to become "Englishmen" or Englishwomen. As Rosenblum's wife puts it, he is a "deliberate assimilator."[18] Rosenblum's internment is very brief, and in the novel its description lasts for a mere four pages; while he is held in a police station, Rosenblum wonders how he has been labeled, at a tribunal, which is not depicted, a category B alien, that is, of possible security risk. As the narrator puts it, "With his knowledge of marmalade and Royal Family History going back to Ethelred the Unready, it scarcely seemed possible that he could be anything other than a 'class C' (loyalty to the British cause not in question)."[19] By what is almost a fairytale plot device, Rosenblum is rescued by a fellow refugee, who has bought his categorization as a category C refugee, and thus his liberty, in exchange for handing over Rosenblum's carpet business to the British war effort. The space of the internment camp is not represented in this text. The reason for this comic approach is generic, since Solomons' novel is a comedy of refugee manners rather than an exploration of its difficulties or ambivalences. It is for such generic reasons that the historical record, which makes clear that refugees in all three categories were interned, has been elided. Yet Mr Rosenblum's equating "marmalade and the Royal family" with Britishness is not simply comic, but an acknowledgment of the linked difficulties of categorizing refugees and of defining Britishness, as is apparent in the titles of the earlier memoirs.

Like Frederick Cohn's *A Lucid Interval*, Ruth Borchard's *We Are Strangers Here*, planned as part of a longer work that was never completed, is a novel based on the author's experience of internment, although one written in the immediate wake of that experience in 1942. The novel's focus is on the subjectivity of Anna Silver, a young refugee from Berlin who is interned in Holloway prison before being sent to the Isle of Man. Anna is imprisoned as a German and the wife of a Jewish refugee but one who is not Jewish herself, by contrast to Borchard's own case, in an alteration necessitated by the plot. The other internees suspect Anna of being a Nazi sympathizer, since she is not Jewish, giving a political substratum to her fears of rejection and wish for a community to replace the loss of marital intimacy.[20] The novel opens surprisingly and directly with Anna's emotional concerns, in a way that emphasizes from the outset the dual identity of imprisonment as a record of events and as the projection of an inner state: "Anna knew that her husband was about to become unfaithful to her. Indeed, she could even understand why it had to happen."[21] Her separation from her husband Bert itself has a symbolically positive aspect, and makes Anna's experience in Holloway prison, despite the uncertainty and privation, resemble being at university or at boarding school, as she puts it. Before their internment, Bert refers to the possible "ruin" of their new life in Britain, but Anna is relieved to discover that her husband refers to internment, not infidelity: "Nothing more than that?"[22] as she asks in relief. Conversely, internment gives the opportunity for thwarting the affair, as Anna thinks of Edith, the young woman to whom Bert is attracted: "Where was she now? Anna certainly had no objection to her being put behind barbed wire."[23] The difference between Britain and Germany in Borchard's novel is summed up in such personal terms: while Anna's baby son died during his parents' flight from Germany, in Britain her little daughter is returned to her on the Isle of Man.

Like Borchard's *We Are Strangers Here*, Alison MacLeod's novel *Unexploded*, which was longlisted for the Booker Prize in 2013, views the war and internment in relation to the effect of extreme events on personal relationships, as the title suggests: danger comes from the leftovers of conflict in every sense. *Unexploded* opens in Brighton in May 1940, exactly the moment when the fall of France led to the fears of invasion that prompted mass internment. Philip Beaumont, the eight-year-old son of the protagonists, Geoffrey and Evelyn, believes that Hitler will use the Brighton Pavilion as his British headquarters. This is a detail that is designed to shock, consisting of the imagining of quintessentially British institutions not just juxtaposed with, but overrun and inhabited by, the Nazis. Such a trope is a threat which is not fully realized in MacLeod's novel: although Philip's notion arises from contemporary rumors based on Lord Haw-Haw's broadcasts, such a notion remains imaginary. By contrast, C. J. Sansom's novel *Dominion* (2012) is set in a Britain that is a satellite of Nazi Germany, 12 years after its surrender, again in 1940, in which the domestic implications of such a counterfactual occurrence are fully fleshed out. Here we learn that Senate House in London is used as the German embassy, bedecked with a giant swastika flag, its basement the Gestapo interrogation center; the television cook Fanny Cradock demonstrates how to cook sauerkraut; and the Isle of Wight is a transit camp for Jews en route to being deported to the east. Similarly, in Len Deighton's much earlier novel *SS-GB* (1978), a fictional British concentration camp is situated at Wenlock Edge in Shropshire. Like the Isle of Wight, this particular location is cleverly chosen, as an already over-determined signifier of Britishness. Wenlock Edge features in a section of A. E. Housman's poem *A Shropshire Lad*, a composition by Vaughan Williams, and several drawings by L. S. Lowry; as a limestone escarpment, it is even made of the same stuff as Dover's white cliffs. Yet readers might wonder whether such fictional "third space" devices as imagining what everyday British life would look like under

TRACING TOPOGRAPHIES

Nazi rule, as we see in *Unexploded*, or situating fictional British camps in the Isle of Wight and Wenlock, as in *Dominion* and *SS-GB*, strike a cautionary note, or one that is full of bravado: does the apparently violent incongruity suggest that this is what might really have happened, or show it to have always been impossible?

In *Unexploded*, Evelyn thinks in just such a way about the threat of invasion, as a kind of Nazi uncanny in which the familiar becomes malign:

> Everyone said it was unimaginable, but she could imagine it: flint-eyed soldiers lining the London Road; officers, impeccable in their dress uniforms, in the boxes at the Theatre Royal … Jews – had she ever known a Jew? – writers, artists and intellectuals disappearing in the night; public executions at the Town Hall.[24]

There is a significant slippage here between the domestic details of what Nazi occupation might look like, and those of a murderous racial policy if it were introduced into Britain, since the possibility of genocide in Britain is for the most part not fully imagined in any of these texts. Yet Evelyn's rhetorical question to herself, "had she ever known a Jew?" turns out to merit an ironically affirmative answer. Not only does she learn that she first met her husband as the result of an antisemitic act on his part, but she falls in love with Otto Gottlieb, a German Jewish internee in the camp at Brighton racecourse. This geography has a psychic meaning, since it is Evelyn's husband Geoffrey, in peacetime a bank manager, who is the camp "superintendent." Evelyn's revulsion at her husband's political behavior, and his "slavish" obedience to orders, results in her affection going elsewhere, toward the foreign "other," the artist Gottlieb. It is hard to prize apart the elements of the metaphor here, and to decide whether war is a figure for romance or vice versa. As MacLeod has said in an interview, suggesting that each conveys the other, "I am really interested in writing the intimate, but I am also interested politically. I think wars do get into the cracks and crannies of our home."[25] Indeed, it seems that Geoffrey, who turns out to be less estimable and dependable than his wife had believed, is a figure for Britain itself, and the possibility of national disappointment and betrayal: as Evelyn thinks, "Geoffrey was a man respected for his sense of fair play, for his decency and good sense, yet he harbored an irrational contempt for a whole race of people."[26]

However, there is another reason why Evelyn falls for Otto Gottlieb, which arises from MacLeod's debt to Virginia Woolf. Woolf is herself enlisted into the geographical symbolism of *Unexploded*, revealing the lack of a clear difference between what is and what is not British. Woolf appears in the novel as both character and stylistic forebear. Hearing Lord Haw-Haw's voice on the radio interrupts Evelyn's reading of Woolf's novel *The Waves*, prompting her to think of the danger of invasion in terms of "Mrs. Woolf who had a Jewish husband; a Jewish husband in the Sussex countryside, just beyond Brighton. Were they at this moment listening too?"[27] It seems that this "Jewish husband" is what Evelyn herself wishes for, even including the act of Woolf's suicide, which she views as motivated by Woolf's horror of the Nazis' arrival in Britain. It is as if the implied author herself also wishes for a Woolfian influence, not only in relation to the novel's stylistic interest in the subjective states of memory and internal monologue, but also its plot. In *Unexploded*, like Woolf's *Mrs. Dalloway* of 1925, a woman who is distant from her husband comes into contact with a man who has been traumatized by war: in *Mrs. Dalloway*, this is the shell-shocked Septimus Smith, who dies at the novel's end, instead of her, it is implied. Anthony Cummins' review of *Unexploded*, commenting on Otto Gottlieb's similar fate, could equally have been written about *Mrs. Dalloway*. He claims that there is "something unpalatable about how [the novel] puts an exotic stranger on the rack just so the heroine can feel more alive."[28] The life of the female protagonist in each case is saved at the cost of that of a male outsider.

In David Baddiel's 2004 novel *The Secret Purposes*, a different version of the same trope of juxtaposing British with Nazi elements is apparent. The novel, based on the history of Baddiel's maternal grandparents,[29] focuses on the German refugee Isaac Fabian and his internment on the Isle of Man. The novel opens with a map of Konigsberg in 1934, all of its seven bridges individually named; as the reader learns, the Nuremberg laws in that city meant that Jews could not cross any of them. The map offers both a historical foundation for the novel, which Baddiel describes in the postscript as a "collage of fact and fiction,"[30] and also a contrast from its outset between Nazi tyranny and British tolerance, since the novel's second section opens with a map of Cambridge, all the bridges of which are open to Isaac. Yet the contrast is not so simple, in a novel that Eva Figes described in a review as "an antidote to British smugness."[31] Britain is sufficiently similar to Germany that, as Isaac thinks to himself, from the perspective of his job in Cambridge and in a perception that conceals trepidation within apparent nostalgia, "Sometimes, looking up at the spires of the chapel from the windows in the college kitchens, Isaac could convince himself he was still in Konigsberg."[32]

The attitude of *The Secret Purposes* to Britishness and the notion of Britain as a safe haven for Jewish refugees is thus initially ambivalent. During the war, an émigré friend of Isaac's wife Lulu warns her against seeming "too English"[33] lest she is considered a spy, and observes that she has heard "'more thoughtless anti-Jew comments'" in Britain than she ever did in Germany, leading her to conclude that "'[t]he only difference is that, here, they come wrapped in a gentlemanly distaste for doing anything about it'."[34] By contrast, it seems to be uncomplicated praise that Isaac, when he has become a citizen, ruminates fondly on the "sweet stability"[35] of life in Britain. Both utterances allude to a notion of British inaction rather than ethical superiority.

In yet another twist, however, even despite the opening of the novel's third section with a map of the Isle of Man internment camps, and a description of Isaac's difficult experience there, *The Secret Purposes* does conclude by emphasizing the difference rather than the similarity between wartime Britain and Nazi Germany. This is accomplished by means of a series of images from refugee life in wartime Britain, behind which is visible a shadow version of what existence might have been like for these refugees in Nazi-occupied Europe. Isaac's inamorata June Murray sees husbands and wives reunited from their separate internment camps on the Isle of Man:

> She watched, as husband found wife, and wife found husband; she felt the squeeze of each embrace, and the amazement of each kiss; she saw the unbelieving, joyous recognition, the mutual, infinite smiling, and the outstretched arms.[36]

Being brought together in this way is the opposite of the deathly separation of men and women in the Nazis' camps, which can only resemble being reunited in the backwards world of a novel like Martin Amis's *Time's Arrow*:

> As matchmakers, we didn't know the meaning of the word *failure*; on the ramp, stunning successes were as cheap as spit. When the families coalesced, how their hands and eyes would plead for one another, under our indulgent gaze.[37]

When he takes part in a failed attempt to assassinate a Nazi in the camp, Isaac "forgot which country he was in, and thought they were going to be shot, there and then,"[38] while later in the novel, June recognizes Isaac "immediately" due to the fact that he is wearing striped clothing, but in its British setting this is on account of a pajama top and not a camp uniform.[39]

Deportation

In Sansom's counterfactual novel *Dominion*, the process of discrimination against and preparation for the deportation from Britain of the "last free Jews" of Europe in 1952 threatens to take place as we read, and we learn that these individuals are to be deported to the Isle of Wight and thence to the East. However, this process is represented in relation to the small social details of British life rather than as a fully-fledged enactment. Lyons Corner Houses have been renamed British Corner Houses, so that any trace of their Jewish ownership is expunged; and, following the census of 1951 in which Jewish parents and grandparents had to be declared, Jews now have to wear "a little Star of David lapel badge ... very British and discreet."[40] The one Jewish character who briefly appears in the novel claims that he never thought they would really be "shipped off," holding up to scrutiny the very same phrase that Evelyn questioned in relation to her husband: it would run counter to "'British fair play'."[41]

Although in the world of *Dominion* the government has already expelled foreign-born Jews and is about to deport the British ones, in a version of what took place under the French Vichy regime, their fate appears as a signifier for the cost of British surrender rather than as an effort to consider the Holocaust itself. It is a way of revealing the responses of the protagonists to the new world order, in particular that of the resistance member David Fitzgerald and his wife Sarah. David is, according to the Nuremberg Laws terminology which has been introduced into Britain, "half Jewish," and thus we as readers fear for his "secret" being found out. By this means, suspense is created without commitment to constructing a self-identifying Jewish character. The closest the novel comes to imagining the detail of genocidal policy in Britain occurs when a round-up takes place in London's Tottenham Court Road. David's wife Sarah has a political epiphany when her friend Mrs Templeman tries to protest at this public round-up, and is killed. But Sarah's realization is one concerned with the dangers of resistance and her friend's death, not the deportation itself. The Jews are thus a supporting cast in every sense.

There is potential in Sansom's novel for a kind of moral defamiliarization, looking forwards as well as backwards, including reference to the danger represented by Britain's real-life UKIP (United Kingdom Independence Party), and Sansom devotes a large part of his afterword to the dangers of nationalist politics as represented by the SNP (Scottish National Party). In the novel, no-one protests much at the round-ups, in part because Britain seems to be a nation of bystanders, but also because the plot does not require it. Indeed, the fate of the Jews is simply a distraction from the main narrative, as we see for instance when the Nazi protagonist Gunther wants to find a locksmith to get into a suspect's house, and is told they are all busy securing the property of deported Jews from looters. The Jews' fate constitutes simply a pretext for delay in the novel's main plot, which is not concerned with genocide. At another moment, Sarah is taken to the Senate House basement to be questioned about her husband's activities in the resistance, and we learn that the SS drag past her in the opposite direction "an elderly man in a rumpled suit with a yellow badge."[42] Again, this is a symbolic movement of a Jewish character away from the main action, encapsulating the concerns of the novel *Dominion* as a whole. Sarah later realizes that "she had hardly thought about the Jews over the last few days,"[43] and the same is true of the novel.

Sansom's novel is thus a thriller with Nazi occupation simply as a backdrop, and its satirical concern is with British political and imperial history and not that of the Holocaust. Surrender after the 1939–40 war, as it is called, has entailed Britain's holding onto its imperial possessions, and British history of this kind is invoked in *Dominion* in reference to the shooting of strikers, unemployed settlers being sent to Kenya and displacing the local people, the denial of independence to India, and New Zealand taking a dim view of its antisemitic policy. Even David Fitzgerald's "half-Jewish" identity takes on a symbolic aspect since it is thought by other characters that with his "dark, curly hair" he is "Irish looking."[44] Just as the Nazis in the novel look to South African apartheid for some hints at how to deal with the Russian population, so the history of Irish emigration to the mainland is invoked in relation to the Jews: a soldier commands the Jews being marched away down Tottenham Court Road to sing, "It's a Long Way to Tipperary." The song's expression of homesickness on the part of soldiers in the First World War makes its appearance here rebound ironically against any positive construction of Britishness. Yet *Dominion* has a rather cursorily described happy ending, and Churchill's eventual return to Downing Street means that the Jews in the Isle of Wight camp are sent no further, but allowed to go home and their possessions are restored to them. Thus, although *Dominion* insists that British exceptionalism and immunity to fascism is a myth, it remains agnostic about a British propensity for genocide.

Auschwitz

Like *Time's Arrow*, Martin Amis's 1990 novel about a Nazi doctor, his *The Zone of Interest* of 2014 aims to match form to content. In this way, the construction of the camp is a self-consciously literary one, and the novel's status as a specifically British representation arises from the anachronistic effects this generates, including the Anglophone narrative voice. *The Zone of Interest*'s formal innovation consists of dividing the narrative between three characters: that of Auschwitz Commandant Paul Doll; the "desk perpetrator" Golo Thomsen, who is in charge of developing the Buna rubber substitute factory; and a camp prisoner, Szmul Zachariasz, a Sonderkommando member who buries his writings "in a thermos," as did his real-life original, Zalman Gradowski, and "under a gooseberry bush,"[45] as if this material points to a new kind of birth. It is because of Doll, who is named perhaps in an echo of the prisoners' nickname for the deputy commandant of Treblinka, Kurt Franz,[46] that *The Zone of Interest* has been described as an office comedy about middle management, in which the office is Auschwitz.[47] In the novel, the camp functionaries are all concerned with the petty details of hierarchy and self-advancement, and with the form of things rather than their substance. For instance, using the phrases of corporate discourse, Doll takes people "off the payroll," and says of extermination that "somebody's got to do it"; he tells Szmul to "put a date in his diary"; describes arrivals at the camp as "detraining"; and refers to himself as "your humble servant." It is as if deploying such phrases might lead

TRACING TOPOGRAPHIES

directly to the Nazi euphemisms that Doll also relies upon, including "pieces" for bodies, "Little Brown Bower" for the gas chambers, "Behandlung" for a gassing. We might be reminded of Hannah Arendt's observation about Adolf Eichmann, that "his cliché-ridden language produced on the stand [at his trial], as it had evidently done in his official life, a kind of macabre comedy."[48] In Amis's novel, Doll complains that he has to undertake menial tasks:

> Of course, muggins here *did* have to go down to Katowicz to fetch more petrol refuse. I motored there (with 2 guards) in my 8-cylinder diesel Steyr 600, heading a convoy of trucks.[49]

In this particular combination of self-pity with boastfulness and entirely missing the point of his actions, Doll resembles his much less entertaining original, Rudolf Hoess, who similarly notes in his autobiography:

> Yes, I even had to visit the farms in order to collect straw. Since I could expect no help of any kind from the Inspectorate, I had to make do as best I could on my own. I had to "organize" the trucks and lorries I needed, and the fuel for them. I had to drive as far as Zakopane and Rabka ... .[50]

Indeed, this apparent debt on Amis's part to Hoess's autobiography might make us view his novel as an effort to reproduce in comic form the real-life Nazi's combination of petty discontent with immersion in work-related detail at the expense of any moral awareness. About the Battle of Stalingrad, a disaster of which he seems unaware, Doll berates a junior, as if he is talking about embarrassing sales figures of which he has not been told:

> I lost no time in bearding [young Prufer], saying:
> "Did you *know* they were encircled?"
> "Yes, they've been encircled for well over a month."
> "Why didn't you tell me? I looked a real ... "[51]

When the fictional Doll criticizes the Sonderkommando members for "going about their ghastly tasks with the dumbest indifference,"[52] it is ludicrously transparent hypocrisy, but when the historical Hoess "is quick to describe the brutality and indifference" of the Jews who were "assigned to get rid of the corpses," it constitutes the "most repugnant pages" of his autobiography, as Primo Levi puts it in his introduction from 1985.[53] It is hard to know how to approach Amis's grotesque, carnivalesque, and of course fictional version of the historical horror, and it might seem that representing the commandant of Auschwitz as a middle manager is to present a functionalist comedy, in which the structure holds responsibility for the escalation of genocide. Perhaps Rebecca Abrams is right to suggest that the comedy itself is the greatest ethical challenge to the reader, since it makes us respond as if pleasurably to real and genocidal enormity.[54] Comedy in *The Zone of Interest* thus has the same effect as reverse narrative in *Time's Arrow*, in making us dwell on the details of Nazi policy by slowing down our conception of them, in a way the Russian Formalists would argue that only literature can do. In demonstration of this idea that the reality itself has the effrontery of comedy, Doll's wife Hannah, like several female characters in these novels, mounts a satirical rebellion against Nazi policy during a dinner party conversation listing the Jews' evil-doing. Hannah uses antisemitic discourse to mount an implicit attack on a Nazism which she judges has failed to fulfill its promises:

> "Well, it's a basic point," she said. "There's no avoiding it. I mean the talent for deception. And the avarice. A child could see it ... They promise you the earth, all smiles, they lead you down the garden path. And then they strip you of everything you have."[55]

Even the assembled SS officers notice that "the words seemed to equivocate" since the referent of "they" is not identified: as Hoess's case shows, it is the Nazis who commit the very crimes for which they demonize others.

Amis's commandant Paul Doll is not only based on Hoess's autobiography, but also has a different kind of literary forebear, that of Paul Celan's poem "Deathfugue." Amis seems to have been influenced specifically by John Felstiner's experimental translation of the poem, in which German phrases progressively creep back into the English.[56] Paul Doll anachronistically quotes Celan when he describes a former girlfriend as "the golden-haired Marguerite,"[57] while the Sonderkommando Szmul's wife is called Shulamith, invoked in "Deathfugue" as representations of, respectively, German and Jewish history. Szmul denies that the Germans are the Devil, but claims that they are Death. This discourse can only remind us of Celan's poem as rendered by Felstiner:

> Black milk of daybreak we drink you at night
> we drink you at midday and morning we drink you at evening
> we drink and we drink
> a man lives in the house your goldenes Haar Marguerite
> your aschenes Haar Shulamith he plays with his vipers
> He shouts play death more sweetly Death is a master from Deutschland ...
> he plays with his vipers and daydreams

Doll's wife Hannah again voices disgust at her husband using just these terms:

> "Do you know who you are?" she whispered ... "You're a fucking chump of a Brownshirt who, tired of thinking dirty thoughts and playing with his Viper, falls asleep in his bunk and has the worst of all possible dreams ... Then you wake up and you find it's all true."[58]

Hannah goes straight for a buried meaning in Celan's poem: alongside the Biblical associations of the viper, Felstiner describes his choice of words to reproduce the "treble alliteration" in the original German phrase. He translates "der spielt mit den Schlangen der schreibt" as "he plays with his vipers he writes," since this "ties vipers to writes, uncovering something deadly in the act of writing,"[59] not to mention the echo of the Yiddish-language body part "schlong" in "Schlangen," to which both Hannah and Amis also make implicit reference.

But, yet again, we might ask to what end *The Zone of Interest* cites Celan, and whether it is effective to have macabre comedy alongside, and even to incorporate, witness poetry. Amis's novel also adopts not Celan's, who wrote in German, but Felstiner's poetic practice of making us understand the language of the original poem and its cultural background through its translation into English. Although Szmul seems to quote "Deathfugue" in his observation that immediately after the invasion of Poland, he was put onto a transport, "to Deutschland supposedly,"[60] elsewhere the eruption of German seems, almost inevitably, to have a comic function. Paul Doll wants to locate Szmul's wife in the Lodz Ghetto, and the reader learns that, "[t]o locate a Jew in a Polish ghetto one casually turns to the Uberwachungsstelle zur Bekampfung des Schleichhandels und der Preiswucherei im Judischen Wohnbezirk."[61] The effect of such satire, in its reliance on the excessive titling of bureaucracy, simply domesticates the idea of mass murder and that its object is corporate discourse, or even German as a national language, and not the Nazis. Furthermore, this is clearly not an accurate citation. Although Doll's phrasing approximates to the name of a Nazi institution – that is, the Control Office to Combat Black-Marketeering and Profiteering in the Jewish Residential District – in its novelistic setting it is missing all its umlauts and should be instead: *Überwachungsstelle zur Bekämpfung des Schleichhandels und der Preiswucherei im jüdischen Wohnbezirk.* The umlauts are strategically omitted. Their absence makes the novel's German quotations into what Mikhail Bakhtin calls the artistic image of a language and not the real thing,[62] in another example of the novel's stylization of both literary and historical detail into a contemporary and Anglophone form.

Conclusion

There is no canon of British Holocaust literature to match the extent or renown of that in Europe or North America. This is in part due to Britain's location "on the edge of history," in Natasha Solomons' phrase, in relation to the fate of the Jews in the Second World War, as well as the existence of an otherwise triumphalist national wartime narrative.[63] This position is shown by the prominence in British literary history, rather, of refugee and Kindertransport narratives, such as, respectively, Judith Kerr's 1971 novel *When Hitler Stole Pink Rabbit* and Karen Gershon's 1966 memorial compilation *We Came as Children*, in place of memoirs or novels about the camp experience. Exceptions to this tendency include Anita Lasker-Wallfisch's 1996 memoir *Inherit the Truth*, about her imprisonment in Auschwitz and Bergen-Belsen, as well as some examples of fiction which, although set in the camp world, deploy it for other symbolic or ontological concerns. Novels of this kind include John Boyne's *The Boy in the Striped Pyjamas* of 2006 and John Donoghue's *The Death's Head Chess Club* of 2015. In Howard Jacobson's 2006 *Kalooki Nights*, tragedy arises from British-Jewish over-identification with the victims of Nazi antisemitism, despite living at a great distance from the European topography of genocide. As Jacobson's narrator, the Mancunian Max Glickman, is reminded by his mother, "'The only camp you ever went to was Butlins'."[64] The existence of particular representations of British internment and European extermination camps, some of which I have analyzed here, makes clear the kind of material that has not yet been portrayed, including British internment camps on Cyprus, slave labor on Alderney, or, counterfactually, the existence of anything other than a transit camp located on British soil, including an extermination camp or site of mass shooting.[65] As we might expect, even when internment or a counterfactual textworld implicitly brings British into comparison with Nazi camps, the object of fear remains the Germans, and the resentment against Britain arises from the "muddle and confusion," rather than the "system," in Anna Silver's words, implicit in such acts as mass internment.[66] These testimonial or fictional revisitations of Britain's wartime record as it stands, or as it might have been, thus appear to offer the "third space" of questioning British moral and historical superiority, yet conclude by affirming it even in the act of such scrutiny.

TRACING TOPOGRAPHIES

Notes

1. Bhabha, quoted in the introduction to the present volume, 141.
2. Cesarani and Kushner, "Introduction," 1.
3. Bhabha, quoted in the introduction, 147. See Charmian Brinson, on the extreme psychological toll of internment in relation to such writers as Livia Laurent and Ruth Michaelis-Jena, in her "Autobiography in Exile," 14.
4. Cohn, *A Lucid Interval.*
5. Burt, *Animals in Film*, 11.
6. Cesarani and Kushner, "Introduction," 10.
7. Brinson, "'In the Exile of Internment'," 74; Kühn, *Gertrud Kolmar*, 274.
8. Kushner, "Loose Connections?" 53.
9. Cesarani and Kushner, "Introduction," 8. See also Pistol, "Enemy Alien and Refugee," 42.
10. Cesarani and Kushner, "Introduction," 4.
11. Lynton, *Accidental Journey*, 80.
12. Brinson, "'In the Exile of Internment'," 79; Uhlman, *The Making of an Englishman*, 227.
13. Uhlman, quoted in Brinson, "'In the Exile of Internment'," 83.
14. Uhlman, *The Making of an Englishman*, 224.
15. Cesarani and Kushner, "Introduction," 4–5.
16. Nelki, quoted in Brinson, "'In the Exile of Internment'," 82; Igersheimer, *Blatant Injustice*, xxix.
17. On the literary adoption of the "Helpful Information" leaflet, see Vice, "British-Jewish Holocaust Fiction."
18. Solomons, *Mr Rosenblum's List*, 7.
19. Ibid., 10.
20. Mark Lynton notes that had any of his non-Jewish fellow internees confessed to Nazi sympathies, it would have been "tantamount to a death-wish." *Accidental Journey*, 83.
21. Borchard, *We Are Strangers Here*, 19.
22. Ibid., 30.
23. Ibid., 35.
24. MacLeod, *Unexploded*, 20.
25. MacLeod, interview with *Sussex Life*.
26. MacLeod, *Unexploded*, 178.
27. Ibid., 81.
28. Cummins, "Review."
29. See the BBC's "Who Do You Think You Are?" episode devoted to Baddiel, 23 November 2004.
30. Baddiel, *The Secret Purposes*, 405.
31. Figes, "Behind Barbed Wire."
32. Baddiel, *The Secret Purposes*, 29.
33. Ibid., 98.
34. Ibid., 103.
35. Ibid., 368.
36. Ibid., 294.
37. Amis, *Time's Arrow*, 132.
38. Baddiel, *The Secret Purposes*, 324.
39. Ibid., 334.
40. Sansom, *Dominion*, 16.
41. Ibid., 245.
42. Ibid., 444.
43. Ibid., 580
44. Ibid., 357.
45. Amis, *The Zone of Interest*, 270.

46. Arad, *Belzec, Sobibor, Treblinka*, 98. However, by contrast with the baby-faced Franz, the fictional Paul Doll's visage is said to resemble a "huge and unwashed strawberry" (Amis, *The Zone of Interest*, 154).
47. See Guest, "Review."
48. Arendt, *The Life of Mind*, 4.
49. Amis, *The Zone of Interest*, 111.
50. Hoess, *Commandant of Auschwitz*, 129.
51. Amis, *The Zone of Interest*, 88.
52. Ibid., 67.
53. Levi, Introduction to Hoess, 24.
54. Abrams, "Review."
55. Amis, *The Zone of Interest*, 51.
56. Felstiner, *Paul Celan*, 36.
57. Amis, *The Zone of Interest*, 125.
58. Ibid., 228.
59. Felstiner, *Paul Celan*, 36.
60. Amis, *The Zone of Interest*, 204.
61. Ibid., 179.
62. Bakhtin, "Discourse in the Novel," 359.
63. Solomons, Interview.
64. Jacobson, *Kalooki Nights*, 472.
65. On Cyprus, see David Hughes' novel *My Son the Enemy*; Caroline and Kevin Sturdy-Colls cite some first-person accounts of the Alderney camp in their "Reconstructing a Painful Past."
66. Borchard, *We Are Strangers Here*, 117.

Disclosure statement

No potential conflict of interest was reported by the author.

References

Abrams, Rebecca. 2014. "Review." *Financial Times*, August 29.
Amis, Martin. *Time's Arrow*. Harmondsworth: Penguin, 1990.
Amis, Martin. *The Zone of Interest*. London: Cape, 2014.
Arad, Yitzhak. *Belzec, Sobibor, Treblinka: The Operation Reinhard Camps*. Bloomington: Indiana University Press, 1999 [1987].
Arendt, Hannah. *The Life of Mind – Thinking – Willing*. New York: Harvest, 1978.
Baddiel, David. *The Secret Purposes*. London: Abacus, 2004.
Bakhtin, Mikhail. "Discourse in the Novel." *In The Dialogic Imagination: Four Essays*, translated by Caryl Emerson and Michael Holquist, 269–422. Austin: University of Texas Press, 1981.
Borchard, Ruth. *We Are Strangers Here: An "Enemy Alien" in Prison in 1940*. London: Vallentine Mitchell, 2008.
Boyne, John. *The Boy in the Striped Pyjamas*. London: David Fickling, 2006.
Brinson, Charmian. "Autobiography in Exile: The Reflections of Women Refugees from Nazism in British Exile, 1933–1945." In *German-Speaking Exiles in Great Britain*, edited by J. M. Ritchie,

TRACING TOPOGRAPHIES

1–22. The Yearbook for the Research Centre of Austrian and German Exile Studies no. 3. Amsterdam and Atlanta, GA: Rodopi, 2001.

Brinson, Charmian. "'In the Exile of Internment' or 'Von Versuchen, aus einer Not eine Tugend zu Machen': German-Speaking Women Interned by the British during the Second World War." In *Politics and Culture in Twentieth Century Germany*, edited by William Niven and James Jordan, 63–87. Woodbridge: Camden House, 2003.

Burt, Jonathan. *Animals in Film*. London: Reaktion, 2002.

Cesarani, David, and Tony Kushner. "Introduction." In *The Internment of Aliens in Twentieth-Century Britain*, edited by David Cesarani and Tony Kushner, 1–24. Abingdon: Routledge, 1993.

Cohn, Frederick G. *A Lucid Interval: A Young Poet behind Barbed Wire*. London: Premier Fois, 1999.

Cummins, Anthony. 2013. "Review." *Daily Telegraph*, August 20.

Donoghue, John. *The Death's Head Chess Club*. London: Atlantic, 2015.

Felstiner, John. *Paul Celan: Poet, Survivor, Jew*. New Haven, CT: Yale University Press, 1997.

Figes, Eva. 2004. "Behind Barbed Wire." *The Guardian*, July 31.

Gershon, Karen. *We Came as Children: A Collective Autobiography*. London: Gollancz, 1966.

Guest, Katy. 2014. "Review." *Independent*, August 24.

Hannam, Charles. *Almost an Englishman*. London: Scholastic, 1979.

Hoess, Rudolf. *Commandant of Auschwitz*. London: Phoenix, 2000 [1959].

Hughes, David. *My Son the Enemy*. London: Papercraft, 2010.

Igersheimer, Walter. *Blatant Injustice: The Story of a Jewish Refugee from Nazi Germany Imprisoned in Britain and Canada*. Montreal: McGill-Queen's University Press, 2005.

Jacobson, Howard. *Kalooki Nights*. London: Jonathan Cape, 2006.

Kerr, Judith. *When Hitler Stole Pink Rabbit*. Harmondsworth: Puffin, 1971.

Kühn, Dieter. *Gertrud Kolmar: A Literary Life*. Translated by Linda Marianiello. Chicago: Northwestern University Press, 2013.

Kushner, Tony. "Loose Connections? Britain and the 'Final Solution.'" In *Britain and the Holocaust: Remembering and Representing Genocide*, edited by Caroline Sharples and Olaf Jensen, 51–67. Basingstoke: Palgrave, 2013.

Lasker-Wallfisch, Anita. *Inherit the Truth, 1939–1945: The Documented Experiences of a Survivor of Auschwitz and Belsen*. London: Giles de la Mare, 1996.

Levi, Primo. *Introduction to Hoess, Commandant of Auschwitz*. London: Phoenix, 2000 [1959].

Lynton, Mark. *Accidental Journey: A Cambridge Intern's Memory of World War II*. Woodstock, NY: Overlook Press, 1998.

MacLeod, Alison. Interview with Sussex Life, 10 April 2014, http://www.sussexlife.co.uk/people/how_alison_macleod_s_novel_unexploded_was_inspired_by_the_brighton_pavilion_1_3541888.

MacLeod, Alison. *Unexploded*. London: Hamish Hamilton, 2013.

Pistol, Rachel. "Enemy Alien and Refugee: Conflicting Identities in Great Britain during the Second World War." *University of Sussex Journal of Contemporary History* 16 (2015): 37–52.

Pettitt, Joanne and Vered Weiss. "Introduction." *Holocaust Studies* 28 (2016): 141–150.

Sansom, C.J. *Dominion*. London: Macmillan, 2012.

Solomons, Natasha. Interview. Accessed October 24, 2015. http://www.penguinrandomhouse.com/books/310276/the-house-at-tyneford-by-natasha-solomons/9780452297647/readers-guide.

Solomons, Natasha. *Mr Rosenblum's List, or Friendly Guidance for the Aspiring Englishman*. London: Sceptre, 2010.

Sturdy-Colls, Caroline, and Kevin Sturdy-Colls. "Reconstructing a Painful Past: A Non-invasive Approach to Reconstructing Lager Norderney in Alderney, the Channel Islands." in *Visual Heritage in the Digital Age*, edited by Eugene Ch'ng, Vincent Gaffney and Henry Chapman, 119–46. New York: Springer, 2014.

Uhlman, Fred. *The Making of an Englishman*. London: Gollancz, 1960.

Vice, Sue. "British-Jewish Holocaust Fiction." In *The Edinburgh Companion to Modern Jewish Fiction*, edited by David Brauner and Axel Stähler, 267–278. Edinburgh: Edinburgh University Press, 2015.

Afterword

Joanne Pettitt[a] and Vered Weiss[b]

[a]Department of Comparative Literature, School of European Culture and Languages, University of Kent, Canterbury, Kent; [b]Program in Jewish Culture and Society; and Comparative and World Literature Department, University of Illinois at Urbana-Champaign, USA

This volume originated as a conference, held at the Jewish Museum in London (6–8 January 2015), designed to commemorate the seventieth anniversary of the liberation of Auschwitz. The event was organized because, we decided, this important date needed to be marked somehow – a simultaneous attempt of respect and mourning. Yet this sincere aim does point to a particular peculiarity in the way in which we remember the Holocaust because, despite the fact that Auschwitz was one of many camps erected for the incarceration, torture, or murder of the Jews and others who were deemed somehow dangerous for the "Master Race," it has come to symbolize the entire scope of the Nazi enterprise within our cultural imagination. This is so much the case that, as has been pointed out within the volume, Auschwitz is often filmed using aspects of other camps which are themselves deemed to be a less potent symbol of Nazi atrocities. Actually, one might well argue that the metonymic function of Auschwitz points to a reduction of the complexities of the genocide, especially in the way that it is remembered. In fact, and of particular relevance here, the Holocaust Memorial Day – during which we are encouraged by the Holocaust Memorial Day Trust to "remember the millions of people killed in the Holocaust, Nazi Persecution and in subsequent genocides in Cambodia, Rwanda, Bosnia, and Darfur"[1] – occurs each year on 27 January, the date of the liberation of Auschwitz. The singularity of this event is thus reified as an emblem of genocidal suffering in a much broader sense. Just as the Holocaust Memorial Trust aims to construct a commemorative discourse that extends beyond the borders of Auschwitz-Birkenau, so too do the contributors of this volume move away from this unilateral perspective and seek to consider a range of "Nazi 'spaces" and their influence on the shaping of collective memory.

Holocaust memorials also have a significant spatial dimension. The *Holocaust-Mahnmal* in Berlin, for instance, is designed to disorientate those who walk through it because of the varying dimensions of its blocks and the slightly off-kilter construction of its grid. Similarly, Berlin's Jewish Museum, designed by Daniel Libeskind, is designed to embody the void that has been left by the Holocaust; it culminates in the Holocaust Tower – a dead end. Libeskind deliberately created spaces that are highly oppressive, forcing the visitor to engage with the Holocaust through physical sensations of disorientation. These are just two examples of a particular spatial metaphor that proves itself to be significant in the construction of post-Holocaust memorial experiences. Yet the disorientating effects that are built into these structures are consciously employed as structural devices designed to encode a particular mode of encounter, but this is not always the case (and, in any case, such designs are not without their problems). One of the difficulties that this volume seeks to consider is the role of the camps themselves as memorial sites. Such spaces have the added advantage of connoting "true" experiences since these are the sites at which the original horrors occurred; yet the way that we remember and experience them as memorial sites is both highly subjective and, as several of the articles in this volume indicate, precisely mediated. Thus we are left with questions as to how we might usefully engage with these sites in a way that is both respectful toward and conducive to appropriate reflections about the Holocaust.

A potentially problematic aspect of these spatial considerations – and one that is, again, dealt with in some of the articles collected here – is the political dimensions that are inevitably attached to certain spaces. Indeed, the very notion of the liberation of Auschwitz – the place from which this entire project began – entails an understanding of the Auschwitz space as one in which a particular geo-political binary of "right" and "wrong" was constructed: the arrival of the Axis powers heralded the triumph of good over evil. Of course, there is no genuine debate about whether Hitler had been morally wrong or not (the culpability of the Nazis is so obvious that it hardly seems mentioning); yet the victory over Hitler – and, by extension, the liberation of the camps – facilitated the perpetuation of a discourse of Allied superiority which, as Sue Vice notes, is not entirely unproblematic.

In short, this volume took as its starting point the liberation of Auschwitz 70 years after the event. But it was not intended as – nor did it become – a mere examination of the Auschwitz-Birkenau complex. Instead, it deals much more broadly with the relationship between geographical spaces and the shaping of collective memory. Despite, or perhaps more appropriately because of, the variety of considerations offered here, the volume does not intend to answer all the questions it has raised, some of which have been discussed in this Afterword. Rather, the collection is conceived of as a starting point for further discussions surrounding the mediation of memory through space and time. This is especially important now, in 2016, as the Holocaust slides out of living memory and begins to exist primarily in the spaces – and the gaps – that it has left behind.

Note

1. http://hmd.org.uk/page/about-hmd-and-hmdt (accessed 1 May 2015).

Index

Note: **Boldface** page numbers refer to figures and tables. Page numbers followed by "n" refer to footnotes

Accidental Journey (Lynton) 165
Adler, H. G. 155–7
Adorno, Theodor 154
Allgemeine Jüdische Wochenzeitung 40
Almost an Englishman (Hannam) 166
Alter, Hermann 40
Anschauung 21
"*Arbeit Macht Frei*" 48
Arnold-de Simine, Silke 149
Arrow, Time's (Amis) 169
Aryan Couple, The 108, 109
Auschwitz (Cutler) 136; anticipation of encounter 137–8; cognitive dissonance 140; collecting objects 141–2; experience of arrival 138–9; notion of being "different" 138; writing about Auschwitz 142–3
Auschwitz-Birkenau State Museum 65n42; aesthetics and "good" photography 51; annual report 46; aspects of 50; commemorating the dead 53–4; definition of 46; education and visual reminders 52–3; Facebook page **47**; hope and tolerance 56–8; iconic images 48–51; "morbid voyeurism" 46; notion of 53; prisoner brothels at **70,** 71–4; sympathy and empathy 54–6; for tourist destination 48; visitors, photographs taken by 45–6, **46,** 63–4; "With my besties in Auschwitz" 58–63; *World at War, The* 50
"Auschwitz-land" 60
Auschwitz Museum *see* Auschwitz-Birkenau State Museum
Austerlitz (Sebald) 8, 149–50; Bibliothèque nationale in Paris 153–5; Iver Grove, "curious confusion" 150–3; Terezín, ghetto of 155–9
Auster, Paul 8, 143–5

Balogh, Ákos 59, 60
Barker, Jennifer M. 117, 120, 124, 127

Bartetzko, Dieter 40
Barthes, Roland 50
Benjamin, Walter 4, 154; 'dialectics at standstill' 151–2, 159n13
Bergen-Belsen, Auster's encounter with 143–5
Bhabha, Homi 4
Bibliothèque nationale in Paris 153–5
Blut und Boden 22–4
Bogue, Nicole 7
Bottrel, Felipe 51
British camps: deportation 170–1; internment 164–70
Brook, Peter 96
Brück, Wolfram 35–6
Brumlik, Micha 35, 38, 41
Bubis, Ignatz 33, 35, 37, 38, 40, 42n2
Burt, Jonathan 164

camp brothels *see Sonderbauten*
Carney, Martin **49,** 50, 55
Celan, Paul 173
Cesarani, David 165
Chmielewski, Artur 51, 65n43
Chronicle of Amorous Accidents, A 109
Cinquegrani, Maurizio 8
Claassen, Henk 55, **56, 58–9,** 59, 60
cognitive dissonance 134, 135, 140
Cole, Tim 47
Collins English Dictionary, defines sympathy 55
Cowan, James L. 150
Cronin, Joseph 6
Cutler, Angela Morgan 8, 137–43
Czarne Chmury 113

Dalton, Derek 139
Dalziel, Imogen 6–7
Darrè, Walter 22, 24
Das KZ-Bordell (Sommer) 68
Debbie S. 57, 60
De Cesari, Chiara 119
Delbo, Charlotte 89
Demski, Eva 39

181

INDEX

Der ewige Jude 113n14
Des Pres, Terrence 91, 93
Diamond, Matt **61,** 62
Diary of a Young Girl (Frank) 94
Didi-Huberman, George 136
Diner, Dan 38, 39
Doll, Paul 173, 174
Dominion (Sansom) 167, 170
Durkin, Keith 62

empathetic photography 54–6
Erll, Astrid 3
Eshel, Amir 151
Ezrahi,. Sidra Dekoven 5

Facebook 47, 64n15
Fassbinder, Rainer Werner 33
Feder, Gottfried 19
Federman, Raymond 137
Feehily, Claire 153
Feldman, Jackie 139
Festinger, Leon 140
Fight and Martyrdom monument 111
Finkelstein, Norman 47
Fitzgerald, David 171
Foley, Malcolm 45
Fragility of Empathy after the Holocaust, The
(Dean) 94
Frankfurter Allgemeine Zeitung 33, 38
Frankfurter Häuserkampf 40
Frankfurt's Jewish community: Brück, Wolfram
35–6; Brumlik, Micha 35, 38, 41; Bubis, Ignatz
33, 35, 37, 38, 40, 42n2; "ghetto" in 32, 37,
38, 41n1; journalist and museum 39; and
Kirchheim'sche Stiftung 33–5; Wallmann,
Walter 36–7
Friedländer, Eli 151
Friedman, Michel 35
"functionalistic" interpretations 16

García-Moreno, Laura 149
geo-bio-political dispositif 16
German *Geopolitik* 12
Gisel, Ernst 34
Glajar, Valentina 117
Gradowski, Salmen 134
Grimm, Hans 12
Grosser, Alfred 38

Habermas, Jürgen 37
Haltof, Marek 105, 118
Haushofer, Karl 12, 13–14
Hay, James 104, 105
Herf, Jeffrey 14
Hessischer Rundfunk 33, 34
Hicks, Jeremy 109
Himmler, Heinrich 12, 17, 24
Hirsch, Marianne 130n19, 134–5

Hitler, Adolf 12, 13, 24
Hoess, Rudolf 172, 173
Holocaust: industry 47; photography at 51;
victims and survivors 54
Holocaust and the Literary Imagination, The
(Langer) 1
*Holocaust Literature: A Handbook of Critical,
Historical, and Literary Writings* (Klein) 2
Holocaust memory, films and 116–19;
see also Kornblumenblau

iconic images 48–51
iconic photographs 48–51
Igersheimer, Walter 166
Imagine This 92
Instagram 47
Iver Grove, in *Austerlitz* 150–3

Johnson, Mark 159
Jordanova, Ludmilla 71
Judengasse 37, 38, 40

Kafka, Franz 51
Kaynar, Gad 90, 92–3
Keilbach, Judith 48
Keil, Chris 89, 90, 95, 98, 102n49
Kershaw, Baz 97
Kirchheim'sche Stiftung 33–5
Kirton, Sarah 48, 52
Kjellen, Rudolf 12
Klein, Dennis 2
Klopfleisch, Margarete 165
Kornblumenblau 117, 128–9; archival skin
121–4; color overlays in 124–6; confronting
gas chamber 126–8; film body in 117–18, 120,
125; "missing Jew," concept of 122–3; Polish
Holocaust memory 118–19; as transcultural
experience 119–21, 129n5
Korn, Salomon 33, 34, 37
Krauzenberg, Joseph 108
Kristeva, Julia 125
Kugelmann, Cilly 39
Kulturboden 19
Küppers, Hans 34
Kushner, Tony 164

Lakoff, George 159
Lalonde, Solange **52,** 53, **57**
Langer, Lawrence 1–2
Lanzmann, Claude 50
Lebensraum ideology *see* Nazi "*Lebensraum*
ideology"
Lemoine, Henri 153, 154
Lennon, John 45
Levinas, Emmanuel 120
Levi, Primo 1
Levy, Daniel 117, 119
lieux de mémoire 2–3

INDEX

Liulevicius, Vejas 17
Lu, Andong 104
Lublin: Commemoration at Majdanek 109–10
Lublin's Jews, cinematic city and destruction of 104–14
Lucid Interval, A (Cohn) 164, 166
L'Univers Concentrationnaire (Rousset) 5, 7

Majdanek: Cmentarzysko Europy 109, 110
Making of an Englishman, The (Uhlman) 165, 166
Marks, Laura U. 117, 120, 121, 123
Martinez, Keila 53, 55
Mass, Sandra 21
Meier-Arendt, Walter 40
Menschen Dinge: The Human Aspect of Objects (Shalev-Gerz) 141–2
metaphorical reality, Cowan's notion of 150
Mickiewicz, Adam 119
Miles, William F. S. 46
Milton, Sybil 71
"missing Jew," concept of 122–3
Mitchell, Breanna 61–2, 90
Mitschke, Samantha 7, **61**
"morbid voyeurism" 46
Mr Rosenblum's List (Solomons) 166
Mrs. Dalloway (Woolf) 168
Murphy, David 14
Murray, June 165

Nachmann, Werner 40
National Library of France *see* Bibliothèque nationale in Paris
Nazi "*Lebensraum* ideology": *Blut und Boden* 22–4; Coda 24–5; concept of 12; "functionalistic" interpretations 16–17; genealogy of 13–16; by *Geopolitik* project 13–16; key expression of 13; life-world 20–2; notion of 12, 24; *Raum* in 16–20
Nelki, Erna 166
Neumann, Boaz 20–1
Neumann, Robert 165, 166
Nicely-Borland, Julia 54, **54**, 55
Night and Fog (1955) 114n26
Nora, Pierre 41, 110
Nuit et Brouillard 114n26
Nünning, Ansgar 159

Ognim i Mieczem 113n15
150 na godzine 113n15
Ostforschung 14

Pan Tadeusz (Mickiewicz) 119
Penck, Albrecht 19
Penz, François 104
Photographing the Holocaust (Struk) 47
Polish Catholicism 74–5
Polish Film Chronicle 109
Polish Holocaust memory 118–19

Polska Kronika Filmowa 109
post-witnessing concentration camps 134–6, 145n2; Auster's encounter with Bergen-Belsen 143–5; as "cognitive dissonance" 134, 135; Cutler's encounter with Auschwitz *see* Auschwitz (Cutler); "postmemory," Hirsch's definition of 134–5; stages in 137

Quirke, John 61

"race contra space" approaches 13, 15
Ratzel, Friedrich 12–14
Raum: embodiment of 18–20; emergence of 17–18
Ravensbrück *Gedenkstätte*, prisoner brothels at **70**, 71–4
Reader, The 110, 111
Reimer, Robert 113n14
Rettet den Börneplatz see "Save Börneplatz"
Reunion (Uhlman) 165
Rigney, Ann 3, 119
"Romantic Auschwitz": Auschwitz-Birkenau State Museum *see* Auschwitz-Birkenau State Museum
Rosen, Martin 164

Sammy's Follies: A Criminal Comedy 92
Sanyal, Debarati 3
"Save Börneplatz" 33, 36, 37, 39, 41
Schindler's List 116, 129n2
Schwinghammer, Georg 40
Sebald, W. G. 149–61
Secret Purposes, The (Baddiel) 165, 169
Seitz, Stephan 149, 153
Sekret Enigmy 114n27
Shalev-Gerz, Esther 141–2
Shaviv, Miriam 94
Shropshire Lad, A (Housman) 167
Sicher, Efraim 6
Simon Konianski 111
site-specific performance at Auschwitz: overview of 88–90; "profane" performance 90–4; "sacred" theatre 94–9
Slesin, Aviva 94
Smith, David Woodruff 23
Soldiers of Freedom 106
Sonderbauten 68, 75–6; academic works 68–9; Auschwitz-Birkenau State Museum **70**, 71–4; Ravensbrück *Gedenkstätte* **70**, 71–4; *System Sonderbau* 75; *Zwangsprostitution* 75
Sontag, Susan 45, 47, 50, 51
Spring 1941 108, 109
SS-GB (Deighton) 167
Steinlauf, Michael C. 105
Strasser, Petra 152
Struk, Janina 47
sympathy 54–6
Sznaider, Natan 117, 119

INDEX

Terezín 150, 151, 155–9
Tetno 113n15
Third Reich: on Eastern Front 14; "geographical imaginations" 14; for racial and ethnic reordering 11
Time's Arrow (Amis) 172
Tragic City of Lublin, The 106–7, 110
Tyminski, Kazimierz 118

Uczniowie Widz¹cego z Lublina 106
Uhlman, Fred 165–6
Unexploded (MacLeod) 165, 167, 168

Vergangenheitsbewältigung 75
vexata quaestio 15
Vice , Sue 9
Victims, Heroes and Survivors (Gertjejanssen) 69
völkische Flurbereinigung 17
Volk ohne Raum 12
Volksboden 19
Volksgemeinschaft 17
Volkskörper 21, 22
Volks und Kulturboden 19
Volz, Wilhelm 19

Wächter, Kirsten 48
Walden, Victoria Grace 8
Wallmann, Walter 36–7
Wall of Death in Auschwitz I 51, 63
Walter, Benjamin 51
Wasylewsky, Vicky **50,** 57
Waves, The (Woolf) 168
We Are Strangers Here (Borchard) 166, 167
Weikart, Richard 23
Weimar Republic: *Lebensraum* 16
Werkbund, German 37
Willis, Emma 94
Winter Journal (Auster) 136, 143
"With my besties in Auschwitz" 58–63
Wosiewicz, Leszek 116–30

Young, James 71

Zabłocki, Maciej 53, 58, 64n16
Zelizer, Barbie 47
Zimmerman, Andrew 14
Zone of Interest, The (Amis) 171–3
Zwangsprositution 75